INSIDE AGT

THE UNTOLD STORIES OF
AMERICA'S GOT TALENT

SEAN DALY
ASHLEY MAJESKI

Roundup Publishing, Inc.
LOS ANGELES, CA

DISCLAIMER: *INSIDE AGT* was compiled using exclusive interviews with dozens of contestants and other individuals associated with the television program *America's Got Talent.* It contains both original, independent reporting and previously published material.

This book is not endorsed by, or affiliated with NBC-Universal, Fremantle Media North America or Syco Television.

Roundup Publishing, Inc.
507 7th Street, Suite #104
Santa Monica, CA 90401
www.AGT-Book.com
Email: Editor@AGT-Book.com

Inside AGT / Sean Daly & Ashley Majeski —1st ed.
ISBN: 978-1492203605

CONTENTS

SEASON BY SEASON

STORIES THAT TOUCHED OUR HEARTS

A CONVERSATION WITH...

"There aren't even categories for some of the things we have seen. What is more amazing to me than even the level of talent is the level of audacity people have. I don't know if they are delusional. I don't know if they are crazy. I think in order to make it, you have to throw everything by the wayside."

— HOWIE MANDEL

Mel B. (L) and Heidi Klum attend auditions for season 8 of *America's Got Talent*.

Photo: Helga Esteb (Shutterstock)

My Guilty Pleasure

BY SEAN DALY

EVERYONE HAS A GUILTY PLEASURE. I found mine on June 21, 2006 while channel surfing with the new 50-inch flat-screen my wife and I received as a wedding gift just weeks earlier. At the time, I hated – and I mean hated – reality television. I would have rather put hot pokers in my eyes than watch a minute of backstabbing strangers voting each other off an island – or cheer for a fame-hungry singer to win some phony baloney record deal. But something about *America's Got Talent* – a colorful, over-the-top mash-up of variety schmaltz and carnival freakdom – sucked me right in. At first, it might have been the comical idea of David Hasselhoff, the butt of a million show business jokes, critiquing this motley crew of jugglers, unicyclists and dancing animals. There was also a natural curiosity about Piers Morgan, a virtually unknown British fellow – at least on this side of the pond – who appeared to be not-so-subtly channeling his inner Simon Cowell.

What I learned over the past eight seasons was that *America's Got Talent* isn't like all the other "voice" shows cluttering up the prime time dial. It's the amateur hour to end all amateur hours – a nostalgic throwback to the days of vaudeville, where the limits of entertainment were restricted only by a performer's imagination, and in some cases, tolerance for pain. Over the years, *AGT* has provided a stage for hundreds of acts that simply wouldn't fit in anywhere else. (Hello, Leonid The Magnificent!) Yet with the discovery of a few bona-fide stars – like ventriloquist Terry Fator and classical crossover prodigy Jackie Evancho – it has evolved from nutty sideshow spectacle to cultural phenomenon and taken over the great stage of Radio City Music Hall.

There are lots of reasons to love *AGT*.

1.   **THE TALENT.** Season after season, producers manage to find acts that are even more unusual and outrageous than anything we've ever seen before. That very first episode in 2006 included performances by professional finger snapper Bobby Badfingers, 65 year-old male stripper Bernie Barker, and a guy whose body was covered with dozens of rubber horns. Six years later, a single dad from Pennsylvania was getting whacked in the groin by wooden boards and bowling balls – on the same stage where a Los Angeles musician later played the world's largest Earth Harp.

2.   **HOWARD STERN.** Much of America reacted with outright shock and horror at the announcement that the controversial "King of All Media" would be taking control of Morgan's buzzer during the show's seventh season. The fear, presumably, was that Stern – a show business professional for more than three decades – would somehow forget where it is appropriate to talk about sex positions (his satellite radio program) and where it is not. Stern's critics couldn't have gotten it more wrong. His wife, Beth, tells me that everywhere they go now her "shock jock" husband is approached by young children who recognize him from the show. Though Stern's celebrity seemed at times to overshadow the rest of the judging panel in his first season, he is easily one of the most constructive and knowledgeable arbiters of talent anywhere on the dial. Howard appears genuinely sympathetic to how difficult it is to bare your soul in front of an audience of millions and offers straightforward criticism without kicking contestants while they are down. Perhaps his dirty-minded, self adoring public persona is nothing more than a brilliant and well seasoned act, which he can turn on and off at exactly the right moment. If so, that truly qualifies as "talent."

3.   **THE OTHER JUDGES.** Assembling a dais of celebrity judges is a lot like fielding a championship basketball team – you need precisely the right balance of knowledge, talent and chemistry. (Just ask the producers of *American Idol*.) With the exception of Stern, *AGT* has never traded on the celebrity status of its panel. It has, instead, filled the seats with colorful personalities who sometimes agree – often don't – but never allow the focus to stray too far from the talent on stage. The chemistry has always been next to perfect, with Sharon Osbourne's sensitivity perfectly balancing out

Piers Morgan's matter-of-fact commentary for five seasons. Howie Mandel was a brilliant addition to the show in season four, after David Hasselhoff stepped down. In addition to the cornball comedy that only he can pull off, America's most famous germaphobe brought years of in-the-trenches show business experience to the table along with a genuine sense of compassion and respect for the acts that stand before him. Toss in supermodel-next-door Heidi Klum and "Scary Spice" (token Brit Mel B.) and – voila! - you've got a team of experts that are as compelling to watch as the starry-eyed hopefuls whose dreams they could make or break.

4. NICK CANNON. Mr. Mariah Carey is prime time's ultimate carnival barker – squirting flower and all – and the lovable goofball that holds the whole production together. He's a perfect foil for when the judges become too serious, a comic sidekick to acts in need of a "volunteer" and a compassionate shoulder for heartbroken contestants to cry on after they are eliminated. On a show as unpredictable as *AGT*, driving the bus for two hours is a fine art. In the end, Nick just wants to see everyone have fun – and that's what makes him so fun to watch.

Over the years, I have written literally hundreds of stories about *America's Got Talent* – first as the west coast TV reporter for the *New York Post* and later as editor of *AGTNews.com*. During the summer of 2013, I decided it was time to tell the complete story of this groundbreaking program with the help of the very people responsible for its success. I reached out to more than 70 winners, finalists and fan favorites from the first eight seasons and assembled a must-read collection of memories, personal updates and behind-the-scenes gossip from TV's ultimate talent show.

For the first time ever, the biggest names in *AGT* history are telling all. We found out which grand prize winner gave all his money away, who once tried out to be "Hannah Montana" and how accused "fake soldier" Tim Poe became a hero again overnight. In his very own words, one street performer tells us how he used to rob houses for fun, while a young dancer talks about her brave battle with terminal illness and a beloved runner-up admits he once contemplated suicide.

If you've enjoyed the show for the past eight seasons, get ready for the ultimate trip down memory lane. These are the true, unauthorized stories of *America's Got Talent*.

Sharon Osbourne spent six seasons judging dancers, singers, jugglers and acrobats - but always had a soft spot for animal acts.

Photo: Helga Esteb (Shutterstock)

CHAPTER 1

The Greatest (Talent) Show On Earth

THIS WAS THE MOMENT that Jackie Evancho had waited for her entire young life. The blue-eyed fifth grader from rural Pennsylvania stood motionless under a bright spotlight on Stage 36 at CBS Television City in Los Angeles. Eight feet away, her good friend, bluesy soul singer Michael Grimm, also waited nervously as host Nick Cannon prepared to reveal the $1 million winner of *America's Got Talent*.

Jackie, just 10, emerged as an early favorite to take the season five crown after delivering a you-had-to-see-it-to-believe-it performance of Puccini's "O mio babbino caro" on the NBC show's *YouTube* audition special. To not end up on top, judge Piers Morgan joked days earlier, "she would have to lose her voice or catch a cold. Jackie is probably going to be put in an incubator to make sure she doesn't get a sniffle."

On September 15, 2010 – after months of buzz-worthy auditions, over-the-top performances and teary-eyed eliminations – America ultimately cast its vote for Grimm. But Jackie would go on to become the show's biggest global star – even after failing to get past her first audition during the previous two seasons. "She just grew in a very short time as a performer until she was right and ready to do it," executive producer Jason Raff explained for a 2011 story in the *New York Post*. "There is something about auditioning, especially for young kids. You can be on video and be quite spectacular – and her videos were quite spectacular – but she never sent a video in before." Despite her earlier rejections, Jackie never drifted off the show's radar, Raff said: "The producer who initially saw her – when we saw the videotape come in for the *YouTube* show – was like 'Oh my God! That is that girl. This is pretty spectacular!'"

And at the end of the day, no show celebrates the spectacular quite like *AGT*. Unlike *American Idol, The Voice* and other prime time competitions, the modern day *Gong Show* has never been afraid to pander to the least common denominator – or too proud to trade on its contestants' hard luck stories.   "When I got the call to do this show it was like a dream come true," judge Howie Mandel shared at the start of season 5. "It covers all ends of the spectrum. There aren't even categories for some of the things we have seen. What is more amazing to me than even the level of talent is the level of audacity people have. I don't know if they are delusional. I don't know if they are crazy. I think in order to make it, you have to throw everything by the wayside and there are just people who have what could be construed as ridiculous ideas. And then they just explode onto the screens. So I get to watch these people go on this journey. They come from obscurity and they can end up being the next $100 million act on the Vegas strip!"

The *Got Talent* brand – which includes local shows in 55 different countries and multiple languages – was created by record executive-turned-television mogul Simon Cowell in 2005. "*AGT* is an important program in the history of American show business," says Robert Thompson, head of the Bleier Center for Television and Popular Culture at Syracuse University. "[Ventriloquist and season two winner] Terry Fator to me is the best example of what a show like *America's Got Talent* can do that none of these other shows can do. That kind of act hasn't had any place in this country since 1930. What *America's Got Talent* brought back was all that fringe stuff. If you could come up with a seven-minute act – no matter how incredibly stupid it was – and you could do it well, you used to be able to make a decent living. When vaudeville went away that whole art form of crazy acts died off. This show brings it back."

The series was set to appear first on British television as *Paul O'Grady's Got Talent*, but when its host split with network ITV, the production was put on hold after just one rehearsal. It was launched two years later as *Britain's Got Talent*.

America's Got Talent, the first full series of the franchise, premiered June 21, 2006 on NBC with Regis Philbin as host. The original judging panel featured British tabloid newspaper editor Piers Morgan, *Baywatch* actor David Hasselhoff and R&B singer Brandy Norwood.   (Despite Cowell's involvement in the show's production, his contract with *Idol* prohibited him from appearing on camera.) The debut attracted more than 12 million viewers, setting *AGT* up to become the top-rated summer show for eight seasons in a row.

"It was the bull market for talent competition shows," says former NBC programming chief Kevin Reilly, who green-lit the summertime variety series in early 2006 after Fox passed on it. "*Idol* was absolutely at its height and it felt like NBC was at its bottom. We were really struggling. Certainly Simon Cowell was blazing hot, so the opportunity to get into business with him was great. But right from the get-go, it felt like this show was going to truly operate in its own space and it felt like a very cohesive vision of something that would have its own set of rhythm and competition to it. Right from the get-go it kind of felt good. And it has been surprising. It was never a monster, but it has constantly performed all along." Reilly – now the head of programming at Fox – tells us he didn't hesitate for a moment after hearing Cowell pitch the idea. "The dark charms of Simon, he can sell you anything," he says. "But when he is locked on and believes in something, it is quite convincing. He really believed that there were so many different acts that you could discover outside of singing – and, in fact, that was true."

CHAPTER 2

Making TV Magic

WHAT YOU DON'T SEE ON TV!

PROFESSOR SPLASH HAD SUCCESSFULLY performed his death-defying high dive trick dozens of times before landing in front of the *America's Got Talent* judges during season six. He would routinely suffer minor bumps and bruises belly-flopping from 30 feet or more into a mere 12 inches of water. But never once did the silver-haired stunt diver fail to get up and walk away. Still, when it came time to attempt a world record jump (36 feet, 7 inches) during the quarterfinals in Los Angeles, producers weren't taking any chances. A grown man plunging to his death on live television would be a public relations disaster for NBC and its top-rated competition show. So on July 25, 2011 – the night before *AGT*'s two-hour live performance episode – the crew, judges and a small, handpicked audience gathered in the parking lot of CBS Television City to record the stunt in advance. You know, just in case...

Pre-taping is just one of the many clever maneuvers *AGT* producers employ that go almost undetected by viewers at home. Runner-up Cas Haley (season 2) remembers one uncomfortable episode that took place backstage during the audition rounds. "We were all in the green room, waiting to go out and perform and there was this young girl from Hawaii who was with her mom," he says. "She was practicing [her singing] and was really good, I thought. She went out and auditioned and while she was out there, a producer came back to the holding room and told us, 'OK, she made it, let's give her a big hand when she comes back in here.' So, of course, we all cheered for her when she came through the door and she just burst into tears. It turns out she didn't actually make it, they just told us that so we'd cheer and they'd get a reaction out of her. That was the first time I realized I couldn't trust these people. [The show is] not what people think. It's all for ratings. That's what they're looking for."

"I don't think a lot of people understand that this is a heavily produced TV show," says illusionist Murray Sawchuck (s5). Murray – who now performs a nightly show at the Tropicana in Las Vegas – contends that producers have a master plan for who they want to see advance throughout the competition and, ultimately, into the finals.

They will try to ensure certain acts are eliminated by pitting them against more popular opponents, he says. "You are handed the date and the time and who you are up against. There are only 12 acts in each episode, so if I am up against nine 10 year-old singers and a little guy who plays the violin, good luck. But if I am up against a 70 year-old harmonica player, I am probably going to kill, even doing a coin trick. I don't think people understand that it isn't random at all. They have to produce an entertaining show to keep people watching for two hours. You need to have an interesting [balance of] acts." Back in the executive producers office, Murray says, "they sit down and have their meeting with these lovely judges who make $25,000 an episode and they say 'Here is the deal: he is in, he is out.'" In some cases, he believes, the powers that be will subtly sabotage a performance to increase the chance an act will be eliminated. Several former contestants have told us producers manipulated them into performances they were not comfortable with. On other occasions, singers have reported their songs were switched out at the last moment.

Murray tells us he knew he would be sent home hours before a trick where he made a 1918 steam train locomotive vanish on stage. "Somebody told one of my stagehands 'He can make the space shuttle disappear right now, but this is his last night,'" the performer remembers. "I knew it was the end for me the moment I started my act when my music was [only] at 10 percent volume. I went 'Son of a bitch. I am the guy they are doing it to tonight!' I know numerous friends on that show who would rehearse with full monitors – EQ'd perfectly – then when they do their live performance, the monitors would drop off so the performers can't hear themselves and they sound off key. That is a fact. I thought because I brought my own team in, none of that was ever going to happen to me. But I wasn't going to get through either way. They put [another magician] Michael Grasso through because they knew they could get rid of him before the final four."

What else goes on behind the scenes of TV's biggest talent show? Several former contestants provide answers to some of our burning questions:

AUDITIONS

Where do the acts come from?

Open call auditions are usually held in a half dozen cities across the United States each year, beginning a month or two after the conclusion of the previous season. But most of the acts who typically advance to Vegas Week and beyond are personally recruited by *AGT* talent scouts and producers and never wait in line. Some are discovered on *YouTube*, others in comedy clubs and performance venues. Casting crews will also reach out to dance studios, agents, local talent bookers and anyone with their finger on the pulse of who is hot and buzz-worthy in each city. The acts they find – most of which have years of professional experience – are invited to a local hotel or conference space to perform privately for a panel of producers. "When I made it to the Top 20, I couldn't believe that I was the only one that really came from an open call audition," says country singer Julienne Irwin (s2). "I was the only one that hadn't been a professional performer."

What is the audition process like?

The experience is a bit different for everyone, depending on the type of act, audition spot and whether or not the performer was recruited. Everyone begins by filling out a multi-page application to give producers as much information as possible about their act and personal life – including work history, education, arrests, previous television appearances and more. "People would be surprised how long the [audition] process really is," says singer Daniel Joseph Baker (s6).

Only a small percentage of the hopefuls who line up at cattle calls ever make it before the judges. Those who do – like church singer Queen Emily (s3) – often wait all day in a holding area before first performing for one or more lower level producers. "I remember I was in that big waiting room for maybe 10 to 12 hours, just sitting in there," she says. "They were going around with the cameras trying to find someone special in the crowd, someone with a real special story that they could talk to," she remembers. "They wanted someone who wanted this really bad, someone that felt like it was their turn and that they deserved it – and that was me."

Acts that are selected to audition in front of the celebrity judges are sometimes not notified for weeks. The show arranges – and pays for – their transportation and lodging in the agreed upon audition city. At the theater, the acts wait together for hours in large holding rooms. "Most people would go out near the bathroom and if they are a singer they will practice their songs in there," says teen singer Christina Christensen, who advanced to the Top 10 with her sister Ali (s6). "Dancers would find anywhere they could in the hallway to practice. It was kind of squooshy, but it kind of made people bond and get to know each other." Most contestants got ready in their hotel rooms, says Mary Joyner (s7): "You don't get hair and makeup until the live shows so you have to come camera ready."

Do the judges know who is going to walk out on stage?

Yes. The judges are briefed before each act performs so they know what types of questions to ask and what to expect. It's "basic information about the acts - their name, age, background and talent," Piers Morgan tells us. "But nothing that suggests if they are good or bad."

THE CONTRACT

What kind of agreement do the acts have to sign before appearing?

Fifteen minutes of fame comes with a lot of strings attached. Each act must sign a very detailed 45 page contestant agreement which stipulates that they surrender control of their life stories – and, in some cases, their future careers – to the show's producers and their affiliates. "You are pretty much signing away your life," one former contestant says. "It's almost non-negotiable." In exchange for being seen by millions of viewers each week, everyone must agree that producers can trick, exploit and embarrass them – and even depict their personal stories in a manner that "may be factual or fictional" – and they can't sue for any reason. "I further understand that my appearance, depiction and portrayal in the program may be disparaging, defamatory, embarrassing...and may expose me to public ridicule, humiliation or condemnation," the agreement states.

Among the other terms and conditions:

*Hidden cameras may be used to film contestants in bedrooms, bathrooms, dressing rooms or "any other area in which a person under other circumstances might have a reasonable expectation of privacy."

*If an act is disqualified, "Producer and the Network may make any explanation or announcement, on-air or otherwise...as to the reason why."

*Participants and their families agree to a penalty of $5 million for providing false information to the show.

*Producers and NBC can require talent to participate in additional unscripted, "reality based" programs for up to one year.

The contractual demands are not unique to *AGT*. The creative teams behind *American Idol*, *The Voice* and *X Factor* have similar "talent holds" and options for management and record deals on their contestants that can last for up to one year. "The management company [they made me sign with] did nothing," says season 5 winner Michael Grimm. "It was a horrible, horrible management company that they set you up with. That is not a good situation. The guy they assigned me to was a green horned rookie. He had no experience in the music business at all. And I do. I have way more experience than this manager that was assigned to me. I was telling him how this business works. He was learning from me. That is not good."

The *AGT* contract also requires that all acts reaching a certain point in the competition (usually the Top 10) be available to participate in a live stage show for a small, predetermined salary. One contestant from season 5 revealed the compensation to be $1500 for approximately three performances each week.

"When you do the show, you make a deal with the devil," comedian and runner-up Tom Cotter (s7) told *Laughspin.com*. "I'm not saying *AGT*'s the Devil – they've done a lot for my career and my price is up there now and it's going to be good. But the deal with the Devil is when you sign on the dotted line you're saying that you are available for them to do a show in Vegas after the last episode airs."

After becoming the highest finishing comic in *AGT* history in 2012, Cotter honored his commitment to host the *America's Got Talent Live* show at the Palazzo Resort Casino for seven weeks – which forced him to cancel numerous pre-booked engagements. "So not only have I pissed off those people, I'm taking a big pay cut because they're not paying me a lot to go out there to Las Vegas," he said at the time.

VEGAS WEEK

Most acts only appear before the judges for a few minutes all week. What are they doing the rest of the time?

"They have you in these rooms for days doing B-roll, background stuff and interviews," says dancer Snap Boogie (s6). "You have to prepare your mind mentally for it. You really can't do too much else. There was no time for the pool. I figured anybody who had time for the pool, they wasn't gonna get through. They definitely work you like crazy. They made me stay inside the room all day, just sitting down. We had nothing to do, so the performers would just talk to each other. It almost felt like one of those other reality shows where they just give you little bits of food... And we were getting shitty ass food! I was like "What the fuck is this shit?" But it was one of the most fun times, too. I am a street performer, so after I was done, I was like 'I need to go release this energy and go outside and dance. So I went outside and made some money."

What is the mood like among the contestants in Vegas?

"Vegas was the most pressure of my fucking lifetime," Snap says. "You don't really know who is going to get picked, who the producers like, you just know that a lot of motherfuckers are going home. You are thinking about your life and you are thinking about what can happen and what the reality is all at once."

Is everything as dramatic as it looks on TV?

"No. It was such bullshit," says singer Tim Hockenberry (s7). "It was total staged drama behind the scenes. They basically filmed me with this group of standby singers and they were all killed off. They just put me in that group to make me squirm because they knew I was going to make the semi-finals. They were like, 'Try to look more nervous. Can we get you pacing up and down the hall?' And the staff was so mean to everybody. They've got some 21-year-old girl telling me I can't go out and play with my kid in the casino. I'd say 'I need to go help out my girlfriend with the baby' and she'd say 'No, you've got to sit down.'"

Singer Mary Joyner (s7) says her experience in Vegas was "completely different than what you see on TV. Parts of the manipulation were hard to grasp, mostly backstage. I felt like it was an interesting way they got me to react certain ways. My reactions that they showed for certain things weren't the real reactions I had for those situations. They would edit them so that it looked like I was reacting a certain way to something. I was embarrassed. I mean, who wants to see themselves crying on national TV?"

THE LIVE SHOWS

Where does everyone live?

Contestants stay at a hotel within a mile or two of the main stage. When production was based at CBS Television City in Los Angeles, acts were put up at the Hotel Sofitel on Beverly Blvd. (Fun fact: season 6 finalists POPLYFE were booted from the hotel for making too much noise!) When the show moved to Newark in 2012, performers stayed at the Best Western Robert Treat Hotel, across the street from the New Jersey Performing Arts Center. "I was floored at how bad the hotel was," Tim says. "The staff just hated us. And the rooms were really bad. Probably in its day it might have had something going on. That corner where the hotel is sort of like a destination spot for single, middle class black people. There were singles parties in the hotel we were staying at for old black people. Then down the street was a biker club. On weekend nights, that street that ran into the venue was filled with Harleys and not a white person on the street. A lot of the kids were afraid to go out at night. It is a funky hotel for sure." Acts with more than one member (of the same sex) are required to double up in rooms. Talent is transported back and forth to rehearsals, meetings and performances by an *AGT* shuttle van. They must, however, rely on public transportation for personal errands and commitments.

What is a typical work day like for contestants?

In a word, "brutal," says former subway busker Alice Tan Ridley (s5). "You start out early in the morning around 6:00. And it would go until 9:00 or 10:00 at night." In that time, there are meetings with producers, choreographers, vocal coaches, hair and makeup stylists and more. In addition to rehearsals, each act can spend 10 hours or more each week filming interviews and "reality" segments that air before their performances. Minors are required to spend at least two hours per day with tutors, attending to schoolwork.

"You felt like you were in prison," adds Damien Escobar, half of the hip-hop violin duo Nuttin' But Stringz (s4). "They kept us in this holding area forever, like 19 hours, until it was our time to rehearse. We'd get about four hours of sleep and be up at 5:00 AM to do it all over again. They made us sign a waiver that said 'This show can kill you and we're not liable. You can die from stress or whatever...' They weren't lying! We had a nurse on set everyday that was giving us vitamin B, vitamin K shots. It was crazy. It was one of the things where only the strongest survive. There was a therapist backstage. I got a vitamin B shot because so many people were sick. That kept me healthy. We'd get them every single week."

What do the contestants eat?

Meals and snacks – including lots of donuts and chips – are provided throughout the day. "Everybody complained at one point about the food," says runner-up and opera sensation Barbara Padilla (s4). "But honestly, I didn't. You could chose between a cheese sandwich or a ham sandwich or a turkey sandwich. And every day we had that. But it was for free. It was a very small price to pay. I only remember it because it was such a big deal for some people. "Oh, my God, another sandwich! Not again!" A performer from the following season tells us, "They either had Corner Bakery or pizza every day. A lot of pizza. For me, I love pizza, so it was nice." Each contestant is given a small per diem (usually $25 a day) to spend on snacks and sundries. "Some people would eat the food in the artist tent and pocket the cash," the insider reveals.

Who decides on the song, act or routine?

Each act in the competition is assigned a producer who is responsible for helping coordinate their performances. An individual producer may be working with four or more other acts at the same time. Most artists we spoke with say they were given input into each performance, but ultimately the final decisions were made (or approved) by the show. "You sit down with the production designer and the producers and they have a design for you and a stage set up," says Kehlani Parrish, lead singer of POPLYFE (s6). "The next day you will have a fitting with the costume designer. Then you go to the makeup person and they talk about what your makeup is gonna look like, then you go to the hair person. As far as the music – you have to pick from a list of songs that have been cleared [for use on television]. We were one of the only groups to ever get a Beatles song."

Still, "there is a lot of stuff you just don't have control over," says John Quale a/k/a Prince Poppycock (s5). For starters, each act must work within the parameters of a pre-set budget that the executive producers decide for them. Budgets – which are used to pay for costumes, dancers, special effects and more – vary from act to act and week to week. In some cases contestants are allocated as much as $30,000 to produce a 90 second performance. "Whether or not you are going to be in control of that budget is up to each contestant." Quale says. "I was a real bitch. I really was. I didn't let them steamroll me. They really try to steamroll each contestant and tell them what they want out of them. They end up ruining a lot of acts because of that. [They get] vocalists to do weird song choices. They wanted to make these big spectacles because it makes for good television. For that, luck was in my favor. I wanted spectacle. Then on "Nessun Dorma" they said "Your budget is going to be even bigger for this one and you have just a few days to produce it. We had like four days. They said I was going to come in on a horse and have a fly rig on and I was going to be able to go up to the princess. Then all that stuff just got cut and there is nothing you can do about it." Several comedians also tell us they were required to submit their jokes to producers in advance, to make sure they clear network standards and practices and did not clash with the show's family friendly values.

Sand artist Joe Castillo (s7) says even his patriotic and faith-based artwork was subject to censorship. "For the last three performances I had prepared more spiritual themes but was told by the producers that I could not present them," he says. "It is, after all, their show and I for the most part acquiesced. My semifinal performance was to end with Jesus holding a small child. During rehearsals I was asked to remove the beard, which really made Jesus look like a generic male. Once on stage for the live show I included the beard making it obvious who I was drawing which sparked the fascinating interchange between the three judges. It was fun."

Is there a dress rehearsal?

Yes. During most seasons, a full dress rehearsal is held approximately 24 hours prior to the live performance show. There is no studio audience. Stand-ins are used in place of the judges, who see the final performances at the same time as the home audience.   Some acts, like Professor Splash, which are either too dangerous or complex, are not required to participate in the run-through.

How competitive is it backstage among the contestants?

Although acts are competing against each other for the top prize, most people tell us there is a great camaraderie between contestants backstage. "You will see certain people break down and cry when their friends get eliminated," Kehlani says. "When Daniel Joseph Baker (s6) got eliminated, I cried. When Avery & The Calico Hearts (s6) got eliminated, I cried. I was sad because I had relationships with these people. Plus, I wanted to see them go far because they were so cute." Says magician Landon Swank (s5): "I didn't notice any animosity. It seemed like everyone wanted everyone else to do their best. When someone messed up most people seemed to feel genuinely bad for them. I'd say everyone wanted the competition to be good, they just wanted to do a little better themselves."

Who counts the votes?

The votes are collected and counted by an independent third party called Telescope, Inc. They also tally results for *American Idol*, *The Voice* and *X Factor*.

ELIMINATION

What happens after you get eliminated?

Once acts are eliminated they are given the opportunity to speak with the media, usually for the first time, about their experience on the show. Afterwards, they are taken back to the hotel and given instructions about travel arrangements home. In some cases, contestants are referred to speak with an onsite therapist prior to leaving. "They shipped us to a shrink for legal reasons, I suppose," says singer Eli Mattson (s3). Damien Escobar of Nuttin' But Stringz says he and his brother weren't required to speak to the counselor, "But my mom did when we lost. She was so pissed off. I remember I was in the back doing interviews after the show, and I hear my mom screaming. You would have thought that [she] lost. She was screaming at the top of her lungs, and I was like, 'Oh god, my mom would be the one that went to the therapist!'"

CHAPTER 3

Deadly Audition:
Who Killed Laura Finley?

Joe Finley and wife Laura renew their vows in 2009
Photo: Splash News

AMERICA'S GOT...A MURDER MYSTERY! Hours before season 6 auditions were scheduled to begin on October 23, 2010, the lifeless body of 48 year-old Laura Finley turned up at the bottom of a stairwell inside L.A.'s Millennium Biltmore Hotel. The Los Angeles County Coroner concluded that Laura died of multiple blunt force injuries. Her skull separated from the spinal column during a severe blow to the head, an autopsy revealed. Her top was missing, pants turned inside out and diamond rings removed. The spirited mother of three had accompanied her husband of 29 years, musician Joe Finley, to the hotel where he was invited to try out in front of producers. Which he did – even after learning of his wife's death.

Joe, the owner of a spring-manufacturing business, told *TMZ* that he and his wife Laura had been popping ecstasy pills and drinking wine in the hotel bar just hours before she died. Around 3:00 A.M., he claimed, Laura got up and left their room – presumably to get ice. When he awoke in the morning, she wasn't there, and he called hotel security before heading downstairs to perform.

The aspiring rock star – who has since remarried and had another child – was questioned by detectives for several hours before ultimately being arrested for drug possession. Joe was labeled a "person of interest" in his wife Laura's death, but never charged. Three years later, the mystery remains: Did Laura jump to her death? Was she pushed – as her family believes? Or, as police appear to have concluded, was it merely a tragic accident?

Joe's own brother, Tim, believes the truth has yet to come out. And when it does, he insists, it will lead straight back to Joe: "There's no way that my brother didn't have a hand in [the murder]." Tim (who recently changed his name to Mitch Finn in an effort to disassociate himself from the family) says he believed his brother's story at first, but changed his mind after visiting the scene of crime. Here's what he told us in July 2013:

Before the murder, what was the relationship between Joe and Laura like?
They had their ups and downs. They had been together and had a family and it wasn't great...but it was OK. Laura was awesome. She endured a lot with Joe. He wasn't physically abusive but definitely mentally abusive to her.

What do you think happened that night?
If he's home, then it's harder to do. He obviously had to pay someone else to do it. They interviewed the limo driver twice...and nobody else. To me it's a situation where he paid someone to do it.

What motive would Joe have in killing her?
He didn't want to be with her anymore. If they got divorced it would be 50-50 [division of assets] and also she's relentless. She wouldn't put up with him. Laura would never

let it rest. So he was thinking of the long-term life. He knows how she is. He told her before if she tried to leave that he'd kill her. Many people have witnessed that. Her sisters have heard that. She had thought about leaving him a few times but would never do it. But he did say that. He said, "You're not getting 50 percent and taking my business and my house." He had a very good life from that business. Very lucrative. It basically pays for him to be a pretend rock star and make people believe that he's somebody that he's not. He wouldn't conform and that's why he wasn't successful [as a musician]. He's very talented, though.

Did Joe tell you about the *AGT* auditions?

I didn't even know he was going to audition. None of us knew anything about it. Usually he makes a big fanfare about everything. He loves to show off. So that's weird that we didn't know. He wanted to audition. He's said that. He's actually really very talented. He writes beautiful music and is a great musician.

What do you remember about that day?

We first heard she was missing, so I traveled from Palm Springs to Rancho Cucamonga to be with the family. We thought it was weird. I don't remember who told us that she was missing. Shortly after that they said she was dead. Joe was in jail for four hours being interrogated so I didn't see him that day. He didn't really talk to me that day about anything because there were so many people around. He called the news people, *TMZ* and all that, himself. The cops wanted to keep it on the down low but Joe was calling all the news people and acting like they were coming after him. Everything he did totally describes sociopath.

You went to live with him after the murder. What was that like?

He'd go out partying every night, after the murder. Every night. Having his band play at his house, instantaneous after the murder. When I told him I went to the Biltmore, he was all freaking out because he knows I'm kind of intuitive. I told him I was close to figuring out who did it. I left it at that and about a week and half later he kicked us out of the house. He's my brother, we were pretty close my whole life. We're both into music, had a lot of common interests. That's why it was weird that we didn't know anything about [him auditioning for] *AGT*. My mom would pay us to go to any gig that he had and then all of a sudden he doesn't want anyone to know he's going?

How has your family treated you since you turned against Joe?

The last time I spoke to anyone from my family was February of [2012]. They all wanted me to shut up. My mom kept sending me money and stuff. At one point she just said, "Joe didn't kill anyone...." I took Joe to small claims court because he told me he'd compensate me for coming to live with him but he didn't do it. I told my mom I was going to call all the press and open my mouth. They got restraining orders against me but they were never able to serve me. I live an hour away and don't have a car. They didn't follow through with it. They didn't want me to talk.... [I'd be happy if] I'd never see him ever again in my entire life. I feel the same way about my mom. I'm gay, and that made me and my mom so close. I was her gay son. We lived with her while we were building her house, she knows Craig my partner very well. It's totally sad. It's a terrible thing.

What about the rest of your family?

My stepdad lives in San Diego and he's kind of out of it. He raised us since we were little. They're not together anymore. I briefed him on everything that happened. My other brother's a sheriff and never said anything. He has cancer and didn't want to get involved. We weren't that tight anyway. He always did his own thing. He follows the law and says the courts will convict him if he did it, but I know he knows [the truth] in his heart, and so does my mom. I have said that to her a million times. He's responsible as much as the people who did it. He commissioned it.

We reached out to Joe through his daughter, Lauren, who declined multiple requests for an interview. "What happened to us is tragic," she said. "I know what my uncle has to say about everything. He has been a meth addict my entire life and nothing he says is true or real." The Finley family did, however, walk the red carpet of the Los Angeles Music Awards less than a month after Laura's death. In an interview with *Real TV Films*, Joe said he and his children "have been hounded by all kinds of media and haven't responded because we choose not to respond to negativity." He described Laura as "the love of my life" and noted: "We have been together since I was 15 years old. We are very, very proud of our family. Regardless of what anybody thinks, we stand united. We are strong. We will not break."

In early 2011, Joe posted a video on *YouTube* titled "Murder at the Biltmore So Out of Touch." It contained a rap written for Laura by their teenage son as well as a scrolling text message from Joe that appeared to be directed to the police:

"The LAPD has been consistently calling Laura's death a tragic accident. At the same time they continue to publicly name me as a person of interest. What if someone were to suggest that her killer was at the crime scene when the police arrived? Even further that he had been watching Laura for some time waiting for his opportunity to strike. As I slept, Laura's voice was forever silenced. Instead of notifying me of this heinous act, the LAPD decided to follow me for hours. Not until I made contact with HOTEL SECURITY did they approach me... I was later stripped down and handcuffed to a chair. Screaming in physical pain and mental anguish. I had agreed to polygraph and never got the opportunity. They instead transferred me to county jail. Since my release, Laura, myself and our children have been pursicuted [sic] by the press. I have been advised not to speak, yet I still do. We will not remain silent. Please do your job and just bring this sick murderer to justice. Maybe then our family can begin to heal."

Joe filed a wrongful death lawsuit in March 2011, claiming the Biltmore's head of security, Arthur Smith, "took a gruesome death picture of [Laura] and disseminated that photo to the general public." He charges that Arthur also showed off the topless photo at the hotel bar for "no investigative purposes, but for macabre effect."

In the suit, Joe says he believes a homeless man or "uninvited third party" walked through an unsecured first-floor door and killed his wife while he slept. According to court documents, he also claims that the hotel failed to warn guests about security issues related to remodeling work being done on the first and second floors. "Transients followed guests into their hotel rooms," the complaint alleges. "Open alcohol bottles, empty food containers, filthy clothing, cigarette butts, wrappers, bottles of urine and dirty blankets" could be seen along the floors that were being remodeled.

He is seeking unspecified damages for emotional distress and invasion of privacy.

Everyone else is just seeking the truth.

CHAPTER 4

Embattled 'Fake Soldier' Tim Poe Weds, Saves Gunshot Victim

TIMOTHY MICHAEL POE – the stuttering soldier accused of lying about military injuries during his season 7 audition – has emerged as a hero after all. The embattled country singer was instrumental in saving the life of a shooting victim in Hurst, Texas, his wife, Carrie, says.

Tim and his bride of just 10 months were unloading a moving truck at their new home in April 2013 when a domestic dispute turned tragic a few hundred feet away. "A lady down the street was shot in the head and the chest," Carrie remembers. "Tim ran straight toward

Timothy Michael Poe and Carrie Morris
Photo: Courtesy (Carrie Morris)

the gunshots and actually saved her life. He gave her first aid until the paramedics got there and then held her head and chest until she got into the ambulance. Tim is very confused about everything that happened to him [in the past], but overall he is a really good person."

Numerous news reports confirmed that Lenar Corales, 32, was arrested and facing attempted capital murder charges for gunning down his ex-wife and her new boyfriend. "I was pretty much unconscious," victim Alicia King, 33, tells us. "I do know that he helped save my life. He provided emergency medical care until the ambulance could come." King, who works as a phlebotomist at a nearby hospital, was shot in the forehead and chest. "My sister was there helping Tim at the same time," she says. "Between him and her, they were the ones that helped keep me alive." None of the official police reports mentioned Tim by name. But that's not entirely surprising, since the war veteran has been keeping a low profile in the wake of his controversial appearance on *America's Got Talent*.

During his televised audition in San Antonio, Texas, Tim told judge Howie Mandel that he endured serious brain damage during an explosion in the line of duty. "I spent 14 years in the military, but my career was ended in 2009," he recounted. "I got hit by a grenade in Afghanistan. It broke my back and gave me a brain injury. That is the reason I stutter a little bit."

Tim said he had volunteered to help clear out buildings and tend to the wounded when the explosion occurred. Video of his story – and near flawless performance of the Garth Brooks hit "If Tomorrow Never Comes" immediately went viral. But within 24 hours, dozens of his fellow soldiers came forward alleging Tim was a fraud. His problems were compounded when a photo he supplied to the show – claiming to be of himself – turned out to be another serviceman.

National Guard spokesperson Kevin Olson publicly discredited Tim's story, telling *AGTNews.com*: "Sgt. Poe's official military records do not indicate that he was injured by a grenade in combat while serving in Afghanistan in 2009, as he reports. The Minnesota National Guard can also confirm that he was not awarded the Purple Heart Medal for wounds sustained in combat."

The very public scandal cost Tim custody of his son and nearly ended his new marriage. In November 2012 the couple appeared on an episode of the *Dr. Phil* show, during which Tim claims he was "ambushed" and is now planning to sue. "When we got back I told him 'I don't know if I can do this anymore,'" Carrie admits. Eventually, she got clearance to speak with one of Tim's attending doctors at Brooke Army Medical Center. "He told me that everything Tim said was true."

We spoke to Tim in June 2013 to get a further update:

What is the latest on the allegations against you?
They found out that the Sergeant that brought me to the medical center ended up telling my unit that I left Afghanistan for an ear infection. He is no longer in the military. My National Guard record didn't match my active duty record, so luckily I had all of this stuff on my medical records... I went on the *Dr. Phil* show because he said he was going to help me clear my name and it was a complete ambush. It was pretty much just to promote his book. So I have been talking to an attorney and I am going to file a lawsuit against the *Dr. Phil* show because I lost my son over that and almost lost my wife. My wife ended up talking to the chief medical doctor over at Brooke Army Medical Center because she didn't believe me about what had happened.

How did you convince her?
She ended up talking to the head of the Traumatic Brain Injury Clinic and he told her that everything I said was true. Now I did go see a doctor and he explained it to me like this: he said that my brain is like Swiss cheese. And what I did was remembered bits and parts of things and filled in that Swiss cheese with American cheese. So some of the stuff that I remembered wasn't actually what happened. So that is about it.

What are you doing now?
I have just kind of tried to stay out of everyone's way. I am going to go back to school. I am going to become a golf teacher. I want to start a program for kids with Cerebral Palsy. Golf is one of those things that disabled kids can play for the rest of their lives. It is not a sport that they have to play against anyone but themselves. So they don't have to worry about the team picking on them. Plus it teaches great hand-eye coordination. So that is my goal.

How long do you have to go to school for?
It is a 17-month program. You have to go through all the PGA stuff. Everything from running a tournament and running a golf course to the building of a golf club to learning all the machines... The next goal is to get your PGA card and become a pro. Once you become a club pro, you can teach golf.

You and Carrie also own another business, Great Guns of Texas...

Yes. It was actually Carrie's dad that started that 25 years ago. I don't really do anything with it.

Do you have any other source of income?

I have my military retirement [fund] and Carrie is becoming a real estate agent.

By the way, congratulations on getting married.

Thank you. June 23 [2013] we had our one-year anniversary.

How was the first year?

Well, considering everything that happened... If we can get through that, we can get through anything.

Did you have a big wedding?

It was pretty decent. We got married at the church. Lots of family and friends. Nothing huge.

Looking back, was there any upside to everything that you went through with the show?

Yeah. It definitely brought Carrie and I closer together. I learned a lot about myself and started seeing a psychiatrist and trying to clear up everything that is messed up inside my head.

Terry Fator and second wife Taylor Makakoa in Las Vegas.

Photo: Shutterstock

CHAPTER 5

Terry Fator Finds Love Again
After Ugly Divorce

NEW BRIDE IS HALF HIS AGE!

TERRY FATOR DIDN'T SPEND MUCH TIME looking in the rear view mirror. Just months after the comic-ventriloquist and *America's Got Talent* champ opened his ongoing show at the Mirage hotel in Las Vegas – a gig that reportedly netted him $100 million – he traded in his wife of 18 years for a sexy on-stage assistant, half his age. Terry's very public and messy divorce from Melinda Fator, 40, wasn't finalized until November 2010 – hours before the 45-year-old entertainer tied the knot with Taylor Makakoa, 22, at Sin City's Lily of The Valley Chapel.

"We are so happy and looking forward to spending the rest of our lives together," Terry told the *Las Vegas Review-Journal*. "We want three kids and Taylor's already named them. She wants a boy, girl, boy." Ironically, children may have been exactly what tore Terry and his first wife apart.

"Throughout our entire marriage, she never wanted children," he confessed to reporter Steve Friess on *TheStripPodcast.com*. "When I got to be about 30, I began to get those feelings of 'Oh my gosh, I wonder what that feels like to have a child, to have children.' That was a big issue. I'm here at the Mirage. I have a stable life. I don't have to travel every day. I can have children. And now the prospect of having a house full of kids and dogs and having a family is the sweetest prospect of all."

During the May 2011 interview, Terry said his marriage had been unraveling for some time – mostly because of Melinda's toxic relationship with his family. "[She] refused to allow them to enjoy the success that I had achieved," he said. "I just really had to make a choice between my family and my mom, my brother and my sister and their families and my ex-wife. I don't regret that decision, haven't regretted it one day because to sit and watch my mom who was not able to take part in any of the *America's Got Talent* stuff because of my ex-wife, who was not able to take part in my first show in Las Vegas because of my ex-wife...to have my mom come to town and look at her face and see how proud she is sitting out there in the crowd."

Terry insists he never cheated on Melinda, and in fact waited "several weeks" after their separation to put the moves on Taylor. "She was looking for a guy who would love her and not cheat on her, and I'm that guy," he said. Their first date was on her 21st birthday.

Melinda has said she was "blind-sided" by Terry's actions and insisted that she and her ex-husband agreed up front not to have children. "He knows the truth; I know the truth; he knows I know the truth," she told Friess in a follow-up interview. "Whatever he chooses to put out there is his business. I've never bad-mouthed him in the press. I will not bad-mouth him in the press."

Terry reportedly met the current Mrs. Fator at an audition for his show – which began at the Las Vegas Hilton – in late 2007. Though Melinda said she wasn't shocked by his new relationship, the comic says he was. "I didn't think there was a chance in Hades that she would be interested [in me]," he told *Las Vegas Review-Journal* gossip columnist Norm Clarke.

The courtship lasted just over one year. On October 17, 2010, Terry planted a four-carat custom-made diamond ring inside a seashell along Haleiwa on the Hawaiian island of Oahu. When he led Taylor to the spot, "She (playfully) kicked it," he told Clark. That's when Terry got down on one knee, picked it up and popped the question.

After the Vegas nuptials, the couple returned to the island for a traditional Hawaiian ceremony with Taylor's extended family. "We are living proof that true love exists," Terry said. "If anyone thinks we're getting married for any other reason than love, we'll see what they have to say on our 50th wedding anniversary."

CHAPTER 6

Nuttin' But Stringz Split Up Amid Baby Mama Drama

Damien Escobar (L) and brother Tourie arrive for the *America's Got Talent Live* show in Las Vegas in 2009

Photo: Splash News

THERE'S BEEN NOTHING BUT DRAMA for Nuttin' But Stringz! Hip-hop fiddlers Tourie and Damien Escobar performed at The White House, the Inauguration of President Barack Obama and on *Dancing with the Stars* after finishing in fourth place during season 3. "You guys do an extraordinary thing," judge Piers Morgan applauded after their semifinal performance. "You bring two totally different worlds together."

But five years later, the act that helped them become international stars is defunct – and the brothers from South Jamaica, Queens find themselves on opposite sides of an ugly child custody fight. "We've taken a break," Damien tells us. "It's like any relationship, you just got to let it breathe. We're always going to be brothers, but at this time in my life we aren't as close as we were." That's the sugarcoated version.

Sources close to the musicians say their falling out is tied in no small part to an ongoing custody and visitation dispute between Tourie and a woman he impregnated while cheating on his wife in 2011. In a 900 word "manifesto" posted on his *Facebook* page, Tourie, 29, says his baby mama, Robyn, has never allowed him to meet their 1-year-old daughter. "You are now responsible for making Ava a fatherless child," he wrote on June 24, 2012. "You are responsible for child abuse and brain washing...Those who have conspired with you to abduct my daughter will all have to face God." It is unclear exactly who Tourie believes is in cahoots with his former side dish, but he does point out in comments below the letter that Robin continues to talk with his brother and mother on a daily basis. "They're no longer my family," he wrote.

Tourie – who has since posted the same letter on different parenting websites – is all too familiar with the effects of growing up in a fatherless home. He and Damien, 27, were raised by their mother, Gloria, a schoolteacher. The boys had little interaction with their own birth father until recently. "My father is a great man," Tourie shares in his missive. "My loyalty lies with him. I will never have anything to do with my biological mother for her role in brainwashing me and talking bad about my father and destroying our relationship when I needed a father in my life."

Luckily, they had music. The Escobar brothers first rosined up their violins in elementary school. "It was a required part of the program at PS 223," Damien told the *New York Post* in 2008. "From there, we fell in love with it." Both earned scholarships and attended the Juilliard School of Music. "Where we come from, hip-hop has a heavy influence," Tourie told the newspaper. "So growing up it was always classical and hip-hop that we had in our minds. When we decided to make music together five years ago, we bridged the two styles and sprinkled in some rock and roll."

Damien briefly attended the Borough of Manhattan Community College, and was a guard on the basketball team. "I played for a year, but got injured and that was God telling me I was supposed to play the violin," he says. The pair dedicated one of their earlier performances on *AGT* to their cousin Mike, who was just 17 when he was "killed in the struggles of being a black man in America," according to Damien.

"Some can get through that and some can't. I hope that our peers – not just black people, but all creeds and races can look at us as inspiration of what we came from and they can do something different in life and achieve (their) goals."

In 2006, Nuttin' But Stringz released its debut CD, *Struggle From The Subway To The Charts.* They were also winners of *Showtime at The Apollo* and earned an Emmy Award while appearing on *AGT*. But, predictably, the show portrayed the duo as if they were showbiz newbies.

"That's how they told that story, and I was like, 'Um...alright. You know what, I'll go with it.'" Damien tells us with a laugh.   "The producers were great on the show. There were a lot of acts that didn't have a great experience on the show but the producers were really, really great. They kind of gave us the freedom to do whatever we wanted to do, to be honest. When it came to creativity, they let us have free reign. A lot of artists (on the show) didn't have that."

Tourie, who also has a young son, is still married and recently moved his family to London. Damien, an unmarried father of two, took most of 2012 off from making music, but released a collection of new songs in May 2013. He is currently pursuing solo projects and hopes to release his first original single in late September 2013. "When you go from being in a well-known group, to going solo, it's like starting from scratch," he says. "[People] didn't know my name. They knew Nuttin' but Stringz, not Damien Escobar. For me it's about starting from scratch and getting a great team together and pushing forward...I haven't been this excited since the beginning of my career. It feels like the beginning again. Towards the end [of Nuttin' But Stringz] I wasn't really happy creating music any more. It was all about money. We made a lot of money. We were millionaires, but it wasn't about music anymore. It was just about a job and making money. I hated that. I've fallen in love with music again."

Here's what else Damien told us in August 2013:

Did you ever regret your decision to do the show?
Absolutely not, that was the greatest decision I ever made in my life. It opened up so many doors. It gave us worldwide recognition. *AGT* gets licensed out to every other country. It kept happening over and over again in every country. We became the thing that was talked about in every country.

Did you have a regular job before the show?

I've been making money from music [performing on] the subway since I was 10. But making really good money was 2005, that's when I moved out of my momma's basement and got my own place. I wasn't rich, I was just a working musician, but I was paying my bills and building.

Were you surprised when you were eliminated from *AGT*?

I personally don't know how we lost. There's certain things I'm bound and gagged and I can't say. We were number one by two million votes every single week. So how did we lose? I knew we weren't going to win because of legal issues. Us understanding entertainment the way that we did, there were certain things that we just wouldn't agree to. Did producers tell us we weren't going to win? Absolutely not. But everything happens for a reason. It turned out to be the greatest thing in the world that we didn't win because when you win they own you, and you're bound by the contract. We were lucky enough that they didn't pick up any options for the show, we put our own thing together, did the world tour, and sold a million records. It worked out and I didn't owe Simon Cowell any money. There are a lot of artists that owe Simon a lot of money, and we didn't owe him anything so it was great.

What was your craziest post-*AGT* gig?

We did a concert for professional bull riders, after the *AGT Live* series. And we got a shit ton of money. It was the biggest check we ever got. We were so excited. It was like $80,000. While we were on set doing that gig, we get a call from our agent, saying they want us to go to Dubai to do a concert for the Royal Family's daughter's birthday. That night! They sent a private plane—not a jet, a full plane—picked us up and flew us to Dubai and paid us $500,000 to do a 20 minute concert! The prince of Dubai was there and he said 'My birthday is next week, I want you guys to come back.' So they gave us another half million dollars to come back. We were rock stars, we went crazy for a couple years.

What are your career goals for the year?

I want to win a Grammy. I've never won a Grammy and I'm hoping this record will turn some heads and push the envelope on music. I want to be at the Grammys. They're coming up in February 2014. We'll see what happens there. But by this time next year I want to be the first instrumentalist in the Top 40. I've done some pretty amazing things as far as breaking barriers and setting trends but that's something that hasn't happened yet. So that's the goal.

Season 1

(June 21, 2006 - August 17, 2006)

Host: Regis Philbin

Judges: David Hasselhoff, Piers Morgan, Brandy Norwood

Winner: Bianca Ryan (singer)

"I think we are all thirsting for some good old-fashioned talent. The novelty acts are fun and they get people talking, but there has got to be more than that."

- Regis Philbin, 2006

SOME PEOPLE NEVER THOUGHT David Hasselhoff was a very good singer – but he sure can spot talent. "That 11 year-old girl, Bianca, there is nobody that can beat her," he predicted in an interview with TV critics a full month before the season 1 finale. "When she sang I had to literally turn away because I had never seen anything like that. She raised the bar." The pre-teen singing sensation is all grown up now. So is the show that made her famous. Since its debut seven years ago, *America's Got Talent* has had more facelifts than a Real Housewife of Beverly Hills. All three judges have been replaced. So has the host. Twice.

In season 1, open call auditions were held in New York, Los Angeles, Chicago and Atlanta, but all the performances were filmed on a soundstage at Paramount Studios in Hollywood. Producers simply changed the backdrop behind the stage each week to give the illusion that they were filming in each city. There was no Vegas Week. Those passing through to the next round were divided into groups of 15. From each group, 10 of those acts were selected to perform for the judges. At the end of each episode, the judges picked one of the 10 to advance to the finals. A second act was voted through by America's vote.

The second and third place finishers were each awarded a 2007 Dodge Caliber RT wagon.

FINALISTS

BIANCA RYAN (Winner)
Singer, 11

Let's be honest: who *didn't* think the tiny redhead with the big booming voice was going to win? Her very first audition – a roof-raising rendition of *Dreamgirls* anthem "And I Am Telling You I'm Not Going" – was the gold standard by which every other performance was judged during season 1. It also quickly became one of the most watched music videos ever on *YouTube*. Bianca [who is named after Mick Jagger's ex-wife] "is potentially one of the best singers I have ever heard in my life," executive producer Simon Cowell professed just weeks before signing the young wunderkind to a multi-year recording deal in September 2006. It's a deal that almost never happened.

Bianca Ryan in 2013

In fact, Bianca admits she nearly walked away from *AGT* without belting out a single note. "I went to the audition [in New York] and sat down and there was actually a lady with a beard who was juggling these sticks that were on fire," she recalled in a 2012 interview with *The Scene*. "My dad said 'I think we should leave.' And I was like 'Yeah, this is getting weird.' Then we saw the prize was for $1 million and I was like 'I think I can deal with this lady for a little bit...'"

Bianca – the only minor and only female to ever claim the show's top prize – was the second of five children born to Shawn and Janette Ryan of suburban Philadelphia. She began singing Hilary Duff songs into a hairbrush in her bedroom at age 8. Within a year, she auditioned for the touring cast of *Annie* and performed "The Impossible Dream" from *Man of La Mancha* on *Star Search* (but was eliminated by a 10 year-old gospel singer named Spensha Baker).

"My dream is to be a famous singer and hopefully have my own TV show and not just 15 minutes of fame," she told *AGT* viewers in a pre-taped interview. But after the show, the singer – whose ancestry is Irish, German, Italian and Japanese – chose to focus on singing instead. Bianca's self-titled debut CD was recorded in just two weeks, immediately following her victory and was released November 14, 2006. Two holiday-themed EPs quickly followed.

Bianca returned to the studio in 2013, just before her 19th birthday, to begin work on a new collection of songs. She is also set to make her acting debut in the independent movie *We Be Kings*. In 2013, Bianca will begin her freshman year at University of the Arts in downtown Philadelphia. "I'll be studying jazz and vocal performance," she tells us. "I got accepted to Drexel, but I realized that I kind of want to stay involved in the arts and people who kind of have the same passion as me."

Though she continues to live with her family, Bianca says she has recently been yearning to spend more time in Hollywood. "I would really like to go out there and do some auditions and meet a lot of people," she says. "I fly out to L.A. and go to New York a lot to do a couple of performances, but I don't usually stay for long. So I would love to go and live out there temporarily, maybe for a summer or something."

❖ ❖ ❖ ❖

THE MILLERS (Runner-Up)
Musical Brothers, 12 – 21

Piers Morgan brought young L.D. Miller to tears. "There comes a time in every potential superstar's career when you've got to make very tough decisions," he told the pre-teen harmonica sensation in front of a live television audience. "You are not going to like this, but I think you have got to sack your brother." Piers got it wrong. The blues duo from Lafayette, Indiana ended up riding their talent and boyish charm all the way to the finals, posing the biggest threat to eventual winner Bianca Ryan. "It's kind of hard to split brothers up," Cole tells us. In fact The Millers – who recently shortened their name to Miller – have since added their older brother, Clayton, 31, to the act as well.

Cole Miller, L.D. Miller and Clayton Miller
Photo: Courtesy (Miller)

After years of touring – "we were doing 250 shows a year before *AGT*," Cole says – the summer of 2013 was about taking a break from music. L.D., now 19, spent several weeks as a white water rafting guide in Montana, while Cole, 28, enjoyed quality time with his newborn daughter, Stella Rose.

"I work at a motocross track when I am home," Cole says. "I do track work. I groom tracks and make them pretty. I couldn't always do a lot of actual racing because you can't really break bones and play music. But I have always loved motocross. I do a lot of excavating work. I like playing in the dirt."

L.D., meanwhile, continues to hone his harmonica skills every chance he gets. "He always has a harmonica in his pocket," Cole says. "He is constantly playing guitar, bass, synthesizers. We even had a dub step band on the side for fun. But L.D. plays everything. He's been doing it since 5 years old. He's never stopped. He's almost got a whole career under his belt and he is only 19. John Popper [of Blues Traveler] was our celebrity coach on the show. We still hang out with him and play with him. John loves L.D. They are really good friends."

All the brothers are looking forward to creating – and sharing – new music beginning this fall. So far they have held off on releasing any CDs, Cole says. "We haven't had anything that we felt was good enough. We are just trying to do it right."

◆ ◆ ◆ ◆

ALL THAT! (Runner-Up)

Clogging Group

The five male cloggers – who competed against each other for years as solo dancers – first teamed up in 1999. "The name speaks for itself. You guys were all that and more,"

Brandy Norwood declared at their very first audition. David Hasselhoff agreed, and predicted "I think you guys have a shot at winning this whole thing." They came close – then decided to try again a few years later.

"I don't think I have seen an all male – and burly, tattooed males – clogging (group) before," Sharon Osbourne said when the group reappeared on the *AGT* stage during season 7. But some eagle-eyed TV critics – including Andy Denhart of *RealityBlurred.com* – knew something looked awfully familiar. Since 2006 there had been 100 percent turnover of the judges and host. Still, Denhart wrote: "It's impossible to believe that no producers nor network executives noticed that they have an act that almost won the damn show. It's like bringing back Justin Guarini on *American Idol* and never mentioning that he placed second, although that's quite unfair to Justin, since people actually remember him." (The guys were ultimately eliminated by the judges in the Top 48).

The current lineup of ALL THAT! – Mike Curtis, Delohn Collins, Brian Staggs, Mark Clifford, Kenneth Fithen, Brad Berry, Harrison Barnes, Drake Elkin, and Joel Harrison – perform nightly at the Carolina Opry Theatre in Myrtle Beach, South Carolina.

Mike credited much of their popularity to AGT, when he updated us on the group in August 2013.

How many of the original members are still in the group?

Four of the members from season 1 are still with the group. Those are actually the four original members of the group. All eight of the guys that appeared on season 7 are still with the group and we have recently added three new members bringing the total to 11!

Why did you decide to try out a second time?

Since season 1, our dance and our group have evolved in a huge way. Not only has the footwork gotten a ton better, but our imaginations have been running wild! We had so many new ideas that we were dying for America to see. What better way than to make a second run on the biggest talent show in the world?

Some people thought you "cheated" by coming back a second time.

The people that said we were breaking rules, just didn't know the rules very well. There was an act on against us in season 7 that had just made the Top 48 the previous year! They must have had a friend on the show and we looked to be a threat to them! [Laughs] Seriously, we don't let that type of stuff bother us. People are gonna have their opinions and there is nothing you can do about it. It just gives us the motivation to go that much harder the next time we hit the stage!

Any personal milestones since the last time we saw you?

Brian is getting married this September [2013] and Joel just had a beautiful baby boy. Both huge blessings. The other guys haven't changed much.

What was the best post-*AGT* gig you've had?

We have been invited to New York City to perform live in the Macy's Thanksgiving Day Parade! That's huge —2.3 million people will line the streets of New York to watch the parade live and more than 20 million will watch on TV! We can't wait.

What's next for ALL THAT!?

We have several more corporate gigs lined up and several teaching gigs. We also are trying to land a part in the upcoming movie *Step Up 5*! Keep your fingers crossed for us!

Jerry Springer hosted seasons 2 and 3 before leaving to appear on Broadway. He continues to host the *America's Got Talent Live* tour.

Photo: S_Buckley (Shutterstock)

Season 2
(June 5, 2007 - August 21, 2007)

Host: Jerry Springer

Judges: David Hasselhoff, Piers Morgan, Sharon Osbourne

Winner: Terry Fator (ventriloquist)

Terry Fator
Photo: Helga Esteb / Shutterstock

NBC AND CREATOR SIMON COWELL headed into season 2 with a new host, a new judge and the first of many major tweaks to the show's constantly evolving format. Sharon Osbourne - Simon's partner in crime on the U.K. version of *X Factor* – was tapped to replace Brandy Norwood at the judges' table. The R&B singer voluntarily stepped down after she was involved in a multi-vehicle accident that took the life of motorist Awatef Aboudihaj. Facing a multi-million dollar wrongful death lawsuit and the possibility of jail time, "[Brandy] felt she couldn't give the new season the attention and commitment it deserved," her publicist announced in a statement.

Regis Philbin also decided to walk away from the program, citing a grueling weekly commute between his home in New York and the studio in Los Angeles. On March 6, 2007, he was replaced by tabloid talk show host (and former Cincinnati mayor) Jerry Springer. "Jerry is the perfect ringmaster to harness all the incredibly diverse talent under one big tent," the network gushed in its formal announcement. "To say the least, he is known for presiding over an unpredictable show where the unexpected is the typical order of each day."

NBC had originally planned to air season 2 on Sunday nights at 8:00 P.M. beginning in January 2007 but opted instead to give the time slot to another competition series, *Grease: You're The One That I Want*. The premiere of *AGT* was pushed back until June 5.

FORMAT/RULE CHANGES

For the first time, all hopefuls advancing past the first audition were sent to polish up their acts at "boot camp" in Las Vegas. There, they were separated into two categories: music and variety. The judges then chose 35 acts from both groups to make up a "short list." Later, without any additional performances, they cut the field down to just 20 acts for the live shows.

In one other minor change, the judges abandoned the white check marks, which were used to show support for an act they liked. They were still permitted to sound their "X" buzzers at any time.

BROADCAST LOCATIONS

Live auditions were held in Dallas, Los Angeles, Chicago and New York.

The very first Vegas Week "boot camp" took place at Planet Hollywood Hotel and Casino (though contestants were housed at a nearby Sheraton). A total of 70 acts made it to the Las Vegas callbacks. Twenty of them were put through to the live shows in Los Angeles to be voted on by the public.

The live performance shows took place at CBS Studio Center in Los Angeles.

FINALISTS

TERRY FATOR (Winner)

Ventriloquist, 42

Eight months before he emerged as the act to beat on *America's Got Talent*, Texan Terry Fator swung through Las Vegas to test his act out for a trio of the city's top producers and talent bookers. "All three of them told me I was not Las Vegas material and I would not play Las Vegas," he recalled in an interview with *Atlantic City Insider*. "It was very disheartening."

Terry, who discovered magic at age eight and ventriloquism at 10, had been relegated to the fringe of show business for more than two decades and was desperately in need a break

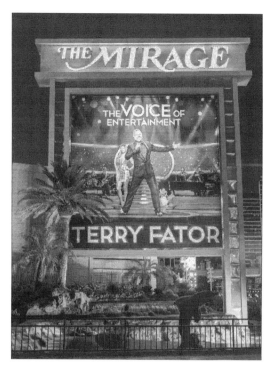

Photo: Jeffrey J. Coleman / Shutterstock

"I was doing fairs, festivals, real small town stuff," he told Larry King in 2010. "Since I was a ventriloquist they always looked at me as a kids act, so they would put me next to the petting zoo or put me with a bunch of clowns. It was always the worst stage in the whole fair. When I got close to about 40 years old, I said to myself, 'I guess the whole thing about being rich and famous is a pipe dream. Nobody is ever going to care about a 40 year-old ventriloquist.' And then *America's Got Talent* came along and changed everything."

Terry was one of the thousands of hopefuls who waited in line for hours to audition with a bagful of hopes and dreams. "I thought I would get on two or three episodes and it would raise people's awareness of what I do," he recalled. "I never in a million years thought I would win it." Neither did a very skeptical David Hasselhoff, when Terry walked on stage for the first time with his singing puppet Emma Taylor. "Oh no, not a ventriloquist," the judge moaned. But after hearing Terry and his puppet belt out Etta James' "At Last," David was sold. "I thought your act was absolutely brilliant," he praised. And Piers Morgan added: "I have genuinely never seen a ventriloquist do impressions of singers. Ever. So I thought that was quite amazing."

"I thought I would get on two or three episodes and it would raise people's awareness of what I do. I never in a million years thought I would win."

- Terry Fator

Terry — a Liberty College graduate and second cousin of *American Idol* finalist Chris Sligh — had been preparing for that moment for more than 20 years. His fascination with ventriloquism began in fourth grade, when he discovered a book called *Ventriloquism for Fun & Profit* by Paul Winchell at his school library.

"When we were kids, my parents owned a janitorial business and when we were emptying trash and vacuuming floors," he told the talk show host. "I decided it was a good time to practice ventriloquism. So I would sing to the radio, but I would do it without moving my lips. I found a little puppet at Sears. It was $20. My mom paid for half and I paid for half. And I started doing little shows for kids around my school and my church. And I decided when I was 13 or 14 that I wanted to be known as one of the great ventriloquists." But there were detours along the way.

In the late 1980s Terry briefly fronted a rock band called Freedom Jam, which performed at hundreds of high schools and middle schools across the United States and Canada. At 23, he became the lead singer of Texas The Band, which featured an early appearance by his popular puppet Walter T. Airedale. The band reportedly turned down a major record deal when Terry refused to cut impressions from their act.

After taking top prize on *AGT*, Terry was signed to a long-term deal in Las Vegas that was reported to be worth $100 million. His second wife Taylor, 25, is his on stage assistant. *Terry Fator: The VOICE of Entertainment* continues to play nightly at the Mirage Hotel and Casino in a showroom bearing his name.

CAS HALEY (Runner-Up)

Reggae Singer, 26

Cas Haley performs at the Taste of Dallas in 2007
Photo: Jeromy via Wikimedia Commons)

He sang "Walking On The Moon" better than Sting. At least that's what Piers Morgan thought. "I was flattered, but I think he's wrong," Cas says, looking back. "I think Sting sings that song way better than I do. Sting is one of my all-time idols so that was definitely a big confidence builder to hear him say that."

Not that he needed an ego boost: Cas – a Texas native with a beachy reggae sound – never had a backup plan for his life. Since age 12 he has always (and only) wanted to be a musician. "Most people don't know what the hell they want to do," he tells us. "I stuck with music through thick and thin. I always have faith that the best is ahead of me." So far, so good. His debut CD, *Cas Haley*, became Billboard's eighth-best-selling reggae release of 2008. Two years and several collaborations later, Cas signed with Easy Star Records and released a second album, *Connection*, which debuted at number two. He continues to tour almost non-stop and recently made his first trip to Europe to promote his May 2013 release, *La Si Dah*.

Back at home, the singer lives a "slow-paced country life" near Paris, Texas with wife Cassie and their two children (Eben, 7, and Nolah, 3) in a house he helped build. Since appearing on *AGT*, Cas says he has finally achieved the dream of supporting his family as a musician. Now, he's helping others do the same.

"I love being a mentor and talking to people and helping young kids map out what they want to do," he says.

BUTTERSCOTCH (3rd Place)

Beat-boxer/Singer, 21

Some girls sing. Others beat-box. Butterscotch does both at the same time. "You were like a one girl show," David Hasselhoff remarked after her roof-raising audition performance of Donna Summer's "Love To Love You Baby." "The sounds coming out of you are effortless, unbelievable. You are not *one* of the best beat-boxers we've ever seen, I think you are *the* best I have ever seen."

Butterscotch
Photo: Courtesy

Antoinette Clinton – who takes her stage name from a song she wrote in high school about candy – has spent the past six years touring the world and performing with world-renowned artists like Wyclef Jean, George Benson and will.i.am. But recently, she has put artistic ambitions on the back burner to spend a little more time caring for her own well-being. "I've been taking a break because some crazy stuff is happening," she told us, offering only cryptic details. "I just have to remember to take care of myself. All these singers or celebs or actors, they get too mixed, too deep. The magic number is 27 [years-old] and I don't want to get mixed in to anything that's potentially harmful to me or my career and my health. It may slow down the process, but it's important. It's a temporary recovery thing I need to do, but I'm planning on getting back as soon as I'm good."

Since her time on *AGT,* the northern California native (and first-ever female international beat-boxing champion) has earned fans all over the world – particularly in Germany, where fans are often shocked by her outgoing onstage persona.

"People think they know you and there's only a part of me on TV," she says. "[AGT] portrayed me as super shy. I am quiet but I'm not anti-social. So people would come up to me and say, 'You really came out of your shell since the show' and I'm like 'I was never in a shell!'

The daughter of a piano teacher, Butterscotch also plays the flute, bass, guitar and saxophone. "Through music, I love myself because I love what I create," she revealed on the show. "[In] high school, I kind of went through a hard time with finding myself and being happy with who I was. [That's when] I began getting into music."

Butterscotch – a beat-box mentor on MTV's *Made* – embarked on her first tour with rapper Pigeon John in 2007. In 2011, she released the single, "Perfect Harmony" and has lent her voice and also collaborated on several recordings – including a cover of "Stand By Me" – with fellow finalist Cas Haley.

❖ ❖ ❖ ❖

JULIENNE IRWIN (4ᵗʰ Place)
Country Singer, 14

Julienne Irwin
Photo: Wikimedia Commons

The Bel Air, Maryland ninth grader – and die-hard Baltimore Orioles fan – always dreamed of being on television. "When I was little I would pretend I was the meteorologist," she remembers. Now 20 and a junior at Nashville's Belmont University, Julienne, a broadcast journalism minor, is finally getting to see the TV news business up close. "I have been interning at WBAL, Baltimore's NBC affiliate," tells us. "I am working at the assignment desk. I always felt like I need to have something to fall back on. Nashville and music is very competitive and I couldn't put all my eggs in one basket."

But Julienne – who told the judges she only sang "in her bedroom" before *AGT* – is not ready to abandon her dreams of becoming a county music superstar. "I live for country music," she wrote on her personal website, *JulienneIrwin.com*. "If it didn't exist, a huge piece of my life would be missing. It wakes me up in the morning and puts me to sleep at night, and it's on my mind 24 hours a day."

Julienne wowed the judges at her New York audition with an a capella rendition of the LeAnn Rimes hit "How Do I Live?" "There is an honesty about you and a sincerity and an innocence that can be honed into something very powerful," David Hasselhoff told her. "You are really raw, but you have got talent." The whole experience of performing for America was "like a big adventure," Julienne says. "I took it seriously, but I don't think I realized at the time how big *America's Got Talent* was. I don't think I realized what I was a part of."

Months after reaching the finale, Julienne was invited to tour for several weeks with Kenny Rogers – one of the highlights of her career. She also belted out the "Star Spangled Banner" in front of 140,000 Nascar fans in 2008.

MORE FAN FAVORITES

JONNY COME LATELY (Top 20)

Rockabilly Band, 15

The high school sophomores from Claremont, California were looking for any excuse they could find to ditch school – so they snuck out and waited in line for 10 hours to audition for *AGT* producers. Their truancy paid off! Even through the quartet had only been together for one year, the young ambassadors of rockabilly, ska

Jonny Come Lately
Photo: Courtesy (Jonny Come Lately)

and soul – Izzy Loya (guitar), Angela Ross (drums), Adrian Johnson (harp/guitar) and Julian Johnson (stand up bass) managed to win over the judges and advance to the live shows.

Five years later, the best friends are still making music together. "They've added a soulful female singer to the lineup," their manager, Patricia Loya says. "The band has infused more ska, R&B, and soul influences to their music, calling their original pieces part of the 'Skankabilly Soul' genre."

Two of the band members, Izzy Loya and Angela Ross, recently graduated from college: Izzy with a B.A. in broadcast news from Pepperdine University and Angela with a double major in economics and sociology from the University of Southern California.

"We still get emails and *Facebook* comments from all over the world [from fans] saying they loved the band's performances on *AGT*," Patricia says. "The band has a large following in Malaysia, for some reason."

Season 3

(June 17, 2008 – October 1, 2008)

Host: Jerry Springer

Judges: David Hasselhoff, Piers Morgan, Sharon Osbourne

Winner: Neal E. Boyd (opera singer)

Host Jerry Springer and the *AGT* judges with season 3 finalists, The Wright Kids.

Photo: Courtesy (Wright Family)

THE GANG WAS ALL BACK as *AGT* rolled into its third season looking bigger and more spectacular than ever. With no changes to the host or judges, producers were free to focus on moving the live auditions to large theaters across America for the very first time. "The number of acts auditioning increased three fold over last season," Jerry Springer revealed shortly before the premiere.

Season 3 again featured a Las Vegas boot camp round, but this time acts were divided into more groups: ventriloquists, female singers, male singers, opera, instrumental music, bands, and other types of variety acts. Of the 113 acts that made it to Vegas, 19 of these acts were eliminated without even being given a chance to perform. The remaining 94 acts were eventually trimmed down to the final 40, which advanced to the live shows.

BROADCAST LOCATIONS

Live auditions were held in New York, Los Angeles, Dallas, Atlanta and Chicago. Vegas Week call back auditions took place at Planet Hollywood Casino Resort. Live performance episodes originated from Universal Studios in Hollywood.

FINALISTS

NEAL E. BOYD (Winner)

Opera Singer, 32

Neal E. Boyd
Photo: Courtesy

The baby-faced opera sensation had just one question after being named champion of season 3: "What has happened to my life?" Thunderous cheers...sudden riches...accolades from personal hero Placido Domingo! It was all a bit overwhelming for Neal – an AFLAC insurance salesman from Sikeston, Missouri – who didn't even try to fight back his tears of joy.

The win – much like Neal's entire journey on *AGT* – was inspired by his mother, Esther, who worked for years at an accounting firm to put food on the table for her two sons. The singer and his older brother, Michael, were raised in a modest two bedroom home in a racially divided mid-western neighborhood where it wasn't advisable to leave your doors unlocked at night. Their father, Michael, (who is black) left the family before Neal was born to pursue singing and a minor league baseball career with the Los Angeles Dodgers. Esther (who is white) would pick up shifts at Walmart during the holiday season so she could afford to buy Christmas presents. "She had to be the mother and the father," Neal says. "We have talked to [my father] over the phone since I was a child, and he has visited off and on since I was 12. He and Mom get along well, but they've both moved on with their lives. I still talk to him for advice to this day."

In 2012, the Boyd family was heartbroken when they learned Esther was diagnosed with breast cancer. "My mother is in remission as of June [2013]," Neal tells us exclusively. "She is a very resilient woman."

The entertainer – who refers to himself as "Half-rican American" – discovered opera by accident at age 13. As the story goes, his brother brought home a CD of The Three Tenors for a homework assignment. The sound of "Nessun dorma!" began to resonate through the house and Neal was instantly hooked! He went on to join the high school choir. Then came state competitions, festivals and local concerts before he eventually earned a music scholarship to Southeast Missouri State University. "I don't wanna say that some of the other singers tended to not like him as much," lifelong pal Shawn Taylor told *St. Louis* magazine. "But it's kinda hard to shine when you're standing next to the sun."

Neal's solo career kicked into high gear when he was invited to sing at the funeral of Missouri Governor Mel Carnahan in 2000. He has since shared his vocal gifts with so many state and national officials that even former President George W. Bush exclaimed: "Mr. Boyd, you are the Voice of Missouri, indeed!"

But that voice was nearly silenced in 2002 when doctors in Boston discovered partial paralysis affecting one of his vocal cords. Neal, who was enrolled in a graduate program at Boston's prestigious New England Conservatory of Music was under doctors orders to rest his voice for six months – which quickly became six years.

Neal has balanced out his love of music with a more than passing interest in politics. After earning one of his degrees in political science, he worked for several local politicians including Missouri senators Kit Bond and John Ashcroft. Other jobs were less glamorous. Just two years before appearing on America's biggest talent competition, Neal was named assistant manager of an Enterprise Rent-A-Car branch in Cape Girardeau. "It was awesome. I had the best time of my life. But unfortunately

I wasn't makin' enough money. And I had a girlfriend [Heather Tomko] I wanted to marry. And I wanted to have a family and kids, so I threw caution to the wind, opposed my family's opinion and went into commission sales, where it was all about personality. Within a couple of months I was one of the top salesmen in the company along with my friend Justin Cox." Today the pair are business partners in the Cox and Boyd insurance brokerage. Neal – who has lost more than 75 pounds since appearing on the show – released his debut CD, *My American Dream*, in 2009 and continues to perform two weekends out of every month. In 2012, he ran as a Republican for a seat in the Missouri House of Representatives, but lost to Democrat Steve Hodges by a two to one margin. Neal is currently in the studio working on an album of Christmas music.

◈ ◈ ◈ ◈

ELI MATTSON (Runner-up)

Singer-Pianist, 26

Eli Mattson still feels a twitch of panic every time he hears the thumping *America's Got Talent* theme music. "That meant you had to be TV-ready," he remembers. "It still makes my heart jump

Photo: Courtesy (Eli Matson)

a little." The singer-pianist from Door County, Wisconsin – just 26 when he auditioned in Chicago – was one of the most memorable contestants of season three. His performance of "Walking In Memphis" left Sharon Osbourne wondering why he hadn't already signed a record deal and Piers Morgan exclaiming: "This show is about finding the next great star in America who can take their moment. You just took your moment. You've got talent!" Despite comparisons to a young Billy Joel ("You tell a story and it comes from the heart," David Hasselhoff said), Eli never quite accomplished the goals many believed he would obtain in the music business. In 2012, the married father of two was forced to put his rock-n-roll dreams on indefinite hold due to a painful spinal condition. But, he insists, "Someday I'd like to get back on the piano."

DONALD BRASWELL II (4th Place)

Opera Singer, 45

Donald Braswell performs in Kerrville, Texas in 2009
Photo: James Avery (via Wikimedia Commons)

Things could have ended up much worse for the multi-lingual opera sensation, who was nearly booed off the stage during his first live audition. Luckily, Donald turned the ship around mid-way through Josh Groban's anthem "You Raise Me Up" and had the crowd cheering for "Vegas! Vegas!"

Donald was, in many ways, the perfect *AGT* contestant. He brought seasoned vocal skills, movie star good looks and a backstory that jerked tears from even the most jaded viewer's eyes. The youngest of four children, Donald was just 32 and on the brink of international fame, when injuries from a hit-and-run traffic accident left him unable to speak for a year. At the time, doctors believed he would never be able to sing professionally again.

Though Donald was sent home during Vegas Week, he eventually returned as the show's first ever "wild card" act when the Russian Bar Trio suffered an injury and was forced to withdraw from the competition.

His favorite *AGT* memory? "We were doing one of the rehearsals - I think it was for the Top 10 - and this guy came down with a white T-shirt and it was Simon Cowell! He walked up to me and shook my hand and said 'You are fantastic. They were idiots to let you go in Vegas.' And I was like, 'Wow, that was cool.'" Braswell, a father of three, is now completely recovered from his injury. He continues to perform concerts as part of a trio of tenors and travel as a motivational speaker. He hopes to have his fifth CD out in time for Christmas, 2013.

◆ ◆ ◆ ◆

QUEEN EMILY (5th Place)

Church Singer, 40

Queen Emily In Las Vegas
Photo: Courtesy (Emily David)

"Queen Emily" David nearly blew off her *AGT* audition at the very last moment. "I remember I got tickets for the Greyhound bus to go to [Los Angeles], and then I changed my mind," she says. "It was my younger daughter that encouraged me to go. She said, 'Mom, do you already have those tickets? Then you need to go.'"

That advice – and a handful of knockout performances in front of a national television audience – changed Emily's life forever. Within months of reaching the finale, the church singer and foster parent from Stockton, California had inked a deal with Malaco Records and a starring role on the Las Vegas Strip. "I did 10 months in *Menopause the Musical*," she tells us. "One of the things you dream of is having your name in lights and I did it. My name was on one of those big signs!" The glitter and glamour of Sin City seemed worlds away from Emily's hand-to-mouth existence years earlier on the streets of Houston. "I remember as a little girl in the projects, I knew that singing was what I wanted to do," Emily shared during her first appearance on *AGT*. "But raising my children as a single parent was very difficult. So I had to give up my dream to care for them. It has been a financial struggle not having anywhere to live, not having enough to eat – while at the same time trying to live a life in front of your children where they could still be proud of you. If I had to do it all over again, I would. But I am ready to get back into singing. So many times I thought it would never happen for me."

And then it did. Her audition song – Aretha Franklin's "Chain of Fools" – wowed the judges and brought the studio audience to its feet. "You have got a great chance of winning *America's Got Talent*," Sharon Osbourne predicted.

But instant fame – especially during her time in Las Vegas – wasn't exactly as she'd imagined. "I spent a lot of time by myself," Emily remembers. "I'd fly one of my daughters in to keep me company, or I'd fly home to Oakland to go to church. There's an upside and a downside to all the fame. I had the money and my name up in lights, but I wasn't in a relationship at the time so I didn't really have anyone to share it with. After smiling for the cameras, I'd go back to this huge suite all by myself. It can be a lonely life."

Like many performers who found overnight success on reality TV, Emily says people came out of the woodwork looking for handouts. "You begin to get a lot of phone calls, and you really don't know who to trust," she says. "People called me names, because they thought I thought I was better than everyone I guess. But that wasn't the case at all. I worked hard for that money. I got off my behind and did what I needed to do, made a life for myself, but a lot of people didn't see it that way."

Emily – who now has a boyfriend – recently moved back to Houston, where she continues to sing in a church choir, attend bible study and plan her next career moves. "Right now I'm working with a *Cirque du Soliel* music producer," she says. "We're getting ready to do an album together."

MORE FAN FAVORITES

THE WRIGHT KIDS (Top 10)

Family Band, 6 - 10

The Wright Kids: Baruch, Levi, Selah and Sage (L-R)
Photo: Courtesy (Wright Family)

These kids are all-Wright! Singing siblings Sage (17), Baruch (14) and Levi (11) have a new addition to their family bluegrass band: sister Selah (9). "She has been performing with them for the past three or four years," their father, Barry Wright, tells us. "She is doing more lead vocals. This is her first year singing harmony. When Sage goes away to college next year, Selah will keep that three part harmony going."

Before auditioning for the *AGT* judges in Dallas, the talented young musicians from Rocky Mountain, Virginia were performing for tips and ice cream at their neighborhood soda shop. The first incarnation of their group included older brother Mason (24), who is now married. The younger kids tried out for the show on their own, not long after he left the band to attend college. "We just did that [audition] kind of on a whim," Barry says. "They sounded quite good, just the three of them." David Hasselhoff agreed, boasting: "You guys have got a huge and long and fantastic career ahead of you and I wish you nothing but the best because you've obviously got talent."

The highlight of their *AGT* experience? Meeting the Hoff, of course! "He signed our copy of the Spongebob movie," Baruch says. "When we went to audition in Dallas we had him sign it because we saw him back stage." Afterwards, Barry remembers, "He was showing off and he hit the floor and gave us 10 push ups!"

Each of the Wright children began music lessons as soon as they were old enough to hold a violin. "My wife and I enjoy music but neither of us are musicians," Barry says. "It just came real naturally to them." Music is now a part of the kids' daily routine. After receiving home schooling, they each practice for about 30 minutes a day on their own and then spend another hour on group rehearsals. "Sage, Baruch and Levi are all classical musicians," Barry boasts. "Each of them are members of the Roanoke Youth Symphony Orchestra. Sage is the concert master. All four are also members of the YMCA swim team."

In 2011, The Wright Kids released their first self-produced CD, comprised entirely of pop cover songs ("Sir Duke," "Stand By Me," "Rockin' Robin.") They hope to release another, Barry says, "in the next couple of years."

Season 4

(June 23, 2009 – September 16, 2009)

Host: Nick Cannon

Judges: Piers Morgan, Sharon Osbourne, David Hasselhoff

Winner: Kevin Skinner (country singer)

Simon Cowell and the *AGT* cast talk to the press in Los Angeles before the start of season 4.
Photo: Splash News

I T WAS NICK CANNON IN, David Hasselhoff out. As Nick took over hosting duties from Jerry Springer – who left to join the cast of Chicago on Broadway – The Hoff was enjoying what would be his last season at the judge's table. His departure from the show after four seasons followed a stint in rehab and an embarrassing drunken video leaked on the Internet by his teenage daughter. Reports in the British media said NBC execs chose not to pick up his option for season 5 out of concern over his personal demons. But David added a different spin, telling *People*: "It's been a rewarding experience and now I'm thrilled to be able to follow my dream to do my own TV show, which will be announced very shortly."

Season 4 offered only subtle changes to the show's format. A total of 160 acts were passed through to Vegas, but unlike in previous seasons, they were not permitted to perform a second time. Instead, judges relied on video of their auditions to cut the field down to 40. At the conclusion of the second "Vegas Verdicts" episode, executive producer Simon Cowell is heard calling the judges as they fly back to Los Angeles. He said he was unhappy too many talented acts were left behind. As a result, two acts are brought back as "wild cards" during each of the four quarterfinal performance episodes.

BROADCAST LOCATIONS

Televised auditions were held in New York, Houston, Los Angeles, Miami, Chicago and Seattle-Tacoma. (Auditions were also held in Boston, Atlanta and Washington, D.C., but were not shown on TV). Vegas Week call back auditions – renamed "Las Vegas Verdicts" – again took place at Planet Hollywood Hotel and Casino. Live performance episodes were broadcast from CBS Television City in Los Angeles.

FINALISTS

KEVIN SKINNER (Winner)

Country Singer, 35

Sharon Osbourne had low expectations when the unemployed chicken catcher first appeared at *AGT* auditions in Chicago. "I thought that you were going to be really hokey and silly," she admitted, "but you're really not. I can tell you are a lovely person. Very, very genuine." Kevin – a father of two from Mayfield, Kentucky – won America over with his heartfelt performance of Garth Brooks' "If Tomorrow Never Comes."

"That was actually my grandmother's favorite song," he tells us. "If I went to her house and had my guitar she would always say to me, 'Sing me 'If Tomorrow Never Comes" before you go. She always wanted to hear that song." His grandmother, Ethel Clapp, passed away several years before Kevin first decided to venture outside of the Bluegrass State and audition for the show. "Before that I had never even been on an airplane," he says.

Kevin Skinner at Planet Hollywood in Las Vegas
Photo: bcbusinesshub (via WikiMedia Commons)

After taking the title in 2009, Kevin appeared on *Ellen*, *The Tonight Show with Conan O'Brien* and *Live with Regis & Kelly*. He also opened up concerts for George Jones and got to meet his childhood hero, Willie Nelson. His debut CD, *Long Ride*, was released on St. Patrick's Day 2010 – just six months after the *AGT* finale. "I knew I needed to get some stuff out there [quickly], but it wasn't really produced the way it should have been," he admits.

Kevin – who has a twin sister, two older brothers and an older sister – has spent much of 2013 helping tend to his aging parents, Jackie and Joe Skinner. In March, Kevin posted a sad note to his family and friends on *Facebook*:

> *Please keep my mom, Jackie Skinner in your prayers please. She is in the hospital with heart trouble following a car wreck yesterday, where she had passed out before being able to pull off the road. I returned to the hospital today to be with her and I sure would appreciate your adding her to your prayer list.*

Kevin admits 2013 was a "slow" year for work. "The economy took a hard hit and that kind of threw a curve at me. It was going real strong there for a while. I had quite a bit of concerts, did quite a few casinos. But with the economy and everything, the way it has turned out, it has got me a bit slowed down right now. I am just trying to write some. Takin' a little time off. I guess everyone needs a little of that time, you know what I mean?"

Barbara Padilla
Photo: Courtesy

BARBARA PADILLA (Runner-up)

Opera Singer, 35

The biggest drawback to coming in second place? The Mexican-born soprano will never be able to compete in another singing competition again. "I just don't want to lose my status as a winner," she jokes. "I can't compete any more unless I know I am going to win. I just don't want to be third place. I am fine with my runner-up status." Barbara – a cancer survivor and mother to adopted daughter, Elizabeth – appeared to be the act to beat going into the season 4 finale. But she refused to buy into the hype. "I don't take anything for granted," she insisted the night before country singer Kevin Skinner was officially crowned champion.

The $1 million prize would have come in handy, Barbara admits: "I could have bought more shoes! [laughs] But I have not had the need for the money. When God wants to give you something, he will give it to you. You don't have to win the competition. I got to where I wanted to be. There was a part of me that was disappointed. You wanted to hear your name. But I think I won, too."

Barbara – who was diagnosed with Hodgkins Lymphoma at 23 – has been in remission for 13 years. She's spent much of her post-*AGT* time speaking and performing on behalf of various cancer-related charities. "When you are healthy, you know you are healthy because you don't think about it," she says. "I like to talk about it because then I realize it is a gift and I don't take it for granted. I appreciate it and I can go back to not thinking about it."

Barbara spent the summer of 2011 working for the NBC station in Houston recapping each episode of *AGT* for their morning news program. "I was getting up at 4:00 AM to do hair and make up then driving myself to the station to be there at 6," she remembers. "I could not believe it." Barbara's new CD, due later this year, is her best work yet, she says. "Everything has evolved. The genre I used to sing before is opera. I recorded this CD with opera arias that I never released because [my sound has] evolved," she says. "It is going to be released soon."

RECYCLED PERCUSSION (3rd Place)

Junk Rock Band

Photo: Courtesy (Recycled Percussion)

Recycled Percussion has managed to do what every *AGT* contestant dreams of: secure a headlining show on the Las Vegas Strip. The "junk rock" band – Justin Spencer, Ryan Vezina, Matt Bowman and Jason Davies – are headlining six nights a week at The Quad (formerly Imperial Palace), following successful runs at MGM Grand, Planet Hollywood and Tropicana.

Formed in 1994, Recycled Percussion had been playing professionally for over 10 years before first stepping onto the *AGT* stage. "We were a small band in New

Hampshire," says founder and lead percussionist Justin Spencer. "We didn't grow up with a lot of money, so it was cool for our parents to get to see us perform live on TV. I think that was the coolest thing, giving our parents the forum to watch us."

Shockingly, the band's Vegas dreams were nearly dashed at their first audition in New York City. "We got two X's – one from Piers and one from David Hasselhoff," Justin remembers. "We were leaving the venue and the producer asked us to come back the next day. I think the producers wanted us on the show so they pulled some strings. It didn't really matter what the judges said." The band was scheduled to fly to South Carolina the next day for a performance that paid $20,000, but decided to skip the gig and give reality TV stardom another try. "We took a big risk doing that but it paid off," Justin says.

The guys were put through to the next round, and even got Piers to change his mind, declaring "These guys *are* Vegas!" Though the former judge Piers has yet to turn up at one of their Las Vegas shows, several other *AGT* alums have – including season 2 and 3 host, Jerry Springer.

❖ ❖ ❖ ❖

TEXAS TENORS (4ᵗʰ Place)

Vocal Trio, 34 - 44

The first trio to combine classical crossover with country music say they owe "99.9 percent" of their success today to *America's Got Talent*. "We talk about our *AGT* experience in every performance," founding member Marcus Collins says. "We never take it for granted!" Collins, a pop vocalist, put the group together with opera singer John Hagen and country crooner J.C. Fisher in 2009, specifically to audition for the show. The voters loved them – and so did the judges: "Vocally and with the harmonies you produce together, it is a stunning act," Piers Morgan cheered.

As of June 2013, the group had performed over 520 concerts (many of them sold out) and has a deal to perform 60 shows a year at the Starlite Theatre in Branson, Missouri through 2017. "Along with our show we perform with our band, we also perform with many symphonies each year including the Cleveland Pops, Phoenix

Symphony, Houston Symphony and others," Marcus tells us. "We have one fan named Vivian who has seen our show 107 times!"

Since *AGT*, John got married (in 2011) and J.C. had a daughter (2 year-old Jennings). He will celebrate his 10th wedding anniversary with his wife Jen in February 2014. Marcus is still single. Texas Tenors' debut album *Country Roots - Classical Sound* (released in 2009) has sold over 100,000 copies. A follow-up CD and PBS concert special *Texas Tenors: You Should Dream* are in the works. In September 2013, the group is scheduled to perform in China for the first time.

The Texas Tenors with former host Jerry Springer
Photo: Courtesy (Texas Tenors)

MORE FAN FAVORITES

GRANDMA LEE (Top 10)

Comedian, 75

Grandma Lee performs in Las Vegas in 2009
Photo: bcbusinesshub (via WikiMedia Commons)

"I had bronchitis and the flu at the same time [The doctor] told me, 'The good news is you don't have lung cancer. The bad news is you have emphysema!' So I quit smoking right away. It has been five months without a cigarette."

- Grandma Lee Strong

Not all of the geriatric joker's stories are funny. Grandma Lee Strong – born May 29, 1934 – was touring with the *America's Got Talent* all-star show in 2010 when she tripped over a table box backstage in Los Angeles. "I fell down and broke my right hip, my right shoulder and my right wrist," she remembers. "I went to surgery and rehab and got home in time to do a Thanksgiving show in my home town!" But Lee's health problems were far from over. In January 2013, the mother of four (and grandmother of 10) landed in a Las Vegas emergency room. Her diagnosis: "I had bronchitis and the flu at the same time [The doctor] told me, 'The good news is you don't have lung cancer. The bad news is you have emphysema!' So I quit smoking right away. It has been five months without a cigarette." Lee – a former school-teacher and phone operator – jokes that she smoked "forever" but never inhaled. "Apparently that wasn't working. I will never smoke again. That was a quick wake up call. I quit cold turkey."

"You may be my favorite contestant this season," Piers raved after her first audition in Houston. Much of Lee's act is loosely inspired her own life experience. "I did invent an ex-husband named Duane," she told the *Florida Times-Union*. "I don't talk about my real husband, but I made up Duane. I say that we were married 35 years and got a divorce. He thought he was God. I did not." In real life, Lee was married for 37 years to former Marine Ben Strong. After he died from cancer in 1995, Lee decided to give stand up a try. Her first time on stage was at the Comedy Zone in Mandarin, Florida. "The first time I went to an open mic night," she told the newspaper, "I knew that this is what I wanted to do with the rest of my life. [After that], we'd get in a car and go anywhere: Orlando, Savannah, for two or three minutes in front of an open mic." After appearing on *AGT*, Lee was recruited for her first acting role in the independent movie *Redneck Roots*. There are also several possible television shows in development, she says. "Somebody called me from L.A. a while back and [said] they are thinking about having a show with me on it. Something about I am in charge of a dating service or something. It is a thing where these women are so busy with their kids and their careers that they don't have time to date. I am kind of setting them up. There is also a guy in Vegas named Cliff that has written a sitcom for me, but I haven't heard anything back about it. I run a bar and I am married to a midget."

And Lee admits she owes much of her success to *AGT*.

"Everywhere I go, somebody will come up to me and say 'I loved you on TV," she says. "Every day. No matter where I go. Sometimes a bunch of times. At the gas station, the Walmart...I love it!"

Photo: Courtesy (Lawrence Beamen)

LAWRENCE BEAMEN (Top 10)

Singer, 34

The judges hailed him as "the new Barry White." Still, success after *AGT* didn't come as easily as the Mississippi-born crooner had hoped. "I got sent through the wringer," Lawrence tells us. "I wasted three years of my life with management companies that claimed they could do this and do that. As smart as I thought I was, they can still come in and manipulate you based upon their lies and representations. Basically I was living out their dreams instead of mine."

The former church singer emerged as a sentimental favorite when he burst out in tears, following a booming baritone version of "Old Man River" at *AGT* auditions in Los Angeles. "What you brought to this show is class, grace, and talent," David Hasselhoff praised. "We have a lot to learn from people like you." Lawrence began singing at the age of six. Ten years later, he was invited to perform for Rosa Parks, the mother of the civil rights movement, and later summoned to the Vatican to sing for Pope John Paul II.

"[*AGT*] has helped me to stay true to my game, true to my craft," Lawrence says. "They had me going kind of everywhere on the show. I am not going to lie. I wasn't peer pressured into singing Barry White, but I honestly believe that if I had stayed with the classical songs I probably would have won that show. Honestly. Because that was my lane. Classical music. I could have pumped out songs like 'Old Man River' all day long. But still, I got top five. And I am happy I did get to that point."

Even more satisfying than reaching the finals, Lawrence says, is the connection he made with a handful of very special *AGT* viewers. "There were so many people who contacted me on their deathbeds," he remembers. "This is true. I have letter after letter from people saying that they were glad to see and hear that style of music before they die. All while I was on the show, I was getting letters from people wanting me to come to their deathbeds while they were dying. I was on the show so I wasn't able to do it. That was the most touching thing. All these people who appreciate this style of music. It was eight people total. I wasn't able to meet any of them, but I did reach out to their families that were calling in or emailing. That is what kept me humble. I would go back to my room and see these touching emails and I would sit and cry. Some of these older people - or people who were dying – they weren't ready to cross over. So when I start singing these songs on the show... There were four funerals that people would follow up and say 'Mr. Beamen, my mom died. It would be a pleasure if you would come out to the funeral.' Those were the moments I appreciated most."

Lawrence recently completed recording his new CD, *Sacred Love* – but its release is on hold because of a dispute with business partners. He will perform a concert at Carnegie Hall in New York City on May 9, 2014 in memory of Paul Robson. "I'll be doing all the songs he recorded at Carnegie Hall in 1958."

Howie Mandel replaced David Hasselhoff
beginning in season 5.

Photo: Helga Eseb (Shutterstock)

Season 5

(June 1, 2010 - September 15, 2010)

Host: Nick Cannon

Judges: Piers Morgan, Sharon Osbourne, Howie Mandel

Winner: Michael Grimm (singer)

NBC DIDN'T HAVE TO LOOK VERY FAR to find the newest addition to the *AGT* judges table. Howie Mandel was already an audience favorite after hosting *Deal Or No Deal* on the network from 2005 to 2009. And it didn't hurt that he was also a huge fan of the summer's biggest TV competition.

"There isn't a better job around," he gushed during his first weeks on the job. "This is a show I watched for four years. I sat on my couch screaming at the TV. I swear to you. I love this show. I love talent. I drop in to clubs. I watch it on TV. I love variety. When I got the call to do this show it was like a dream come true!"

Howie, 54 during his freshman season, admitted he felt "pressure" being the new kid on the block. "It is not so much about filling David Hasselhoff's shoes, because I think he was totally different," he said. "I am not going to try to do anything that he did. But coming on to something that is successful already and everybody knows each other, it makes it not as comfortable to come in."

Perhaps the only addition more impactful than Howie was the new *YouTube* audition round, which allowed tens of thousands of acts to submit themselves to the show online. (In previous years, contestants were permitted to apply via *MySpace*). Twelve acts – 11 selected by the judges and one by online voting – were invited to compete in Hollywood. Many of them ended up being painful to watch, but the novel audition process helped producers finally discover an act with which the competition would forever be synonymous: 10 year-old classical crossover singer Jackie Evancho.

Viewership for the season finale – featuring Jackie, champion Michael Grimm, Prince Poppycock and Fighting Gravity – reached an all-time high of 16.4 million.

BROADCAST LOCATIONS

Live auditions were held in Dallas, Orlando, New York, Los Angeles, Portland and Chicago. Vegas Week call back auditions took place at The Palms Casino Resort. A total of 108 acts participated. Live performances were broadcast from CBS Television City, Stage 36, in Los Angeles.

FINALISTS

MICHAEL GRIMM (Winner)

Singer, 30

The veteran Las Vegas lounge singer could have been disqualified during Vegas Week for ignoring a 90 second time limit on his bluesy rendition of "Try A Little Tenderness." Though Piers Morgan was critical of his performance, Michael kept his focus and eventually was last man standing in the competition. "You are my favorite as far as a singer goes," Howie Mandel told him after one number. "I am such a huge fan."

Michael Grimm performs in Las Vegas
Photo: Joseph Connell

Long before Michael took the season 5 crown, he vowed to use any winnings from *AGT* to build a new home for his grandparents. Thomas and Laura Butters – who raised the singer and his younger sister from the time they were in pre-school – lost their Waveland, Mississippi home in 2005 during Hurricane Katrina. But now they are facing an even bigger setback, Michael confides. Laura is battling colon cancer.

"You are the first to know that she has been dealing with this and having radiation treatment," he told us in June 2013. "We can keep our fingers crossed, but we really don't know (the prognosis). We know that the cancer is at bay right now. They think they have it under control. She is completing some chemotherapy. Everything is looking good. We are just keeping our fingers crossed and praying."

Compounding the family's challenges, Michael's grandfather is now suffering from dementia, he reports. "I am glad I was able to put them into that house. That eases things a little bit. The rest of the family is there helping them out."

The day after his big win on *America's Got Talent*, Michael appeared on the *Ellen* show, where he proposed to longtime girlfriend Lucie Zolcerova. The couple serenaded each other with a duet of "Islands In The Stream" at their wedding less than a year later. Rock legend Bill Medley was among the guests.

"We talk about [having children] all the time," Michael admits. "We are just not doing it at this moment. We want to get ourselves a little more seasoning. And we have time to do that. We have a little more time to get some roots into the ground. Somewhere. We don't know where. Maybe Vegas."

Since appearing on *AGT*, Michael has released a critically praised solo CD and toured the U.S. as an opening act for rock legend Stevie Nicks. As of July 2013, he was performing again at the Green Valley Ranch Resort in Henderson, Nevada.

◈ ◈ ◈ ◈

JACKIE EVANCHO (Runner Up)

Classical Crossover Singer, 10

From the moment Jackie first opened her mouth on the live *YouTube* audition show, Piers Morgan saw the writing on the wall: "We are going to wake up tomorrow and America is going to be going crazy for a little girl who just sang like an angel!" He couldn't have been more right. Millions of viewers – and even judge Sharon Osbourne – couldn't believe their ears. How could a tiny blue-eyed fifth grader pack such a gigantic, pitch-perfect voice? "I have never seen anything like it," Sharon praised.

Jackie Evancho performs
Photo: Joe Duerr (WikiMedia Commons)

Jackie, just 10 at the time, admits she was a bundle of nerves before belting out Puccini's "O mio babbino caro." "I remember hugging my mom before going on stage," she says. "I got on stage and performed the best that I could. I was so surprised that I did better than I imagined I would that I started to cry on stage! I kind of felt on top of the world then – like I could do anything!"

When it was all over, the young schoolgirl from suburban Pittsburgh placed second only to Michael Grimm. And she couldn't have been happier! "If I won, I would have had to do a whole tour and my parents thought it might be too much for me – and it might have been," she says, looking back. "So I am kind of happy I didn't win."

Three years after her triumphant debut, Jackie – who describes her sound as "classical crossover" – is looking more like a winner than ever. She's released four full length CDs (one platinum, one gold!), sung with Barbara Streisand and Tony Bennett and performed for President Barack Obama and the Japanese Royal Family. In 2013, Jackie made her acting debut as Robert Redford's daughter in *The Company You Keep*.

The cyber-schooled teen began performing in 2008 and has never had any formal training. She placed second in her hometown *Kean Idol* talent competition two years in a row (2008 and 2009) and was quickly invited to perform at charities and other events near the home she shares with her father (Mike), mother (Lisa), siblings (Rachel, Jacob and Zachary) and collection of lizards, pigs, dogs and ducks. Prior to her *AGT* debut Jackie had already caught the attention of super-producer David Foster and was invited to sing at New York's Carnegie Hall. In June 2010, she successfully raised $1,000 through a *Kickstarter.com* campaign to fund her second CD. Jackie – an ambassador for the animal advocacy group Mission: Humane – was recently chosen as the face of Guess Kids fall 2012 clothing line.

The young vocalist hopes to continue recording, touring and acting, but says it is unlikely she will take her talents to the New York stage. "I would prefer not to do musicals and Broadway," she told Pittsburgh's *Conversations@WQED*. "Not to offend anyone who performs on Broadway, but I have gotten a lot of [offers] to perform on Broadway and they want me to sing differently. That is my whole thing. I sing the way I want to. I can't really change it or I won't be happy with it."

❖ ❖ ❖ ❖

PRINCE POPPYCOCK (4th Place)

Opera Dandy, 32

Prince Poppycock
Photo: Larry (via WikiMedia Commons)

Prince Poppycock was shocked he advanced to the finals. "I never thought that America would accept a gay nightclub performer into the top four of a very populist competition," he told the *New York Post* moments after the results were revealed. "I guess you can never underestimate the power of shiny things."

Poppycock – the alter-ego of aspiring opera singer John Quale – is what you might expect if Lady Gaga and Boy George had a child: a towering powder-faced concoction of glam-rock, synth pop and light opera wrapped up in flamboyant period costumes that could put RuPaul to shame. His motto: "Over the top is not far enough."

John, who was raised on a Virginia horse farm until age 14, developed the Poppycock character in 2006 so he could perform in a Los Angeles nightclub show. "The club was called Wigged Out, so the only rule was you had to wear a wig," he explained. The openly gay performer admits his parents (Dad is now deceased) were "a little concerned" about his outrageous new persona. "But my mom couldn't be more pleased now," he says.

Quale trained for two summers at Michigan's famed Interlochen Arts Camp and admits his flair for theater and arts made the teen years particularly rough. "I was hazed quite a bit," he remembers. "High school was a very dark point in my life. I dropped out and junior year got my GED. I struggled with depression for most of my life. Poppycock is kind of a remedy for that."

Piers Morgan thought the opera dandy had a legitimate chance to take the crown, but then set off a social media firestorm by buzzing the performer during his final live act.

Since *AGT*, Poppycock has toured the world and performed at countless gay pride functions. Interestingly, he notes: "I don't really have much of a gay fan base. It is mostly straight girls and women. The most vocal part of my fan base are like 40 to 70 year-old women. They have the dollars to be able to fly around. That is just the power of *AGT*. It is not exactly a show that a lot of gay guys watch. They are all watching *RuPaul's Drag Race*." In the spring of 2013, Poppycock officiated his first wedding. "It was a [straight] couple that had seen me perform several times – all the way back to my fetish days at a club called Mask," he tells us. "They went and saw me while they were dating. They got married at the Aquarium of the Pacific in Long Beach [California]. It was pretty rad. I officiated the wedding in front of a giant 50-foot tall aquarium in a neon pink wig. So that was fun."

MORE FAN FAVORITES

TAYLOR MATHEWS (Top 10)

Singer, 18

Photo: Zuri Louis

"Music is a patience game," says the Alexandria, Louisiana native, who relocated to Los Angeles and is currently working on his first full length CD – funded entirely by his fans! Taylor, who was inspired to become a musician by his father, Randy – was about to graduate high school when he won over judges with his unique, acoustic version of "Somewhere Over The Rainbow." "You are an odd little thing, but in a good way," Sharon Osbourne told him. "It makes you so much an individual."

So do some of the scary and traumatic events Taylor experienced early in life. When he was five, Taylor and his family cheated death when they were rear-ended by an 18-wheeler. Months later, the kindergartener was caught inside his own house as it burned to the ground, destroying most of their possessions.

Before his *AGT* audition in Dallas, the biggest crowd Taylor ever played to was in a local coffee shop. "My buddy [auditioned] the year prior, and he invited me out to try with him again," he tells us. "[We] decided to the day before and drove five hours to the nearest audition city, Dallas."

Taylor credits the show with helping him meet his current manager, but insists the rest of his success is from his own day-to-day hustle. "Most of my fans are not from *AGT*," he says. But those who discovered him on the show "would be surprised [to learn] that I cut my hair and I'm wearing skinny jeans."

The singer recently completed his first tour of the U.S. and Canada. "My 'Head Over Feeling' music video also premiered on national television in Canada for about four months," he says. "It was an incredible experience. I had about 900 people a night singing along to every word!"

Taylor admits he set off on the North American trek with a broken heart. "I fell deeply in love with a girl [but] it ended over Valentine's Day weekend before my tour," he shares. "I had a difficult time trying to cope with the separation but I still love her. That'll never change. A good bit of my record will be about our relationship."

❖ ❖ ❖ ❖

MICHAEL GRASSO (Top 10)

Magician, 36

Michael Grasso began doing magic at birthday parties as a teenager. "I was making $175 for a half hour, babysitting a bunch of brats," he remembers. These days, the New Jersey-born entertainer has attained his life-long dream of performing illusions all around the world. "I have a crazy middle eastern following," he tells us. "My biggest fan lives in Kuwait. She paints pictures of me. It's nuts. She came backstage and gave me one. She said 'I'm sorry about the wrap job. My driver gave it to me.' She must be the daughter of some rich oil guy."

Michael amazed the *AGT* judges at his first audition but was eliminated during the semi-finals before eventually returning as a wild card act. He was the oldest contestant (and only magician) in the top 10. Since appearing on the show, Michael married his girlfriend, Stephanie. They welcomed a baby girl in late 2011. "She is so freaking cute!" he says.

Michael also tells us he is healthier than ever. During the show, Michael revealed that he had undergone three kidney transplants since the age of 21. The latest one "functions fine," he says. "It is just one of those things where it might and it might not [last the rest of your life]. You just kind of live with it every day. It could go tomorrow or five years from now or I could be 80 years-old."

❖ ❖ ❖ ❖

MARLEE HIGHTOWER / STUDIO ONE YOUNG BEAST SOCIETY (Top 10)

Dance Act

It was a marriage made in reality competition heaven. Not long after their runs on *AGT* ended, members of the Florida dance troupe began to collaborate with fellow contestants Fighting Gravity. "Our main choreographer, Julie Johnson, has been working with them since the show," says Marlee Hightower, the youngest member of SOYBS, who now leads dance work-

Photo: Courtesy (Marlee Hightower)

shops all over the America. "My first class had 50 people," she tells us. "Now, I'm doing larger workshops. The last one I taught had 300 people, which was amazing!" According to Marlee most of the members of SOYBS "went on to other projects." Meanwhile, she considered a return to the show in 2012 as a solo act. "I was going to go down to Tampa to audition for season 7. I had my scheduled time, and they were calling and really interested. But right before the auditions, I got asked to go on the World Of Dance Tour. I realized I would be so busy performing and traveling, that doing another season on the show would be impossible. It would be cool to go back, but I don't know if I will. Maybe as a singer next time!" Marlee, who now attends cyber-school, recently moved to North Hollywood, California and signed with dance agency Bloc L.A. In 2013 she appeared in a dance show pilot called *Latin Flavah* and made a cameo in the Nick Cannon-produced Nickelodeon show *Party Park*.

Photo: Courtesy (Doogie Horner)

DOOGIE HORNER (Top 48)

Comedian, 30

He may be the only comic to win over an audience by calling them "horrible people." Doogie Horner – a graphic artist who designed book covers by day – was drawing boos at his New York audition before turning the table on his hecklers: "This is the worst crowd I have ever performed for," he declared, immediately eliciting thunderous cheers.

"Ultimately [the show] helped me most by increasing my confidence and proving that my comedy isn't as crappy as I thought it was," Doogie tells us. "I was surprised how positive and optimistic most of the performers were. Before I was on *AGT* I had only hung out around comedians, and most comics are pretty negative and pessimistic. Hanging out with the other contestants taught me to loosen up and enjoy performing more.

"I'm still doing stand up. There have been some great gigs (the Bridgetown Comedy Festival in Portland) and some awful gigs (performing for a bank vault full of dentists at Del Frisco's Double Eagle Steak House), but most of them have been fun."

Doogie moved from his home in Philadelphia to New York City in 2013 when his wife landed a job teaching multimedia art at Farmingdale University on Long Island. "I'll be quitting my job at Quirk [Books] so I can devote more time to standup, a gamble which hopefully will not end in shame and tragedy," he says.

In other Doogie news: "I lost a little weight but gained a few grey hairs. My dog had a bad limp for a while but he's okay now. My wife has been making cool video art and has done a bunch of gallery shows and residencies. My little sister had a baby. My brother bought a kayak and graduated from college. You know, the usual stuff."

SEASON 6

(May 31, 2011 – September 14, 2011)

Host: Nick Cannon

Judges: Piers Morgan, Sharon Osbourne, Howie Mandel

Winner: Landau Eugene Murphy, Jr. (singer)

The Silhouettes
Photo: Courtesy (Lynne Waggoner-Patton)

IT WAS THE YEAR OF DANCERS...and danger! Four dance-related acts – Team iLuminate, Silhouettes, Miami All-Stars and West Springfield Dance Team – made it all the way to the Top 10. But much of the water cooler buzz focused on performers who fearlessly pushed the limits of safety.

"We have had some thrills and spills that I've never seen before — almost near-death experiences," Howie Mandel told reporters at a pre-season press conference. "I don't know if NBC is going to air them. But I'm telling you, it's become the most dangerous show on television!" During an appearance on *Late Night with Jimmy Fallon* days earlier, Howie described how "people broke bones, there's been blood. It's . . . a scary year."

The biggest risk-takers of season 6 included The Fearless Flores Family – which featured a pair of children riding motorcycles inside a "Globe of Death" – and a high diver named Professor Splash, who belly flopped 20 feet into a baby pool filled with 12 inches of water.

While most stunts went largely as planned, some didn't. At auditions in Atlanta, two acrobats tumbled right off the stage during their act, shocking the audience of more than 2,000. "They got so involved in what they were doing, they lost focus," executive producer Ken Warwick told the *New York Post*. "It never happened before in six years. But you get that as the acts push it a little further and a little further."

Luckily, no one was seriously injured during a live semi-final performance when a member of the collegiate tumbling squad Gymkana wiped out and landed next to a large ring of fire. "That was crazy!" Howie exclaimed after the show. "But it just shows you the danger and how far people are willing to go for fame and a million dollars. That is the beauty of our show. Anything could happen."

The accident occurred midway through the routine when one gymnast got his foot caught on the five-foot wide ring, causing the next tumbler to knock the prop over, nearly scorching teammate Warren Hull. The act was immediately aborted and a team member came to the rescue as fire marshals quickly leapt onto the stage.

After the live broadcast, Sharon Osbourne was quick to criticize the show for not responding fast enough. "We have got to be more on our toes," she said. "It took too long" to help him. Howie agreed: "He was lying there and I didn't see anybody with a fire extinguisher. He had a hole in the back of the outfit. In no way do I ever want to see someone get hurt. It was just scary."

The possibility something could go spectacularly wrong is part of what gives shows like *America's Got Talent* much of their appeal. Unlike *Wipeout* or *The Amazing Race*, AGT says it does not require or even encourage acts to try potentially dangerous stunts. With the prospect of serious injury – or even death – always hovering overhead, producers do their best to ensure the safety of all competitors.

Prior to performing on the air, acts are given rehearsal time to become familiar with the stage. A team of medics is also waiting in the wings at all times. And potentially dangerous stunts, like Professor Splash, are pre-taped in case something goes wrong. Live broadcasts are also kept on a five-second delay. "We are ready if and when something happens," executive producer Jason Raff insisted during a 2012 interview, because "even the most professional performers can have an off moment."

BROADCAST LOCATIONS

Live auditions for the judges were held in Los Angeles, Atlanta, Houston, Seattle, New York and Minneapolis. Piers Morgan missed the first day of taping in Minnesota after being caught in a blizzard.

Las Vegas Week took place at the Planet Hollywood Hotel and Casino, which also hosted the *America's Got Talent Live* shows in 2009.

This was the final year that live performance shows originated from CBS Television City, Studio 36, in Los Angeles and the second year, a separate auditions round was also held on *YouTube*, with twelve acts advancing to the quarterfinal round to compete with the Top 48.

CONTROVERSY: DID CINDY CHANG LIE TO THE JUDGES?

The Korean opera singer wiped away tears after her stunning rendition of Puccini's "O Mio Babbino Caro." The audition earned Cindy – who claimed to be a 42 year-old housewife and former technical writer – a standing ovation and praise from Piers. "I can't believe I am here," she told the judges. "I started taking my first voice lessons in my mid to late 20s and my voice teacher said it was too late for me." Cindy's voice, story and bubbly personality might have gotten her a lot farther in the competition – if reports didn't quickly surface that she was not exactly as green as advertised. Cindy apparently failed to mention that she is an accomplished showbiz pro – and member of the Screen Actors Guild – who appeared with Patti LuPone in a production of *Annie Get Your Gun* and in films alongside Kristen Chenoweth, Matthew Modine, John Corbett and Jerry O'Connell.

According to an official biography posted on her agent's website: "Cindy has been able to sing operatically (since) before she was 8 years old." She was eventually eliminated during Vegas Week after a performance the judges described as "warbly."

CONTROVERSY: SHARON CALLS PIERS "HOMOPHOBIC"

Steven Retchless

Male pole dancer Steven Retchless had no idea his performance in the Top 48 would briefly spark a personal falling out between the two of the *AGT* judges. Things got heated when Piers — who has often had a soft spot for attractive female contestants — told the *New York Post* that he was unlikely to vote Steven through in the competition because his act is "weird for guys to watch."

"I am not really into male pole dancers," he said. "It is not my kind of act. Having said that, he is obviously very good at it. He is very talented. I would just personally rather watch a woman do that — which is probably quite sexist, but it is true." That prompted Sharon to blast her fellow Brit's comments as "homophobic." "He is so bloody uptight! Piers is the type that probably wears stockings under his suit," she lashed out. "It wouldn't surprise me if he had suspenders and fishnets on!"

Steven, 24 at the time, was the reigning American Pole Fitness champion.

"The difference between me and other pole dancers is that I have a dance background," he says. "That is something I bring to the competition. I am trying to bring a different dance form with each round." After being eliminated two weeks later, Steven acknowledged that Piers was "entitled to his opinion" but that he "is not homophobic." Steven also offered to provide the sometimes-grouchy judge with complimentary pole dancing lessons at his New York City studio. So far, the invitation has gone unanswered.

JUDGING CHANGES: SO LONG, PIERS!

AGT's longest-tenured judge knew season 6 would be his last, but he waited until November 2011 to confirm that he would be focusing full time on his new CNN talk show, *Piers Morgan Tonight*. "I'm leaving *America's Got Talent* after 6 wonderful years," he announced on *Twitter*. "Turned out that juggling's harder than it looks, so I'm going to focus on CNN. I've loved every single second...I'm going to focus on what will be a huge year here at CNN with the upcoming election." Piers also thanked his "great

Piers Morgan
Photo: Helga Esteb (Shutterstock)

friend" Simon Cowell for the opportunity, and joked that Sharon and Howie would be "relieved to learn they no longer have to work with me." The former British tabloid editor took over the time-slot previously occupied by *Larry King Live* in January 2011 – five months after signing a new three-year contract with *AGT*. In March 2013, Piers admitted he had no regrets about leaving: "I couldn't have done both shows. CNN is an all-consuming show. And it is a nightly show. I tried that one season of doing both and it was impossible to juggle."

Piers answered some of our burning questions about himself and the show when we connected in July 2013.

How did you end up as a talent show judge?
Simon Cowell invited me to try it out. He thought that my background as a newspaper editor was perfect because for both jobs you have to be confident, opinionated, able to

spot future trends and talent, and not be afraid to speak your mind. Or as he put it, "Piers, you're almost as mean, arrogant and obnoxious as I am - that's why I want you for the job!"

Were you cast as the "mean judge" – or did that reputation just develop on its own?

I think it's more that I'm British and therefore less afraid to speak my mind than most American entertainment personalities. We Brits don't think we're rude, we think we're blunt, honest and on point. We also don't mind disapproval. In fact, I quite liked being booed. It fired me up.

How did being a part of *AGT* change your life?

I had never done any TV in America, so this made a huge difference to my life. I lived in the U.S. for four months of the year, and became the kind of 'celebrity' that I had only ever written about before as a journalist. It was a classic case of poacher turned gamekeeper and I loved it!

How much work do the judges do? It looks like they just show up for two hours and give opinions, but there is obviously more to it...

It's actually hard graft. The audition trail usually saw us go to six cities over a period of two months, and we would spend 3-4 days in each place. There would be two audition shows a day, each lasting three hours, and we would see on average 50 acts a day. The live shows were a bit easier, but they were still 10-hour days.

What is written on the index cards that we always see the judges holding?

Basic information about the acts - their name, age, background and talent. Nothing that suggests if they are good or bad.

What happens when you have nothing to say about an act? Is that when you ask "How do you think the performance went?"

Yes, I would have a variety of stock questions for those moments. "Tell me something interesting about yourself," "What's the dream?" "How would you spend the million dollars?" or "Who are your heroes?"

What kinds of things have gone wrong behind the scenes that we would be surprised to learn about?

It was usually very well organized. But I remember one guy who was supposed to jump over a load of metal chairs, and he came up short, crashing into the last one - and knocked himself out. We thought he'd killed himself. Then David Hasselhoff ran over, and the guy jumped straight up. It was the nearest thing to a miracle I've ever seen. Or at least, that's what the Hoff kept assuring us.

Did you really bet your house that Landau Murphy would win after seeing him audition? What made you so sure?

I didn't, no. That was a joke. But I thought he had the perfect combination of a great back story, easy humble charm, and a fabulous natural talent. That tends to be the cocktail for success on a talent show.

What act were you most wrong about over the years?

None. I was always right!

Do you ever regret leaving the show?

No, it was the right time. I couldn't keep juggling two huge jobs.

What is the real story about the famous feud with Howie Mandel? Was it real? And what is your relationship like today?

He remains the single most irritating man I've met in my entire life. But he did, occasionally, make me laugh. Usually without trying to. It remains a great sadness to me that I never got to infect him with any germs.

Would Olate Dogs have won last season if you were still on duty?

Er...No! I loved how Howard Stern poured scorn on Landau's credentials as an *AGT* winner, then he chose a bunch of yapping mutts.

FINALISTS

LANDAU EUGENE MURPHY, JR. (Winner)

Crooner, 37

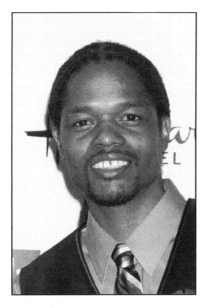

Landau Eugene Murphy, Jr.
Photo: Helga Esteb (Shutterstock)

It was, literally, a rags-to-riches story.

The former car-washer and Frank Sinatra sound-alike – who was raised on welfare and homeless at 19 – staged an amazing comeback and snatched the $1 million prize away from judges' favorite, Team iLuminate.

Landau, the favorite son of Logan, West Virginia, was overcome with emotion and began to shed tears of happiness when host Nick Cannon revealed his name. "Thank you so much for believing in me and letting me be myself," he said before receiving a group hug from the 42 members of runner up act, Silhouettes. "It has been a long hard journey. I have been busting my butt out here doing this for a long time — since I was a kid."

The father of four, who started out as a dancer, impersonating Michael Jackson – emerged as a favorite in the competition from his first audition in New York. But Landau nearly let victory slip through his fingers. Heading in to his Top 10 performance, the judges voiced concern that he was becoming "too much of a Sinatra tribute act." "He has got to be careful," Sharon Osbourne confided backstage. "He shouldn't do another Sinatra song because he is too one dimensional right now. He should move on."

And that's exactly what Landau did, looking more polished and confident than ever as he belted out Dean Martin's "Ain't That A Kick In The Head." "He has his swagger back," Piers acknowledged. "He knew what he had to do. It was infectious. I love him I think he is a tremendous act."

Landau used a portion of his cash prize to catch up on outstanding child support payments. "I got in arrears by trying to put a band together," he says.

Since appearing on *AGT*, Landau has performed to sellout audiences all over the country. In November 2011, he released his first CD, *That's Life*, and is currently working on an album of Christmas songs.

❖ ❖ ❖ ❖

THE SILHOUETTES (2nd Place)

Shadow Dancers, 4 – 18

Who wasn't rooting for the adorable young dance squad from Denver that creates heartwarming stories using shadows, video and a giant screen? Nothing like their act had ever been seen on the *America's Got Talent* stage before

The Silhouettes
Courtesy: Lynne Waggoner-Patton

the 42-member team auditioned in Minneapolis. "That is one of the most brilliant things I have seen in a long time," Piers Morgan told director and creator Lynne Waggoner-Patton. "I think I have seen everything and then this kind of act comes out of nowhere..."

Lynne developed the act in March 2009 using students from her world famous Rocky Mountain School of Dance in Arvada, Colorado. To participate, each member must maintain a strict 3.0 grade point average. After performing their first routine for an NBC-televised event called *SportAccord*, the young dancers caught the attention of *AGT* producers, who invited them to audition in October 2010. Two months later, they were officially selected to appear on the show.

Since coming *thisclose* to the grand prize (which they had pledged to donate to charity), Silhouettes has become a worldwide phenomenon. "We recently did a television commercial for a cement company in Columbia," Lynne tells us. "We made a cement truck [out of the dancers' bodies]. We also did an Internet commercial for the Lenovo Yoga laptop."

Many of the current Silhouettes are the same kids who appeared on *America's Got Talent*, Lynne says – including terminally ill 11 year-old Ellie White, who suffers from a rare genetic disorder called Wolfram Syndrome, which will soon cause her to lose both her sight and hearing. During their time on the show, Lynne had revealed that other children competing suffered from Cystic Fibrosis and Juvenile Diabetes.

In August 2013, two-dozen Silhouette dancers headed to Dublin, Ireland for a three-week engagement. A complete European tour is also being discussed. "They get paid for each show," Lynne says. "It depends on what we book the show for. There are some shows we don't charge for. If it is an event that helps children, we don't charge for that. I would like to get to a point where we can get a bus and stop in every city that we can and meet with children and shelters that help children that are homeless and teach them to dance. We already do that locally. We have free classes for a children's home that is very close to our studio. We are donating to the ISPCC (Irish Society for the Prevention of Cruelty to Children) during our shows in Dublin."

Back home, Lynne says interest in shadow dancing has never been greater – especially with a very similar-looking act (Catapult) earning lots of buzz during season 8 of *AGT*.

"I literally got hundreds of emails," she laughs. "People were angry for me. I'd write back and say 'What are you talking about? This is wonderful.' There is more than one singer in the world. There is more than one touring group of a Broadway show. I think if we helped inspire them, that is wonderful. It gets us back into the media again and gets people talking about us again. It is like any business. Competition is good. It fine-tunes our skills. I appreciate what they are doing. It makes you work harder. We didn't invent shadow work. That has been around for thousands of years. What I did do was bring children into it and we brought the photo overlays to make the shape and the picture comes up on the screen. So we have our own little niche. I am not offended in the least but I think it is funny how many people are. I think they were most upset because Howie said 'I have never seen anything like this before.' We must not be that memorable to him."

◆ ◆ ◆ ◆

TEAM iLUMINATE (3rd Place)

Glow Light Dance Act, 25 - 33

iLuminate performs in New York City
Photo: Courtesy

Columbia University graduate Miral Kotb ended up "hundreds of thousands" of dollars in debt after self-financing the development of technology behind her nine-member dance troupe – which performs its routines in complete darkness wearing computerized, light-up body suits.

"A couple of years ago, I quit my job and put all the money I had into creating this," Miral, a cancer survivor, revealed during iLuminate's incredible run to third place. "It is definitely a start-up made from blood, sweat and tears."

Miral – originally from Clear Lake, Texas – was training to be a professional dancer when she was diagnosed with retroperitoneal sarcoma more than a decade ago. "I found out about it when I went to my doctor and they felt a mass," she told the *New York Post*. "It was wrapped around the muscle and the artery that supplies blood to the right leg, so I am lucky to have a hip and right leg."

Once in remission, Miral put her dreams on hold and took a job as a software engineer at Bloomberg LP, where she could secure heath insurance in case the cancer came back. "Through physical therapy, I was able to dance again, but never at the level that I could before I got sick," she revealed on the show. "I honestly don't think that if I didn't survive it, I would have created this technology."

At their audition in Atlanta, buzzer-master Piers called iLuminate's performance "probably the single most exciting audition I've ever seen on this show," adding: "I have no doubt that we are looking here at a group that is going to be a huge act in Vegas."

After appearing on the show, Miral and her team literally traveled the world — performing in Canada, Egypt, and even South Africa. In the summer of 2012, two different teams appeared nightly at Six Flags amusement parks in Georgia and Texas.

"At any given moment we have four or five performances at the same time around the country or the world," Miral says.

Several members of the original *AGT* team are featured in Miral's first off-Broadway production, *iLuminate: Artist of Light* which began an open-ended run at New York's New World Stages in July 2013.

"The show is about this boy named Jacob who has this magic paintbrush that can create imagery and features that come to life," she explains. "It is kind of how he expresses himself. Then the town bully steals the paintbrush and the beautiful creations turn evil as the bully starts wreaking chaos in the town. So it is kind of about how Jacob overcomes this. You know it is like a good wins over evil kind of theme. I have always wanted to have an iLuminate show – since the conception of the technology I always thought it would be really cool to put it on the stage and actually have a storyline."

As producer, Miral once again finds herself in the position of self-financing her dream – which is to create a national, or international, tour for the show.

"I have been saving up and all the money we make from our performances and putting it back into the shows," she says. "I have yet to pay myself a check."

❖ ❖ ❖ ❖

POPLYFE (4th Place)

Band, 12 - 16

Kehlani Parrish and Dylan Wiggins of POPLYFE
Photo: AGTNews.com

POPLYFE was already building a reputation as the next big thing in the San Francisco Bay area when they first arrived on the *America's Got Talent* stage. And why wouldn't they be? The six talented teens – students at Oakland School for the Arts – were being groomed by producer D'Wayne Wiggins of 1990s supergroup Tony! Toni! Tone!

"We are watching a band that is going to be, I think, within the next two or three years, a huge band in this country," Piers Morgan predicted. After their amazing run to the finals, Oakland mayor Jean Quan declared October 7, 2011 "POPLYFE Day" in the teens' hometown. The group released its first single, "The World Is My Dance Floor," in early 2012, but several months later founding members Dylan Wiggins, Jaden Wiggins and Ali Khan Lochin opted to continue on without the rest of the group – including lead singer Kehlani Parrish.

Kehlani — who the *AGT* judges considered to be the real star of the act – had a chance to ditch her band-mates at their Seattle audition when Piers offered to pass her through as a solo singer. She declined, insisting: "I don't go without my brothers." Now, Kehlani laughs, "Everybody has been saying 'I guess her brothers left her...'"

"It was becoming less and less like a family and more and more like a company," she says. "People's heads were in it for the wrong reasons. Personally I haven't had a silver spoon my whole life, so I know how it is to struggle. I wasn't in it for the money. I am in this because it is what I love to do. I want to be a musician. Other people's heads weren't in the same place." Kehlani eventually re-teamed with exiled POPLYFE-rs Dillon Ingram and Denzel Merritt to form the short-lived trio Contraband. POPLYFE added several new members and spent much of 2012 on the road as the backing band for Disney Channel star Zendaya. They performed together at the 2012 White House Easter Egg Roll.

Kehlani graduated high school early and relocated to Los Angeles to pursue a solo career.

❖ ❖ ❖ ❖

ANNA GRACEMAN (Top 10)

Singer-Pianist, 11

Anna Graceman
Photo: AGTNews.com

She started singing at 18 months, playing piano at four and writing songs at six. So no one was all that surprised when the Juneau, Alaska resident made it all the way to the top 10 of *America's Got Talent* during her first weeks of sixth grade. Anna's audition – a cover of Alicia Keys' "If I Ain't Got You" became an overnight viral video sensation, racking up more than 29 million views!

Now 13, she's a bona-fide *YouTube* celebrity with more than 95,000 subscribers. In 2012, Disney even licensed some of Anna's early homemade videos – which date back to age six – for the "Disney Stars" section of its own *YouTube* channel.

The talented teen – who says she has no cell phone or allowance – has found even more success off-line.   She wrote all 10 songs for her self-titled, self-produced, debut album, which was released in September 2012.   Anna earned rave reviews a few months later for her participation in *America's Got Talent Live*, which ran for seven weeks at the Palazzo Hotel and Casino in Las Vegas.

"The pint-sized charmer is one giant talent," columnist Robin Leach wrote in the *Las Vegas Sun*.   "I know she will one day return to The Strip headlining in her own right. She sings well enough to rival Alicia Keys. She also plays piano as grand as Sir Elton John and writes songs as gifted as Adele and her idol, Taylor Swift."

In December 2012, Anna performed the National Anthem – a song she has said is one of the hardest for her to perform – for 65,000 fans at a Chicago Bears game. And more performances are in the works. In April 2013, she took home an honorable mention at the 2013 International Songwriting Competition for her music video "Showtime," despite being younger than nearly all of the contestants. Her music video also received an award in the contests' Teen category.

ANNA GRACEMAN SOUNDS OFF...

On Life In Alaska: "It's just a little town where I come from. We do a lot of outdoor things. Not shooting bears! But we do go hiking, fish and go to the glacier. I haven't done this but you can go on the glacier and go dog sledding."

On Jackie Evancho: "She is a star. She is absolutely amazing. I feel honored to be compared to her."

On Pre-show Nerves: "Before I go on stage I'm a little bit nervous but, you know, stars have said before that nerves are good. I always think that nerves help me. I just try to block everything out and think 'Oh, I'm just singing to myself in the mirror' or 'I'm just playing in front of my family.'"

- AGTNews.com (September 2011)

MORE FAN FAVORITES: WHERE ARE THEY NOW?

LANDON SWANK (Top 10)

Magician, 26

Wedding Day in Hawaii!
Photo: Courtesy (Landon Swank)

Since spellbinding a national television audience on *AGT*, the Alaska native has taken his illusions to Italy, Spain, Scotland, Ireland, England, South Africa, China, Japan, Taiwan and South Korea. But even more exciting: on November 11, 2011, Landon tied the knot with his onstage assistant – and girlfriend of just one year – Harmony Moniz. "Married life is wonderful," he gushes. "I have a partner to travel and perform with. She's my best friend and sidekick for all the adventures I get to take. That's why her nickname is 'Watson.'"

Nearly 80 people attended their Friday evening nuptials in Oahu, Hawaii (the bride is Portuguese and Hawaiian). "The only thing we would have wanted to change was the wind," Landon admits. "It was a tad bit windy that day. And she forgot to get a garter. So we had to pull a lei off of her leg for me to throw to the guys. Other than that things went pretty cool. She is a singer so one of the ideas we had for table seating was we got like a little flip flop luggage tag thing and right where you would write the name, we wrote a lyric to a song and the song titles would be framed on the tables so you had to figure out which song title your lyric went to. It was pretty laid back and fun."

Landon says it was always the plan to tie the knot on 11-11-11: "It is both of our favorite numbers. That was always my sports number growing up and it was her favorite number. It is one of the random things we had in common and we kind of talked about it the day after we met. We talked about getting married that day."

◆ ◆ ◆ ◆

DANIEL JOSEPH BAKER (Top 24)

Singer, 20

Just weeks after his elimination, the flamboyant singer-pianist-showman was invited to perform as part of "A Swingin' Affair" — a three part gala hosted by Pamela Anderson and honoring what would have been the 95th birthday of Frank Sinatra in Palm Springs, California.

Daniel – who relocated from Texas to Los Angeles – shared the stage with Frank Sinatra Jr., Canadian singer Matt Dusk and

Daniel Joseph Baker in 2013
Photo: Courtesy (Daniel Joseph Baker)

Broadway legend Lainie Kazan. "Since the show, I've been focusing solely on becoming an artist," he told us in July 2013. "I've worked with some very talented producers and musicians, who have taught me a lot as a developing singer-songwriter. My new single 'Well' that I wrote was released worldwide on iTunes on June 25th, and I hope to have my new EP out later this year."

Daniel, who is single ("but really married to my music"), says his five-year plan includes "total world domination. To be honest I would like to be singing and dancing my way through the hearts of all of my fans around the world. To be living my dream and making a living doing so would be the ultimate success for me."

PROFESSOR SPLASH (Top 24)

Stunt Diver, 52

Professor Splash

No one is quite sure how he does it. The Colorado daredevil (real name: Darren Taylor) somehow manages to belly flop from jaw-dropping heights into mere inches of water – and walk away! "That is without any doubt, the most dangerous, stupid, incredible, thrilling, ridiculous thing I have ever seen," Piers Morgan cheered. "Absolutely sensational!" His second jump – pre-taped in a parking lot outside the *AGT* studio – set a new world record: 36 feet, 7 inches.

In the past two years, Professor Splash has taken his breath-taking act all over the world. "I jumped in a white cricket uniform into spaghetti sauce down in Australia," he tells us. "That is on *YouTube*. I also jumped into milk for the *Royal Cornwall* show. Camilla, the Dutchess of Cornwall was there!"

Darren (who is not a real professor, duh!) has also been hired to appear on a half dozen *Got Talent* shows in foreign countries. "I did *Slovakia's Got Talent (Česko Slovensko má talent)*," he tells us. "I went over to Brno, Czech Republic and jumped off the Opera House – a non-record dive for their show. It was like a little mock thing of what [I did] for *AGT*. In Germany I did *Das SuperTalent*. And I did a show called *Minute of Fame* in Russia."

Most of the international talent shows are paid exhibitions, he says: "They are set up. They say 'Oh, sure, we give you an okay to go on to the next round,' but there is no next round. The only real one where someone is getting money [is *AGT*]."

Darren, who is single ["Diving tore my marriage apart"], is already beginning to plan for his life after diving.

"I cook. My specialty is Italian and Mexican," he told *AGTNews.com* after being eliminated. "I had a restaurant about 15 years ago and I am going to go back into that. I've got my recipes in order."

His signature dish: the smothered green burrito.

Mauricio Herrera is one of the highest-placing
Latino acts ever on *America's Got Talent*.

Photo: Courtesy (Mauricio Herrera)

MAURICIO HERRERA (Top 48)

Entertainer, 33

He was an explosion of enthusiasm – the type of over-the-top showman who was born to appear on a Las Vegas stage. "It's so schmaltzy, it's funny," Howie Mandel joked after Mauricio's semifinal performance of the Tom Jones classic, "Delilah." Unfortunately, Sharon Osborne and Piers Morgan disagreed, buzzing him midway through the song.

But that's okay, Mauricio tells us: "Becoming a finalist on the number one show in America catapulted my career to a new level. Anywhere I go *AGT* is my business card. You can't top that! Any radio host, TV or film producer knows about the show so whenever I get the chance to meet one, *AGT* becomes the "Fast Lane Ticket" to be heard and introduced into showbiz."

The Costa Rican singer-dancer recently launched his own television and radio shows and is coordinating *Mauricio's Talent Show Tour* in conjunction with several California school districts. "We will be giving away scholarships for kids who graduate from high school and want to go to college," he says. "We will try to include some of my friends and acts from the show such as Snap Boogie, Dylan Andre, Meet Me At Third & Fairfax and Frank Miles. The tour will take place at the Fox Theater in San Bernardino [California] in late 2013."

Maurico – a father of two sons (Carlos, 13, and Hector, 5) – was also recently chosen to record the new theme song "Otro gol y otro gol" ("Goal and Another Goal") for the Club Sport Herediano, the number one ranked soccer team in Central America. He continues to headline at The Ice House and other top clubs around southern California and returned to Costa Rica in April 2013 for a series of sold out concerts.

"At the airports in Los Angeles, Ontario and Texas, I've experienced that some TSA employees recognize me on the spot," he shares. "I've been waiting in line for the screening scan and they pull me out of the line to tell me, 'I voted for you! You should've won! Can you do the pose you did with Howie!' It's priceless! Even crossing the border by land, the Immigration lady the other day looked at my passport card, then looked at me, back and forward many times and then asked me, 'So when are you going back to television? My husband and I loved you on *America's Got Talent*!'"

Howard Stern has declared himself to be "America's Judge."

Photo: Helga Esteb (Shutterstock)

Season 7

(May 14, 2012 – September 13, 2012)

Host: Nick Cannon

Judges: Howard Stern, Sharon Osbourne, Howie Mandel

Winner: Olate Dogs (animal act)

THE KING OF ALL MEDIA was determined to become the judge of all talent. In a scenario that seemed almost unimaginable just a year earlier, controversial radio personality **Howard Stern** joined the judges' table, filling the seat left vacant by pal **Piers Morgan**. And, predictably, not everyone was excited. The Parents Television Council immediately fired off a plea to 91 different sponsors urging them to distance themselves from the "vile" new judge. In the letter — obtained by *AGTNews.com* — the non-profit group blasted Howard's crude language and humor and insisted he could never be a decent judge of dancers, jugglers and dancing poodles after making derogatory comments about *American Idol* winner Fantasia Barrino.

Prior to joining *AGT*, the outspoken shock jock also took swipes at season 6 winner Landau Eugene Murphy Jr., telling listeners of his Sirius XM radio show: "He looks like a homeless guy who stole a tuxedo. I wouldn't pay 10 cents to see this guy... Maybe he should wash my car while he's singing those songs... Maybe someone should alert him. Nobody buys that kind of music anymore." The addition of Stern was the first part of a much-needed top-to-bottom makeover for the aging variety show. In December 2011, executive producer Simon Cowell announced that *AGT* would introduce new graphics, new theme music and a larger, louder studio audience when production relocated to Newark, New Jersey. He also expressed a desire to incorporate a fourth judge "because it leaves less room for error." But NBC execs weren't ready (yet) to pull the trigger on a fourth panel member. They already had an all-in bet on Stern, who was certain to alienate at least a portion of the family-friendly middle-America audience.

Though Stern turned out to be fair, compassionate, and unexpectedly funny in his critiques, it was immediately clear that he had become the focal point of the entire show. "I am America's judge," he playfully declared on more than one broadcast, completely overshadowing the other judges, as fans in the audience cheered "Howard! Howard! Howard!" Still, many questioned if he was worth the reported $15 million-a-season paycheck and the exercise of moving the entire production – and its many staffers – across the country.

The addition of Stern never provided the ratings bump NBC had hoped for – in fact, viewership for the season premiere took a 16 percent hit from the previous year and never really recovered. Peacock brass blamed the drop on scheduling issues related to the network's broadcast of the summer Olympics. "Because of those 17 days off regular programming, we had to start early, which meant its premiere was against the *Dancing With the Stars* finale," head of alternative programming Paul Telegdy told *The Hollywood Reporter*. "I [regret the scheduling choice], if I am honest."

Former judge Piers Morgan thinks the acts on stage were partly to blame. "I didn't think [season seven] was a good season for talent," he says. "That is always a problem. It has nothing to do with the judges. You can only work with what you have been given."

BROADCAST LOCATIONS

Live auditions were held in Los Angeles (Orpheum Theatre), San Francisco (Bill Graham Civic Auditorium), St. Louis (Long Center), St. Petersburg (Mahaffey Theater) and New York (Hammerstein Ballroom). For the third straight year, acts were permitted to submit videos for consideration via *YouTube*.

Vegas Week was filmed at The Venetian and Palazzo Resorts.

Live performance shows were broadcast from the New Jersey Performing Arts Center.

JUDGING DRAMA: SHARON QUITS!

Hell hath no fury like Mama Osbourne scorned! So when Mrs. O. got into a nasty spat with NBC over the treatment of her son Jack midway through the season, she quit the show and went nuclear on her network bosses in a bombshell interview with the *New York Post*. "I just can't be fake. It's discrimination, and it was badly handled," she fumed, claiming the network booted Jack, 26, from its military reality series *Stars Earn Stripes* after he was diagnosed with multiple sclerosis. While Osbourne remained under contract, "They can't make me do something I don't want to do," she insisted. "All they can do is stop me from being a judge on another network for five years. It's time to move on."

Sharon Osbourne
Photo: Shutterstock

Sharon – who also serves as her son's manager – claimed that an NBC executive offered to pay Jack his full appearance fee to smooth things over but she refused. "He didn't want the money," Osbourne said. "He wanted his gig. It gave him something to look forward to when he was diagnosed. Think of the good that it could have done to show other people who have this [condition] that your life is not over."

A network rep told the paper: "Sharon has been a valuable part of the NBC family. We regret any misunderstanding and wish Jack well." But that wasn't enough to smooth over the rift. "I really don't like NBC," she told the *Hollywood Reporter* a few months later. "That's why I wouldn't go back. They treat their talent like shit! Not that I'm a talent, but I'm an employee, and they treat you like shit."

In 2013, Sharon went back to work for Simon Cowell as a judge on the U.K. version of *The X Factor*.

CONTROVERSY: TIM POE ACCUSED OF LYING ABOUT MILITARY INJURY

It was the biggest reality TV scandal of the summer! Sgt. Timothy Michael Poe, an Iraq war veteran and father of two, stole America's heart with a tear-jerking story of how he was nearly killed in the line of duty – only to have fellow soldiers call his story a fake. Compounding the problem, Poe, 35, said he accidentally supplied the show with fake pictures and lied to the judges about his professional singing past.

Days later, the embattled singer came clean: "It may not have happened exactly like I said it did," he told the *New York Post*. "I really do not remember a lot of things since the accident." Poe maintains that he suffered permanent brain damage in a 2009 grenade blast while helping clear out a building.

"I remember a blast going off by my head and being in Afghanistan and telling one of the sergeants," he said. "It is like a dream . . . I can't remember things exactly how it happened."

CONTROVERSY: ST. PETE'S GETS SNUBBED

Officials from Florida's fourth largest city thought *AGT* producers should get a lesson in geography, when they failed to correctly identify the city where live auditions took place. The show filmed April 3 and 4 at the Mahaffey Theater in downtown St. Petersburg, but host Nick Cannon kept referring to the area as Tampa. "I was disappointed," St. Petersburg Mayor Bill Foster told the *Tampa Bay Times*. "St. Petersburg wasn't mentioned once. But for the fact that I recognized the (Mahaffey), I would have thought that it took place in Tampa." The show reportedly rented the venue for $25,000. "It never crossed my mind that this would turn into a Tampa event," Foster said.

CONTROVERSY: HOWARD STERN BREAKS BOY'S HEART…TWICE!

Amir "Mir Money" Palmer (L) didn't make it through to Las Vegas, but was told he had!

The 7-year-old rapper from Philadelphia had a lot more to cry about than America saw on TV. After stepping off stage at the New York auditions, Mir Money — whose real name is Amir Palmer — was accidentally told he had made it through to Las Vegas! "Then they called us the day he was supposed to leave and said, 'We're so sorry, he's not going,' his mother, Regine Palmer, told the *New York Post*. "He didn't take it too well."

Call it a giant misunderstanding. In all the confusion with consoling the boy, the judges never got around to voting. And when they did, they decided it wasn't his time to move forward. Producers quickly issued an apology to Amir and his family and vowed to make sure nothing like this ever happening again.

Things got off to a shaky start when Amir failed to impress the judges with his original rap called "Commas and Zeros." "Howard hit his button, then hit Sharon [Osbourne's] button as well," his grandmother, Suzanne Degree, told the newspaper. When the young performer became visibly upset with Stern's critique, the shock jock jumped up onstage and embraced him.

"He told me 'You're going to Vegas,'" Amir said in an interview the day after the episode aired. Backstage, the boy received congratulations from host Nick Cannon.

"He told him to look into the camera and say 'I'm going to Vegas,'" Palmer said. "He also told him Howard Stern didn't really know nothing about rap. He told him he likes country music."

Stern got a lot of mileage out of Amir's story as he made the rounds on the talk-show circuit to sell viewers on his "compassionate" approach to judging. "It's difficult to look into the eyes of a 7-year-old and say, 'I am going to give you the X,'" Stern told *The Post* in May 2012. "I couldn't handle it. I felt awful. But this is the job I was given. I am not going to sit there and suck up to a 7-year-old. It is up to the parent to determine whether they can handle being critiqued."

In a statement, NBC said, "We apologized to the family and are looking at ways to prevent this from happening again."

FINALISTS

The judges got their wish: for the first time ever, a singer did not win – or even advance to the finale. Producers, with obvious knowledge of voting patterns, helped ensure there were no vocalists close to the finish line by changing up the format. Unlike previous seasons, there was no Top 10. The field of 24 semifinalists was chopped to six in just two episodes, allowing the judges to select two of the acts (33%) regardless of public voting. Here's how it all ended up:

OLATE DOGS (Winner)

Dog Act, 19 – 55

The Olate Dogs picked the right season to try out for *America's Got Talent*. The adorable dancing pups trained by Nick Olate and his father Richard may not have come out on top if Piers Morgan still had a buzzer within reach. During a visit to *Late Night with Jimmy Fallon* shortly after the finale, the always opinionated Brit offered his two cents on the act – and his replacement at the judges' table: "I love Howard Stern, but I have to laugh because when he took over, he said 'You know what we're not going to get any more of? These terrible acts wining the show. No more Sinatra impersonators...' And who won? A couple of stupid dogs running around! Howard said he was going to find 'world class talent.' I am not seeing them in China, are you? 'Here they are, the winners of *America's Got Talent* – two stupid dogs...' That ain't world class talent, my friend."

In the end, American voters disagreed, and the jumping, twirling, dancing dogs made Richard and Nick $1 million dollars richer. It was a windfall Richard could never have imagined when he was growing up in Santiago, Chile during the 1950s. A third generation circus performer, he was the 21st child in a very poor family of 22. At 12, Richard found and adopted a small puppy off the street and slowly taught it

Nick Olate performs
Photo: Rebecca Olate

to do tricks. After developing an act and adding additional dogs, his mother began to book them into school shows and street fairs to earn extra cash.

Eventually, at age 33, Richard brought his wife Rebecca and their family to the United States. Today he is a U.S. citizen.

"We actually got discovered [by *AGT* talent scouts] off of *YouTube*," Nick tells us. "At first we were kind of standoffish because we've had experiences with TV shows before – nothing bad or anything – it's just that we have a lot of dogs and we always have to take them out to the bathroom, and it's always hard to find a spot. So we weren't sure if we wanted to do it or not."

Luckily, they did. At their audition in St. Petersburg, Florida, Howard Stern declared: "I don't let any animal acts through. Hardly any. Because they have been awful. Every nudnik who has a pet comes out on my stage. You guys are probably going to get to be on my stage for a very long time."

The Olate family celebrated their surprise victory by purchasing a new truck and a super-sized trailer to transport their rapidly growing family of show dogs. "We always drive to appearances," Nick tells us. "We went to Chile when I was 13 and did a tour for a few months, but coming back it was a huge issue with the dogs. That was the last time we ever traveled by air."

The Olate's currently share their home with 27 four legged friends, most of which are rescued from shelters. Every dog is kept as a pet even after they retire, Nick says.

Tom Cotter
Photo: Shuttersttock

TOM COTTER (Runner Up)

Comedian, 48

Tom Cotter's father always wanted him to practice law. "He paid for me to go to prep school and college along with my five siblings," the comic revealed in a 2012 interview with the *New York Post*. "So when his youngest decided to tell jokes in bars about his digestive system, he, of course, was not thrilled." But recently, Tom said, his Dad has had a change of heart: "When I did *The Tonight Show*, he realized I wasn't the waste of sperm he thought I was. Now, he gets that I don't suck."

So does the rest of America. Not only was Tom the first comedian to reach the finals of *AGT*, he was also the highest finishing non-canine act of season 7. "I said early on, 'I don't mind losing to any of the finalists. But if I lose to the [Olate] dogs, I'm slashing my wrists and moving to Canada," he joked to *Laughspin.com*. "I would like to officially withdraw that statement, now. I am not going to kill myself. They are a great act!"

Both Tom and his four-legged competitors spent several months performing together at the *America's Got Talent Live* shows in Las Vegas during 2012 and 2013. The 90-minute show – which also featured Earth harpist William Close and others – gave Tom a chance to connect with his audience for more than just 90 seconds. "The [*AGT* television] format is brutal for comedians," he told *The Post*. "Most comics take 90 seconds just to move the stool and get the mic out of the stand and say hello."

Tom, a former Nantucket police officer, is no stranger to the restrictions of performing on TV. He's already appeared in his own Comedy Central special and on NBC's *Last Comic Standing*. In 2006, Tom and wife Kerri Louise — a fellow comedian — landed their own reality series on the WE network.

Two Funny: Cotter & Louise, which followed the newlyweds as they juggled their careers while tending to their twins — was canceled after six episodes. "It was not my demographic," he says. They told us from the get-go that WE was the third of the female networks, behind Lifetime and Oxygen. We were literally sponsored by Tampax. It was very emasculating. "They kept telling us, 'The people who watch our [network] will not like that.' There was one scene where I was throwing my son in the air and catching him, like every dad on the planet does — two feet over my head. And they said, 'We can't show that. People will be upset.' I was like, 'Are you kidding me?' " The show ran out of money in mid-production, Tom says, "So they literally had film students editing the episodes for free."

The Denison University graduate briefly worked as a private detective in Massachusetts before diving into comedy full-time in 1986. Today Tom is finally able to support himself working full-time as a comedian. He continues to perform corporate, college and cruise ship gigs. "I average two weekends per month, on the road," he told *TheSmokingJacket.com*. "Sometimes it's three, and sometimes it's none. The wife knew what she was getting into when she married me. The boys are somewhat less understanding that the road is how we butter our bread. When we lived in NYC, I would pack the night before, and put my bag by the door so I could just dash to the airport, and the twins would wake up and sit on my luggage crying. That was brutal. I started hiding my luggage. The boys are used to it now, and I often remind them that their uncle (my brother) did three years in Iraq and four in Afghanistan, so in the grand scheme of things it's not that bad."

"That said, I have missed a bunch of Little League games and school plays," he admitted. "The wife, like many women, has made the sacrifice of putting her career on the back burner to stay at home most of the time, to hold down the fort, and keep our three boys in line. She still works, but closer to home. Yes, my children are hilarious. They are genetically predisposed to being humorous. They make me laugh harder than any comedian ever has."

◈ ◈ ◈ ◈

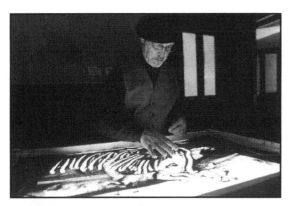

Joe Castillo demonstrates sand art

JOE CASTILLO (Finalist)

Sand Artist, 64

The last thing **Joe Castillo**'s father told his son before he died was "I think you should be an artist." Almost 50 years later, Joe – a native of Mexico City – has done exactly that. Always sporting his trademark beret, the father of four and grandfather of six tells uplifting, motivational stories using light and sand. "I don't know of another human being on earth who can move me the way you do," Howard Stern told him at the Austin, Texas auditions.

Joe – who has a degree in Biblical Studies, but no formal training in art – fell into his unique craft almost by accident. "My wife sent me to the hardware store to get some mulch," he explained before his first live performance in Newark. "I was walking down the aisle where they had bags of sand..." He created his first work of art in the garage with the aid of a kitchen light fixture. And, well, the rest is history.

As one of the top six finalists on *AGT*, Joe was invited to appear in Las Vegas for a live, eight week run at the Palazzo Theater in the Venetian Hotel. "Each day I wake up amazed at the people and places I have performed," he says. "I've been to 43 states, 22 foreign countries, venues as big as the Lucas Oil Stadium in Indianapolis and places as far flung as Kanpur, India. I am thrilled at the journey God has taken me on and the impact I often get to make in peoples' lives. I wouldn't have it any other way."

Almost all of Joe's sand art creations are infused with his deep sense of spirituality. "It is a significant part of life and growth," he tells us. "What changes us more than anything in our lives is what I call divine encounters. My spiritual SandStories touch people on that level and I have seen audiences all over the world brought to tears and healed in ways that the spoken word could not do. I hear personal stories and have folders full of emails, *Facebook* and *Twitter* testimonies of those impacted by my art. *The Passion of the Christ* was actually the very first SandStory I developed. It was an attempt to tell the resurrection story in a fresh and new way. It is still the most powerful and requested performance I do. It is the story that changed my life and changes lives everywhere I go."

WILLIAM CLOSE (Finalist)

Earth Harp, 42

William Close and his Earth Harp
Photo: Courtesy (William Close)

William Close still can't believe he lost to a bunch of dogs. "I am not sure exactly what the voting scenario is on the show, but I know there was a lot of disappointment amongst the producers and the judges," says William, creator of numerous unique instruments, including the mind-blowing Earth Harp. "And there was a public outcry. At least I got an outcry, a lot of disappointment. I think it is frustrating for a lot of people who really believe in the creative voice of the country. To have the country vote for a dog act, it doesn't speak highly of our cultural awareness."

William had one of the most unique acts the show had ever seen – a larger than life musical instrument with strings up to 1,000 feet long that literally ran all the way across the New Jersey Performing Arts Center. "I had given up hope," Howard Stern admitted after Close's breathtaking audition in Los Angeles. "I spent a lot of time watching a lot of nudniks. You walked out here, you looked like a hippie. I said 'If this guy was my son I would sit him down and say listen, you better get a real job.' Then you walked over to this thing. It was totally original. It is why I am here. You turned this whole theater into an instrument. That is originality. I made my career on originality. I bow to you!" William – who appeared in the *America's Got Talent Live* show in Las Vegas last year – created his first Earth Harp in 1999. The instrument is played using violin resin on cotton gloves and musical bows. The performer's hands run along the strings, creating cello-like tones. In the past 14 years, William has created hundreds of custom Earth Harp installations all over the world – from the Grand Theater of Shanghai to Seattle's Space Needle and the *Ka* Theater in Las Vegas.

He lost many of his creations in a devastating house fire 10 years later. In the spring of 2013, William and his girlfriend Sarah were married – on their son Phoenix's first birthday.

DAVID GARIBALDI AND HIS CMYK'S (Finalist)

Performance Artists, 26 - 30

The Sacramento-based "rock and roll painter" brought "controlled chaos" to the *AGT* stage, splattering an array of colorful paints onto a giant easel to instantly create images of American pop culture icons (Albert Einstein, Elvis Presley, Statue of Liberty). "He is a tremendous artist," Howard Stern declared. "The way he presents it is phenomenal. You never know what the final image is going to be till the end."

Once an angst-ridden high school dropout, David turned his life around in 2003 when he moved his graffiti-like art from the streets to canvas. "I was never really inspired to become an artist, it was just always part of my identity to create," he told *Stamp* magazine in 2011. "When I decided to create art professionally, I was definitely inspired by very hard times I was going through. I had lost my job, my car was repossessed, and I was about to be evicted from where I was living. It was then that I made a conscious commitment to start putting my creativity to work in a serious way."

Now 30, David – who has two children (son Chrisp and daughter Mia) with wife, Joy – uses his artwork to both entertain and raise money for charity. At his "Rhythm & Hue" shows, he will frequently auction off the custom-made creations to the highest bidder for $500 to $2,000 a piece. In the past 10 years he has raised almost $1 million.

The father of two – who was once part of a hip-hop dance group – performed for several months at the *AGT Live* show in Las Vegas in 2012. He also painted a portrait of NBA star Jeremy Linn during halftime of a New York Knicks game and was commissioned by Sting to paint artwork that hung onstage during a concert in Paris.

❖ ❖ ❖ ❖

THE UNTOUCHABLES (Finalist)

Dance Team, 8 – 14

The kiddie dance crew from Miami – all ages 8 to 14 – were nearly booted from their Newark hotel just days before competing on the season 7 finale. Guests at the Best Western Robert Treat Hotel say members of The Untouchables were making excessive noise and tossing objects out of windows. "We gave them a verbal warning to let them know if the problem persisted they would be kicked out of the hotel," a rep for the property told gossip site *TMZ*.

The 19-member squad was mentored by Manny and Lory Castro, members of season 6 finalists Miami All-Stars, and featured two of their children. At the Tampa Bay auditions, their "muy caliente" routine to J-Lo's "Get on the Floor" caused judge Howie Mandel to remark, "Your expertise, combined with your youth...was phenomenal!"

The Castro's continue to run Dancetown, their studio in Doral, Florida. During season 8, their son D'Angelo, 11, and daughter Ruby, 8, returned to the competition as members of competing ballroom dance duos. After squaring off against each other at Radio City Music Hall, Ruby and her partner Jonas were eliminated, while D'Angelo and his partner Amanda Carbajales advanced to the semi-finals.

MORE FAN FAVORITES: WHERE ARE THEY NOW?

TODD OLIVER (Top 24)

Animal Ventriloquist, 53

It took an act of God to get Todd Oliver and his talking dogs on the *AGT* stage. "I had just started what was to be a two-year contract with a theater in Branson when it got hit by a tornado," the canine ventriloquist remembers. The unforeseen disaster on Feb 29, 2012 forced the historic Americana Theater to close for nearly three months and scared many tourists away.

Todd Oliver and Irving

When the doors reopened, "I needed to do something to put more butts in seats," Todd tells us. "So I agreed to audition because I figured anything would help." And it did.

A year later, "my show is better than it's ever been," Todd says. "Every day people in the reception line at the show say that they voted for us on *AGT*." *Todd Oliver & Friends* combines ventriloquism and stand up comedy, with many of the punch lines being delivered by his two rescue dogs, Irving and Lucy. When the engagement ends on December 31, 2013, Todd hopes to take the act on the road for a while. "The Branson thing has kind of burned me out," he says.

It's taken a toll on his canine companions as well. Over the years there have been five different Irvings, he reveals. "Irving 5 is five years old. I also have Irving 4 who is nine years old. I switch off, but Irving 4 — his real name is George — doesn't want to work as much anymore. I have a basset hound, Elvis that I use in the show sometimes but [he's] getting older. Usually I'll go to the door and say 'Who wants to go to work?' There are two Lucys and two Irvings. Lucy 2 and Irving 5 are usually the ones that come to the door first and that's who I usually take."

Todd, who is currently shopping a one-hour TV comedy special to networks, is married with an eight year-old daughter – and three foster dogs. "I'll probably do this until I'm close to 70 and that will be it," he says. "I started out as a volunteer when I was 13 and I'd like to end as a volunteer. I just want to make enough money to retire and then I'll go to schools [to perform] and not charge anymore. In the meantime, I have to build my audience on the road, be a dad and husband."

◆ ◆ ◆ ◆

Sebastien performs in San Antonio
Photo: ABC

SEBASTIEN "EL CHARRO DE ORO" (Top 24)

Mariachi Singer, 10 – 30

One of the season's youngest competitors found himself making headlines for all the wrong reasons in June 2013. The sixth grader was bombarded with hateful rants on social media after performing "The Star Spangled Banner" before an NBA finals game between the San Antonio Spurs and The Miami Heat. "This lil Mexican snuck in the country like 4 hours ago now he singing the anthem," one person wrote on *Twitter*. Another commented "I'm highly upset that THIS kid is singing the United States National Anthem. Clearly from Mexico..."

Sebastien — who was born in Texas and resides in San Antonio — eventually delivered a tweet of his own: "Please do not pay attention to the negative people. I am an American living the American Dream. This is part of the American life." In an interview with KENS 5 News, he added: "With the racist remarks, it was just people how they were raised. My father and my mama told me you should never judge people how they look." After appearing on the show, his mother, **Stacy De La Cruz**, said both Disney and Nickelodeon had expressed interest in the young mariachi star, who has been singing since age 7.

❖ ❖ ❖ ❖

SPENCER HORSMAN (Top 24)

Escape Artist, 26

Photo: Courtesy (Spencer Horsman)

Spencer Horsman is just happy to be alive after barely surviving his final trick on *America's Got Talent*. "My cement tank burial was hands-down the dumbest, most suicidal thing I've ever done in my life," he says. "I was just happy to be out of it alive. I didn't care how it looked. I didn't care how it went. I was just happy I didn't die."

Spencer – one of a dozen "wild card" acts – had only practiced the death-defying trick twice before attempting it on live television. He survived but was promptly eliminated from the competition, despite strong support from judge Howard Stern. "He kept saying things like, 'If you kill yourself, you'll really get far in the show,'" Spencer tells us. "He was always cracking jokes like that. All my stuff is dangerous. That's half the fun of it. That's why people watch it, because I *could* kill myself."

Spencer – whose parents were both clowns in the Ringling Brothers Circus – began learning magic at age four and was performing professionally by eight. "I had already done 20 or so national TV shows [including *The Late Show with David Letterman*] before *AGT*."

Though he prefers doing magic and standup, Spencer says *AGT* producers pushed him to compete strictly as an escape artist. "They said, 'We've had plenty of magicians, but we've never had an escape artist before,'" he remembers. Spencer's appearance on the show has brought sold-out crowds to Illusions, a Baltimore area bar-theatre he owns with his father. *AGT* fame has also garnered the young entertainer a Justin Bieber-like following among tween girls.

"I'm 27, but I look 16, which is why a lot of my fan base is 11-17 year old girls," he says. "I have a couple super fans, including a girl from Long Island that drove five hours with her family to my theater to see my show. Since the first episode I was on, she was on *Facebook* and splicing her photo into whatever photo I was in so it looked like she was standing with me. She's very...enthusiastic."

The unnamed groupie will be excited to hear that Spencer recently taped an episode of the TV show *Masters of Illusion*, which will air in November 2013 on the CW network.

❖ ❖ ❖ ❖

EDON (Top 24)

Singer, 14

Edon Pinchot's audition for *America's Got Talent* was also the very first time the suburban Chicago teen ever performed in public. "I was sick to my stomach," he remembers. "I was freaking out!" Edon – who began playing piano at age 9 – was invited the Austin, Texas tryouts after *AGT* talent scouts came across a series of homemade music videos he had posted on *YouTube*. He instantly became a favorite of the judges ("You are so talent, so gifted," Howard Stern said) and young girls around the world who dubbed him "the Jewish Justin Bieber." "It's hard to fathom having

Edon Pinchot
Photo: Courtesy (Pinchot Family)

your own fan base," Edon, a sophomore at Ida Crown Jewish High School, admits. "It is weird that all these people want to know what I am doing every day."

The fourth of five children born to lawyer Dov Pinchot and his wife Laurie, a history teacher, Edon is rarely seen without his familiar knit yarmulke. Faith, he says, has played a "huge role" in his success. "I have grown up as an Orthodox Jew. That is who I am," notes Edon, who attends an Orthodox sleep-away camp each summer in Wild Rose, Wisconsin. "I think part of this process was being able to go out on a stage in front of people and seeing how people would react to that. It was cool to see not only how accepting people on the show were, but also to see my fans – a majority of who probably aren't Jewish – and see that that is something that they can probably put aside. They don't have to look and say 'Oh, he's Jewish. That has really been one of the coolest things, that people kind of accepted me for who I am."

A year after his *AGT* debut, Edon continues to perform. He recently learned to play guitar and is focusing on writing music and promoting his music through social media. In August 2013, Edon released a video cover of Zedd's "Clarity," which was filmed on the 103rd floor sky deck of Chicago's Willis Tower.

Photo: Courtesy (Mary Joyner)

MARY JOYNER

Singer, 22

After a moving tribute to her mother, Olympic star Florence Joyner Griffith, during the audition rounds, Mary looked like she might make it all the way to the finals. But a flubbed note during Vegas Week bounced her from the competition early. Weeks later, Mary was back in top form, performing the "Star Spangled Banner" at Olympic trials in Eugene, Oregon.

"I also did a Leukemia-Lymphoma gala and am releasing a mix tape and collaborating with some rappers," she reports. "I'm kind of changing up my style a bit. I will be releasing an album in the fall and it will be available on my website. I've been writing my own songs, and have been training with my dad to stay healthy, which is a good stress reliever. I'm currently working on my mom's foundation, The FloJo Memorial Foundation. I really want that to grow and reach out to young athletes. I want to keep her dreams going and do things in her honor." Mary has been attending the San Diego Recording Arts Center, studying both music and engineering. "I took some time off to regroup after last year — with *AGT*, the Olympics, and all, it was a huge year," she says. "I needed some time off. But I'm going back to normal school in the fall [of 2013]."

The addition of judges Mel B. and Heidi Klum helped boost ratings during season 8.

Photo: Splash News

SEASON 8

(June 4, 2013 – September 19, 2013)

Host: Nick Cannon

Judges: Howard Stern, Mel B., Heidi Klum, Howie Mandel

"I'm not bringing anything that's different. I'm bringing the same thing I brought last season. I'm going to be an honest judge. You saw how great I was on it last season, and now I'm going to do it again. I'm going to take these 6 and 7 year-olds and make them cry. "

- Howard Stern

AS THE SEASON 8 PREMIERE drew near, producers and NBC executives knew their once-mighty summer juggernaut had reached a fragile crossroads. Would the addition of two new judges – and a change of venue to New York's Radio City Music Hall – be enough to lure back the millions of viewers who tuned out after the addition of Howard Stern? Or would 2013 be the year *America's Got Talent* officially jumped the shark?

"We are going to be making some changes around the way that we do storytelling," newly appointed executive producer Sam Donnelly revealed at a press conference in Pasadena, California. "It's generally a freshening up of the series – about how we tell stories, about some backstage reality. You are going to get to see some of [the acts and judges] in more candid moments, which should be interesting. They don't know that yet. We are filming them a lot."

Indeed *AGT* version 8.0 did have a distinctly different look and feel – from a freshened up logo and abbreviated show opening to the addition of fly-on-the wall moments backstage.   Cameras captured contestants in what appeared to be spontaneous conversations before and after auditions, but insiders tell us most of the dialogue was loosely scripted and often times filmed multiple times. In its early weeks, *AGT* was beginning to look an awful lot like Simon Cowell's other TV competition – *The X Factor*.

Luckily, the new tweaks seemed to be just what the doctor ordered. "The new panel has jelled very well," Cowell bragged to the Associated Press, giving much of the credit for the bump up in ratings to his new E.P. "She's totally revitalized the show. It's by far the best we've done."

At least one critic agreed. Says Linda Stasi of the *New York Post*:

> *Is it even possible that America's Got Talent actually gets more talented with each new year and each new judge? After watching the first few new episodes this season with the two new judges — Heidi Klum and Mel B — yes, the relentlessly entertaining, flat-out best talent competition show on TV just got even better.*

> *For one thing, everybody gets along — even with Howard Stern, who has turned into a funny team player and very thoughtful judge. Who knew he'd become Rodney "Can't We All Just Get Along?" King?*

> *Happily the "AGT" judges have stopped aping for the cameras and have just let the talent fly. In some cases literally. So far this year, I've been amazed, shocked, thrilled, astonished and bewildered. I mean, seriously, a headstand 80 feet in the air without a net?*

Season 8 live auditions were held in New York City (Hammerstein Ballroom), Chicago (Rosemont Theatre), San Antonio (Lila Cockrell Theatre), New Orleans (U.N.O. Lakefront Arena)and Los Angeles (Pantages Theatre). For the first time ever 60 acts advanced from Las Vegas to the live shows in New York. As a result, there was no *YouTube* special or wild card round. (Four wild card acts were selected by the judges to return during the semifinals.)

Among the season's most memorable story lines:

JUDGES FEUD: HOWARD V. HEIDI?

Just in time for the June 4 premiere, the *National Enquirer* broke a (very suspect) story about an alleged feud between Heidi Klum and Howard Stern. "She'll never forget how he made fun of her eating habits and thick German accent and cracked cruel Nazi jokes," an unidentified source told the tabloid. "The last straw came when Howard made fun of her mother."

Heidi reportedly confronted "America's Judge" when they started taping. "He called his remarks 'innocent comedy,' but she's still steaming," the snitch said. "Heidi may be a world-famous supermodel, but she's got her own hidden talent — putting on a poker face. She'll have everyone thinking that she likes Howard, but Heidi says she joined *AGT* to do a job — not make friends."

Not surprisingly, the whole thing turned out to be untrue. In 2012, there were also unsubstantiated reports of a falling out between Howie and Howard. But according to *GossipCop.com,* all the judges "get along great."

◆ ◆ ◆ ◆

HOWIE MANDEL ACCUSES COMIC OF PLAGIARISM

Funny man Greg Wilson got lots of laughs at his live audition in Los Angeles, but did he steal the jokes? Howie Mandel sure thought so, accusing the comic of plagiarizing his entire routine as cameras rolled. Making the whole incident even more uncomfortable, Howie claimed the bit – a reenactment of a wife and husband fighting in a car, but without words – was originally created by the show's audience warm-up comic, Frank Nicotero!

"Everyone involved seemed uncomfortable, and the whole thing felt awkward and unplanned," audience member Peter Sciretta wrote in a blog post on *Slashfilm.com*. "If the producers were involved in a set-up, it seemed clear to everyone at the taping that

Howie, the contestant and Nicotero weren't in on it. The *AGT* cameras tried to get Nicotero, who was off to the side of the theater, to come on stage. Nicotero was pissed and didn't want to be on camera." But later that night Nicotero shared his side of the story in a *Facebook* post:

Tonight I was doing warm up at America's Got Talent and that fat piece of shit Greg Wilson went on tonights taping and DID MY BIT EXACTLY LIKE I'VE BEEN DOING IT FOR YEARS. I rushed to the producers table to talk to the Executive Producers and point blank said he is stealing my bit. I was shaking with anger.

THANK GOD FOR HOWIE MANDEL....Howie pointed out that he's seen the bit before and it's from our warm up guy Frank Nicotero. That piece of shit said, "he stole if from me...I'm a headliner on TV and he's the warm up guy! I have a mic and he doesn't!" Funny thing is I DID Have a mic and chose to not jump in and ruin the show. Needless to say I lost it. That bit is personal. It's the bit people request. It's my "Free Bird!"

No part of Greg's audition – or elimination during Vegas Week – was ever broadcast.

❖ ❖ ❖ ❖

HEIDI KLUM'S BADASS BODYGUARD

Heidi Klum has always been a class act. Her new bodyguard? Well...not so much, according to members of the New York entertainment press. The freshman judge couldn't have been happier to mingle with fans and reporters prior to the first live shows at Radio City Music Hall. But red carpet photographers told the *New York Daily News* that Heidi's bulging new muscle man sabotaged their shots by shining a bright flashlight into their lenses. "Heidi won't be falling for this security guard," one onlooker joked.

❖ ❖ ❖ ❖

MEL B. BOOED AFTER CALLING COMIC RACIST

Mel B. got a face full of angry New Yorkers when she buzzed comic Jimmy Failla for telling an arguably racist joke during his live audition. Failla – a cabbie by day – was setting up a joke about how black taxi drivers are so entertaining when the former Spice Girl X'd him. "I found it really offensive," the first-ear judge said. "There was no need to do a stereotypical black joke. It was not funny." But the audience disagreed, showering her with loud "Boo's." Howard Stern also criticized Mel (who, of course, is black), saying she had no sense of humor. And even Heidi Klum came to the comic's defense, saying, "There will always be jokes made about being black and white."

DID CATAPULT RIP OFF THE SILHOUETTES?

Fans were quick to take sides in the great shadow dancing debate of 2013.

On the season 8 premiere, New York dance artists **Catapult Entertainment** punched their ticket to Las Vegas with a stunning visual performance that many viewers were quick to call "a ripoff" of season 6 runners-up **The Silhouettes**. Days later, the official *AGT Facebook* page threw fuel on the fire by posting a video of the act with the message, "Have you ever seen anything like Catapult?!"

That prompted hundreds of fans to hit up social media and point out the obvious similarities between the acts:

"Yes i have seen..its called silhouettes" - **Cynthia 'Cheng' Sleeman (FB)**

"Yes, they are copy cats or maybe they were around before the Silhounetts, but they are not nearly as good as the Silhounetts. Thought some of their stuff was a little amateur and sloppy." - **Jan Culbertson (FB)**

"The [Silhouettes] were way better I hate it when a copycat comes along and gets praised as if they are an original." - **Tony Dunlap (FB)**

Others stuck up for the newcomers, who many believe delivered one of the best auditions of the season.

"This act was amazing!! Slightly similar to Silhouette, except even better" - **Tabitha Howard. (FB)**

"Who cares if they ripped off the Silhouettes? The show is about talent. Whenever a singer comes on and sings a famous song no one says "hey you copied that song" they have talent so shut up" - **Phill Prew (YouTube)**

"The Silhouettes wasn't 100% original either. People did shadow dances like that for years. This has more action, which I enjoy more." - **iAstro129 (YouTube)**

MAD HOT BALLROOM RIVALRY

From the moment tween siblings Ruby and D'Angelo Castro auditioned with different dance partners – and began talking smack about which of them America would love more – we all kind of knew someone would end up in tears. And that is exactly what happened on August 21, 2013 when 12 year-old D'Angelo (and partner Amanda Carbajales) and 9 year-old Ruby (and her partner Jonas Terleckas) stood eight feet apart waiting to find out which duo America liked better.

It was almost painful to watch young Ruby burst into tears when Nick Cannon awarded the final spot in the next round to her brother. Not surprisingly, fans and members of the press began to wonder aloud if producers had exploited the young kids to create a dramatic TV moment.

"I understand that the kids knew they'd be competing when they first auditioned separately, but did the producers *really* have to make them stand side-by-side as the results were announced?" Andy Swift wondered on *HollywoodLife.com*. "Poor Ruby looked so sad, and poor D'Angelo wasn't even allowed to look happy about his victory. We watch reality TV for intense moments, and I'm sure the producers figured they'd struck gold with this opportunity, but I think it was a major misstep."

5 QUESTIONS FOR HEIDI KLUM

The first year judge told us why she was the right girl for the job when we caught up at the Los Angeles auditions in April 2013.

Photo: Splash News

What makes you the perfect judge for *America's Got Talent*?

I always judge people. Yesterday I told someone who didn't really want to have a haircut, but I thought they needed one. He ended up doing it. And he looks so much better. I think I have always judged people. I have been judged for 20 years being in this industry. And I feel like because I have traveled the world being a model and I am very interested in dance and theater and opera... I danced for 15 years before I started modeling. I have seen a lot of things. I am interested in this kind of stuff. I feel like if someone has it, I feel it and I want to push them forward. If someone doesn't have a tune, I can hear when someone can't sing...

After a decade of *Project Runway*, how have you altered your judging style?

I am definitely not as afraid anymore. When I did *Project Runway* the first year I was definitely scared. "Is that okay to say? Is that not okay to say?" I didn't want to hurt people's feelings. And I think now I am more free. It comes to my head and I say it. Obviously I don't like to put salt in some wounds. If someone said already something negative, I am not going to hack on that and be nasty. There is no reason to be nasty to people. There are some people who have done some silly things. There was a woman on roller blades and she was making orange juice out of her bra and I am like, "Why are you wasting our time?" But I don't get angry and mean.

How do you feel about young children competing?

I think every mom and dad have to make that choice. I wouldn't do it for my children, but if others feel differently that is what they should do. But they should also know, the parents, that if they put them out on the stage in front of four judges, they will be judged. They might tell them they are not very good and they might have their little hearts broken.

Does that make for good TV, when little kids cry?

I think it makes for great TV when kids come on and they are actually very good! There are some kids that are super talented. I have seen more than 300 acts already. And I remember certain kids vividly because they were so good. They were dancing so perfectly. They love it so much. Their facial expressions and the way they light up on stage. I think some kids are made for this. They really love it. Sometimes you see moms that push their kids out and that is sad.

What talents do your kids have?

My kids are great dancers and they love to sing. Obviously I am super proud of them and I think they are fabulous. Not really for this kind of stage. More for the living room stage.

CHRISTINA & ALI

(Season 5)

'CYSTIC FIBROSIS DOES NOT DEFINE US'

Christina (L) and Ali in 2013

THEY WERE NEVER SUPPOSED TO BE ABLE TO SING. But Christina and Ali Christensen – a pair of determined, young sisters from eastern Idaho – were not going to let their dreams of pop stardom get crushed by Cystic Fibrosis. The incurable, genetic lung disease, which eventually makes it impossible to breathe, had already claimed the life of their older sister, April, in July 2009. She was just 25. "It gets worse with age," 19 year-old Ali – then the reigning Miss Idaho Falls – revealed in a televised interview before the girls' emotional season 5 audition in Portland. "Your lungs can get really tight. The average life expectancy is mid-to-late 30s. But we can enjoy every minute together that we have. If we pursue our dreams it will give us something to look forward to instead of dwelling on our disease. Cystic Fibrosis does not define us. We define ourselves."

Christina, who will graduate high school in 2014 and hopes to attend Brigham Young University-Idaho (just like her sister!), says the girls never thought twice about sharing their deeply personal story with a worldwide television audience. "We wanted to inspire people and I think that is what we did," she tells us. "Our goal was not only to relate to other people with CF but to everyone around us. It was kind of tough because with CF we were told we would never be able to sing and traveling was kind of hard on our health. But it was definitely worth it."

The sisters originally auditioned as solo singers but were encouraged by producers to team up at the last minute. Just one problem: they had never sung together before, except at their sister's funeral. "We went in the hall and threw a few things together and kind of went from there," Ali recalled in an interview with *Seventeen*. Luckily, the gamble paid off. Christina and Ali's combination of natural charm, raw determination and vocal prowess eventually propelled them into the Top 10 – despite having to cope with constant fatigue and multiple daily doses of medicine. "We had to pack an extra suitcase just for all our [medical gear]," Christina remembers. Today she continues to receive twice-a-day treatment at home and travels to Primary Children's Medical Center in Salt Lake City every two to three months for regular checkups. "It's pretty time-consuming to stay healthy," she says. "We have inhalers and nebulizers and pills and liquid medicine... It is kind of gross."

With their health in check, Christina and Ali were able to participate in the 25-city *AGT* concert tour in late 2010. Shortly after, they launched a *Kickstarter* crowd funding campaign and eventually released the five-song EP, *Love Is Gonna Find You*.

As it turned out, love ended up finding both girls! In August 2012, Ali (Alexa Rae) married her high school sweetheart, Chase Wilde, and moved to Provo, Utah, where she found work at a local restaurant. Christina attended prom with her "kinda" boyfriend Ethan. "It was super fun," she says. "I was in every dance with him...I am definitely not taking life for granted."

Two years after appearing on *AGT*, the sisters continue to enjoy daily reminders of their 10 weeks in the spotlight. "People will come up and be like 'Oh, my gosh, you are that girl from *America's Got Talent*." Christina says. "I am still kind of shy about it. It's crazy how time flies. When I was on the show I had braces and I was so short! I still don't understand how we did that. It is crazy to me. I look back and think 'We stood on that stage and sang in front of America.' Seriously it is so weird. To this day, it still hasn't clicked yet!"

Reality TV fame has allowed Christina and Ali to connect with thousands of young people through nationwide motivational speaking engagements. "It helps me too because I see a lot of people who we touched," Christina says. "It is just the best feeling."

In 2012, Christina decided to give singing on TV another shot. She tried out for *American Idol* and was flown to California to sing for the show's executive producers, but was cut before the televised auditions.

With Ali settling in to life as a newlywed, Christina says she would now like to focus on a solo career. "I haven't put [singing] on the back burner...but I don't know about her," she says. "I want to stick to the inspirational kind of pop-country music. And I want to record my own CD...and maybe even try out for *X Factor*!"

ALICE TAN RIDLEY

(Season 5)

'PRECIOUS' MOM GOES FROM SUBWAYS TO SYMPHONIES

Photo: Courtesy (Alice Tan Ridley)

ALICE TAN RIDLEY PAID HER DUES the hard way – busking for tips in New York City subway stations. But the mother of *Precious* actress Gabourey Sidibe was far from down on her luck, as her appearance on *America's Got Talent* led the public to believe. "Just being on that show, they kind of change your life because they want everyone to have a sob story," she says. "I felt kind of crazy because as far as I was concerned, my story was not a sob story. It was a happy story."

Alice, who turned 60 in 2013, spent 18 years working as a teacher's aid in the New York City school system. "They didn't play that up as much as the fact that I worked in the subway," she admits. In fact, Alice actually quit her day job years earlier because singing for straphangers simply brought home more bacon. "What I was making every two weeks with the Board of Education, I could make in a day or two underground," she says.

The eighth of nine children, Alice was born into a musical family in Georgia and first appeared on stage at age three. "She's got an amazing personality as well as a great talent," judge Piers Morgan praised. "Put those things together plus her sheer determination and the inspiration of her story...the whole package is very powerful."

Despite having no formal training, Alice has had more than a few brushes with stardom: she appeared in the David LaChapelle documentary *Rize*, sang "America the Beautiful" in the Merchant Ivory film *Heights*, and won an Emmy in 2007 for her part in the documentary *Military Families*. In 2002, she collected $25,000 as the grand prizewinner of Fox's short-lived talent competition, *30 Seconds To Fame*.

Alice claims she was originally offered the role of the mother in *Precious*, but turned it down. "Being a mom and teacher, I just couldn't play that part," she told *Us Weekly*. "It was just too hard. I read the book, and I gave it to Gabby. Her friends encouraged her to try out for *Precious*, and she got it." Alice admits, she "lost her identity for a while" and went into her *AGT* audition hoping to get out of the shadow of her famous daughter. "I am down there singing and all I would hear is people whispering 'That's Precious' mother,'" she says. "I was no longer Alice Tan Ridley, I was just Precious' mother."

Since reaching the semi-finals in season 5, Alice has performed multiple shows at the B.B. King Blues Club in Times Square and traveled the world with symphony orchestras, performing to sellout audiences. "I auditioned for [the Broadway cast of] *Chicago* but that didn't really pan out," she says. "Acting really is not my thing. I can do it, but it is not my thing. I am really more about singing. I am not mad about not getting a Broadway thing. I am still traveling around doing concerts. I worked with the Cab Calloway Orchestra. The average person doesn't get to do that." The soulful mother of two (she still lives in Harlem with son Ahmed) first tried out for *AGT* in 2006, but never made it far enough to sing for the judges. "They had an audition here in New York and I made it through three or four different levels of it," she remembers. "But after a while they told me 'We don't need you anymore' and I was off to my job right down there on 42nd street, 'cause I had my equipment with me that day. I just went right down in the subway and did what I do. You try out for stuff and it doesn't always work out. But there is no crying over spilled milk. You dust yourself off and you keep on gettin' up."

Alice Tan Ridley performs in a New York subway station in 2010
Photo: Ouzounova/Splash News

BARBARA PADILLA

(Season 5)

13 YEARS CANCER FREE, NEW CD COMING SOON

Courtesy: Barbara Padilla

HER STORY WAS AN INSPIRATION to everyone who has ever stared in the face of illness. "I am a cancer survivor," Barbara, 36, proudly shared with almost 20 million *AGT* viewers. "I was sick for five years. Now I am in remission and I am here. When you have hope, you keep going!"

The opera sensation and stay-at-home mom from Houston was diagnosed with Hodgkin's Lymphoma at 23, when she was living with her family in Guadalajara, Mexico. Within weeks, Barbara headed north of the border for treatment. Mere hours after being informed she would need a bone marrow transplant, the gifted soprano was awarded a full scholarship to the music program at the University of Houston. Then came the bad news: her bone marrow was too damaged for a transplant. "The doctors told me, 'We're going to give you radiation in the neck area,'" she remembers, "'but you won't be able to sing again.'" They were wrong.

Barbara arrived at *AGT* auditions in her adopted hometown ready to once again defy the odds. This time, her sights were set on the $1 million grand prize. Her performance of Puccinni's "O mio bambino caro," earned a standing ovation from judges Sharon Osbourne and David Hasselhoff – and praise from often critical Piers Morgan: "You have great character to you. Great spirit and determination. I think you have got a voice that could take you quite a long way in this competition." And she did, finishing in second place behind country singer Kevin Skinner.

"After the show I had a lot of performances, especially as a keynote speaker for a lot of benefits and charities connected to cancer research. I was so happy because I wanted to be able to talk about my journey and if I could somehow be an inspiration for somebody, that is what you have to do."

- Barbara Padilla

In the fall of 2009, Barbara performed for 10 weeks with the *America's Got Talent Live* show at Planet Hollywood in Las Vegas. The production then moved for another three-week engagement at Foxwoods Resort Casino in Mashantucket, Connecticut. "After the show I had a lot of performances, especially as a keynote speaker for a lot of benefits and charities connected to cancer research," she tells us. "I was so happy because I wanted to be able to talk about my journey and if I could somehow be an inspiration for somebody, that is what you have to do."

Barbara has been cancer-free since 2000, but reveals that years of chemotherapy and radiation treatment left her unable to conceive. "I can still have children, I just won't get stretch marks," she jokes. In 2005, Barbara and her husband, I.T. manager Kyle Howard adopted their only child, daughter, Elizabeth. "My daughter is great," she says. "She is a gymnast. She is going into second grade. I am so thrilled she had passed to the non-recreational level of gymnastics. I am a very proud mama. I am so blessed by her. I cannot tell you how thankful I am with God that he has given me a very healthy girl."

The couple have talked about expanding their family, "but every time I bring it up, my husband says, 'Yeah, another baby for me to take care of! You are always traveling,' she says. "We would love to. If I got pregnant that would be awesome, but it is a process we can't focus on right now. If I think about having a child, then I am definitely thinking about giving up my career."

For the past two years, Barbara has been recording songs for a new CD she hopes to release in late 2013. "We recorded it last year (2012) with the London Symphony Orchestra at Abbey Road studios," she says. "Phil Ramone helped us with the mixing. He worked on it a little bit before he passed away. We have everything we need. It is so good we are not going to rush it. Right now we are in that precise moment of calm before the storm. I am so ready."

DONALD BRASWELL II

(Season 3)

OPERA STAR DEFIES ODDS, SINGS AGAIN AFTER CAR ACCIDENT

Photo: Courtesy Donald Braswell

DONALD BRASWELL II WAS TOLD he would never sing again. The Texas-born Juilliard graduate – and one-time singing waiter – was on his way to becoming a world-renowned opera star in 1995 when he was struck while riding his bicycle by a hit and run driver just outside of Cardiff, Wales. "I was laying down inside a ditch," he remembers. "The driver stopped for a second and said 'You alright?' Then I heard the car door slam and the motor revving and he took off."

Donald was just 32 at the time, traveling with the Welsh National Opera production of *Madama Butterfly*. And, as the saying goes, "The show must go on." "Believe it or not, I didn't go to the hospital," he tells us. "At that point – except for the fact that I felt like I had a chicken bone in my throat – I didn't feel terrible. I had pain in the side of my neck, but I could still talk. So I went to the opera company and told them what happened and they asked if I could perform. I told them 'I actually think I will be alright. I just need to rest.'"

He was wrong. During Donald's very next performance – the last of the tour – he experienced severe pain in his throat and neck and was forced to leave the stage. "When I went back to New York, I immediately went to the hospital," he says. "They said 'You have a terrible tear. You made it worse by performing. You tore [the muscle] all the way off the bone." His music career was over.

Donald, whose parents were both Broadway performers, was unable to speak above a whisper for almost a year. He became a recluse and experienced severe bouts of depression. "It was a frightening experience for me," he admits. "I felt like I was never going to get better. I had become very lethargic." When Julie, his wife of a dozen years, became pregnant with their first child, the couple gave up their Manhattan apartment and headed back to the Lone Star State to live with her parents and start over.

"My speaking voice came back around late 1997, early 1998," Donald remembers. "I was starting to speak normally, so my desire was to try to get the voice back to a point where I could sing again. But singing professionally and trying to sing are two different things." It wasn't until *America's Got Talent* that Donald would return to the limelight, finishing in fourth place after being eliminated in Las Vegas and returning as a wild card act.

The father of three wowed all three judges with his inspirational story – which suggested that he was singing again for the very first time in 11 years. Not entirely true. Online reports note that Donald had previously performed several dates with the San Antonio Symphony and appeared in a local production of *Camelot*. Looking back, he insists: "My intention always was to make sure everyone understood that I had not sung *professionally* in any way in all those years." At the time of his audition, Donald was managing a car dealership and previously sold auto insurance, he says. "I did everything but be a singer." Donald concedes "there were some liberties taken" with the way his story was presented on *AGT*: "There were some things said that I never did say – but I don't think the intent of how they said it was meant to change the truth of what happened. The truth is I *was* hit by an automobile. I didn't have severed vocal chords like Jerry said. But I tore a muscle off a bone inside my throat, off of the clavicle bone and off of the sternum. It disabled my ability to produce sound for a good period of time. The prognosis from the medical professionals that I had seen at the time were simply that I more than likely would have difficulty speaking normally for the rest of my life and certainly would not be able to pursue a career as a professional singer ever again. So, it was very believable to me for a period of time because I couldn't produce sounds and there was a great deal of pain. Years later, muscle slowly began to grow along the bone point and I was able to recapture my ability to start speaking normally and then be able to start singing again."

In June 2012, Donald returned to musical theater with a lead role in the musical *The Centurion* in Ronks, Pennsylvania. He continues to tour, performing many of his concert dates in Florida. He is also part of a local "Three Tenors" style group and watches proudly as daughter, Aria, appears to be following in his footsteps. "She attends a performing arts high school here in San Antonio," he says. "She was born with the genetics. Her voice was passed down from my mother and father."

Ellie White is the subject of the new documentary film
A Light In The Shadows.

Photo: Courtesy (White family)

ELLIE WHITE of SILHOUETTES

(Season 6)

11 YEAR-OLD BRAVELY BATTLES TERMINAL ILLNESS: 'I HAVE THE DISEASE, IT DOESN'T HAVE ME'

ELLIE WHITE TURNED 10 the night her shadow dance team, Silhouettes, claimed second place for season 6. But just having the chance to appear on the show at all – and share a bit of her brave, personal story – was the best birthday present the bubbly Colorado tween could ever have hoped for.

Ellie – who loves to surf, snowboard and help take care of her baby brother, Matthew – is one of just 50 children in the world known to suffer from a rare genetic disorder called Wolfram Syndrome. In the next few years, it will almost certainly cause her to lose most or all of her sight and hearing. With no known cure, the average life expectancy for a Wolfram patient is about 30 years. "Just getting to tell about my disease on national TV was huge," Ellie says. "I have always wanted to do that. I am trying to tell everybody and anybody I can about it so we can raise money and find a cure."

The young dancer's story is both tragic and inspirational. She was diagnosed with the little-known condition at age 7, after

Ellie and brothers Ryan (l) and Matthew vacation in North Carolina in 2013.
Photo: Courtesy (White family)

years of being treated for Juvenile Diabetes. "There are some breathing and respiratory problems and choking [associated with Wolfram Syndrome]," says her mother, Beth, a research scientist at the University of Colorado-Denver. "So some of the kids die from that at earlier ages. But we just don't know what will happen. Ellie has already dropped about a line of vision each year. She wears glasses, but the glasses don't correct it. And she is colorblind, which isn't correctable. But it is not like she is going to go blind tomorrow. It is a gradual progression."

Ellie is living life knowing that her time is limited. "The thing that just sucks is that more than anything else in her life, she wants to be a mom," Beth says. "And she really wants to grow up and be a scientist, so she can help other people and make a difference. I think that she feels like that won't happen – but she is hopeful that it will. She is studying hard. It is hard to imagine how she could have such a positive attitude about pushing and carrying on. If you knew your life was going to end, wouldn't you just spend all of your money and go to Hawaii?"

Beth admits the stress surrounding Ellie's situation eventually took a toll on her marriage. She divorced the father of her three children [son Ryan is 9] in January 2013, shortly after Matthew was born. "I found out about some things right after the baby was born," she says. "We tried to work it out but just had irreconcilable differences. Now it is extra hard because I am a single mom working part-time with a mortgage and three kids – one of which is terminally ill and one is a baby. With the divorce, it has been really challenging."

But Ellie, who attends public school in the tight-knit rocky mountain community of Coal Creek Canyon, is determined not to let family drama or an ugly, mysterious illness break her spirit. "I try to keep my spirits up by just thinking of things that I enjoy," the sixth grader tells us. "I try to remember that I have the disease, it doesn't have me. It isn't holding me down. I am able to do all the things a normal person does – just with a few tweaks to them."

Wolfram Syndrome is "a dire, horrible, insidious disorder," Beth admits. "But that is not the way we are living our life. We try to keep things as normal as possible. She has chores and she gets in trouble and she is expected to keep her grades up."

Dear Friends,

I would like to tell you about my rare genetic disorder, Wolfram syndrome. Wolfram syndrome is not only life limiting but it is causing me to lose my vision and my hearing and it causes many other severe problems in my body. I have always planned to grow up to be a mommy and a scientist and a dancer. I want to make sure that my disorder doesn't stand in my way.

We're making a documentary movie and starting The Ellie White Foundation for Rare Genetic Disorders. I'm hoping that you will be willing to donate to help me share my story, which will help us find cure for this disease and help others with similar bad problems. I want the documentary to help people of all ages understand the importance of life.

Thank you so much.

Love,
Ellie

Ellie hopes to someday attend Oxford University. "I really enjoy learning stuff from my mom and my family," she says. "We are all pretty much scientists and teachers in my family. So I like learning from my mom and my dad and my grandparents. And I find that really interesting. I get pretty good grades."

When she's not traveling to raise money and awareness on behalf of the Ellie White Foundation for Rare Genetic Disorders, the sixth grader continues to dance up to 10 hours a week with the Silhouettes. "She is just crazy about dance," her mom beams. "So any opportunity to dance she totally embraces. Her two most important things in her life are public speaking and dance."

In early 2013, Ellie was invited to fulfill a lifelong dream of performing on Broadway in the ensemble of *Elf The Musical*. Two weeks later, she attended the presidential inauguration in Washington DC. Ellie is now the subject of an upcoming documentary about Wolfram Syndrome called *A Light in the Shadows*. Producers hope to have it ready for a summer 2014 release.

"We are just carrying on trying to enjoy life and not let this drag us down," Beth insists. "We don't take anything for granted. Our time together is precious and valuable and we try to make sure it is fun and happy. Life is too short to wallow in self-pity."

Alonzo "Turf" Jones still performs in front of Bally's Casino on the Las Vegas Strip

Photo: Jeffrey J. Coleman (Shutterstock)

TURF v. STEPZ

(Season 7)

RIVAL STREET DANCERS, BOTH FROM BROKEN HOMES, FORM A UNIQUE FRIENDSHIP

IT ISN'T EVERY DAY that two rival street dancers from opposite coasts compete head-to-head for one final spot on the *AGT* live shows – and end up becoming best friends. Alonzo "Turf" Jones, 19, and Tyriece "Stepz" Green, 22, had already crossed paths at numerous local competitions before their emotional, tear-filled Vegas Week showdown. "He's known in Cali for being one of the best and I am known for being the best in New York," Stepz revealed in a backstage interview.

Stepz became a father - twice - in the past year.
Photo: Courtesy

But dancing isn't all the young men have in common. Both are also products of broken homes. "When I was six years old, my parents were drug addicts, into gangs and all of that," Stepz shared. "My grandmother asked my mother 'You gonna choose the streets or you gonna choose your family?' And my mother pushed me out of the way and went out the door. Over drugs." He ended up being raised by his grandmother in a gang-infested section of Patterson, New Jersey. Three thousand miles west, in Northern California, Turf was coping with family problems of his own. "I graduated from school and said 'I am dancing' and my mom kicked me out of the house," he told *AGT* viewers. "I haven't spoken to her since." Turf says he was left "homeless on the streets for about two years."

Despite the pressure of direct competition (Turf ultimately won and advanced to the Top 24), both dancers say their mutual respect and friendship grew even stronger thanks to the show. "We were with each other all day, every day," Stepz tells us. "Turf was the only friend I had there really. We'd go down the [Vegas] Strip and do street shows and try to make extra money. Both of us come from low-income backgrounds so it wasn't really a battle between us. We were rooting each other on. He's still one of my best friends."

Before his *AGT* audition, Stepz was working for Victoria's Secret. "During what they called the fragrance season they'd have me dance out front to attract attention and get people to come into the store," he remembers. He tried out for the show as part of a dance team during season 3, but wasn't selected to appear on TV. He was also turned down by *So You Think You Can Dance*. Since his elimination, Stepz has begun to explore acting and appears in the new dance documentary *Flex Is Kings*. He is also a new father. "I have a son and a daughter now," he tells us exclusively. "One is 9 months old [as of July 2013], the other is 8 months. I actually found out they were coming right before I was on the show, maybe a few weeks before. I think that's what pushed me. It was a very dramatic situation. Honestly, I was a little ashamed to even bring it up so I didn't say anything to the producers or people from the show. Now I'm not ashamed. It's a blessing. My son lives with me and my daughter lives nearby. They are the most important things in my life."

When he's not dancing, Stepz is an independent business owner for Amway. "It was introduced to me through my son's mom," he says. "Since the show, I've performed in Vegas a couple of times, Atlantic City. I've teamed up with Illmatic Force in North Jersey and we've won three or four competitions so far. I dance with them and on my own. It's sort of like a partnership. We grew up together and we were like rivals, and we figured if we came together it would be good and turns out we were right.

"I was also thinking about auditioning for *So You Think You Can Dance* again because they seem to be looking into more urban dancers. A few of my friends are on the show, I would definitely audition again." Turf – who describes himself as an "extreme hip hop contortionist" – has relocated to Las Vegas where he performs five shows a week at the Quad Hotel and Casino as the opening act for comic Jeff Civillico.

"I haven't gotten nothing from [AGT]," he says. "I couldn't give credit [for my success] to the show. I still gotta audition for everything. It just let me know that there are auditions out there and if I can audition for AGT, I can audition for anything. I never expected to get farther than one episode. I never expected to win. Then when I saw who did win, it was just totally full of shit anyway. I don't even consider that shit real. That was the biggest point in my life that could ever have been wasted on nothing."

Turf shares an apartment behind the Wynn hotel with his girlfriend of two years and continues to perform for tips on the sidewalk three to four nights a week. "I recently saw my first Turf impersonator," he says. "There's actually two on the Strip and two on Fremont Street. They totally suck. They don't even look like me. I have never seen anybody pretend to be anybody until I came to Vegas. It was very eye-opening. I just tip them $20. I am flattered off of it. I watch and get on with my day. If you can make money pretending to be me, that has got to be the shit. I am not gonna stop you."

VOICES OF GLORY
(Season 4)

ANGELIC SINGING SIBLINGS WAKE MOTHER FROM EIGHT-MONTH COMA

Photo: Adam Hughes

VOICES OF GLORY OWE AT LEAST PART of their success to a fast-talking con-artist named Tammy Clausen who tricked them into moving to Branson, Missouri. The singing siblings – Michael II, Avery and Nadia Cole, whose inspirational harmonies lifted their mother from an eight month coma – were one of 10 acts from across the country contacted by the fake promoter in 2010 and offered an ongoing show in the mid-west resort town.

"She brought us down here and pretty much wined and dined us for a week," Michael remembers. "We decided it was a move we wanted to make. We prayed about it. Then about a month after we moved down here we found out she was a fraud and was brought up on charges up in Chicago! But we felt and prayed that this was something that really happened for God's glory. So we decided to stay here."

It was a wise decision. Today, the teens – who grew up in Highland, New York – perform over 200 dates a year in Branson and continue to expand their ministry across the country. "Every time we do a concert it is always ministering," their uncle and manager Gerard Cole says. "We belong to a church but we don't have a congregation that we perform to every day. Every place we go to we are always ministering. Even here in our concerts. We do jazz, pop, soul and gospel. We try to interject the things that Voices of Glory stands for into the concerts themselves."

The Cole family's incredible story began in July 2005, when mother Felicia – a junior high school science teacher and former Evangelist – was one of five passengers in a minivan that was struck head-on by a drunk driver in North Adams, Massachusetts. One woman, a fellow summer student at the Massachusetts College of Liberal Arts, died at the scene.

"I barely recognized her at all when I saw her in the hospital," her husband, Michael Sr., told the *Hudson Valley Press*. "If the hospital staff didn't tell me the person lying on that hospital bed was my wife, I would have never known." Despite Felicia's unsettling appearance and severe brain injuries, her children never gave up hope of her recovery. For three months, they gathered at her bedside every day to sing and pray until she finally awoke. "I could feel them there, even when I was in a coma," Felicia told the newspaper. "I wanted to be with my children, and I could hear their singing. It made me stronger."

Soon the Cole kids – fifth place finishers during season 4 – were traveling to nursing homes and hospitals all over the state sharing their inspirational messages and sounds. Naturally, concerts followed. "There was one lady that came to us and said 'What do you call yourselves?'" Michael II remembers. "At that point we just said 'The Cole Family.' After that we sat in the car and decided that Voices of Glory was the name that we wanted. Ever since it has grown to something that, honestly…right now we are very surprised about where it is going and we are so grateful for the leaps and bounds that God has allowed us to make."

But it was *AGT* that put them on the national radar. The group became a viral video sensation within hours of their audition in New York. The touching rendition of "God Bless America," brought Sharon Osbourne to tears. And the audience of 3,000 rose to its feet when Felicia was wheeled out to join her children on stage. "You are the pride of America tonight," Piers Morgan declared. Four years later, Felicia remains in a wheelchair but is showing signs of improvement. "I am getting better every day," she tells us. Still, Michael admits, it is unlikely that she will ever make a complete recovery. "She can take some steps, with assistance. She is just not able to walk fully," he reports. "We are praying for complete restoration and that she will be able to get up and be walking just as much as anybody else."

In the meantime, Voices of Glory continues to sing, inspire and make the most of the unique opportunity they believe God has given them. "We believe that if a door closes or something bad happens that something good will come out of it," Michael says. "Whether it is a lesson learned or another opportunity that we wouldn't be able to take if it wasn't for that door being closed. We feel like all things happen for a reason."

ANDREW DE LEON

(Season 7)

TEEN OPERA SENSATION EMBRACED GOTH LIFESTYLE IN MIDDLE SCHOOL

ANDREW DE LEON COULDN'T BELIEVE how many people were touched by his personal story – and amazing vocal talent. "I am so used to being hated that I thought that was what was going to happen," he told *AGTNews.com* immediately after being eliminated (for the first time) during Vegas Week. "But it means everything to me that I was able to touch people's hearts and reach through and help other kids."

Fans of the 19 year-old Goth-opera sensation went crazy when he was first bounced from the competition, starting an online petition demanding his return. It worked! The makeup artist – who worked on low budget horror films in Austin, Texas — was back on stage in August as a wild card act, only to be eliminated again in the semi-finals.

Andrew DeLeon

Photo: Courtesy (Andrew De Leon)

Andrew first embraced the alternative lifestyle in middle school. "(That's) when I saw the first Goth kid I had ever seen," he says. "I was horrified of this person. But through that I got to know this person. And I was inspired by that. Then I found out that we had the same interests. Through that I started to develop an interest in heavy metal music and gothic music and literature. And from there it just started to evolve." By high school, Andrew said, he grew angry and began to suffer bouts of depression. "For a good while there, I was kind of a horrible person. I was mean to everybody."

Those days are behind him, Andrew says. He continues to perform and is getting ready to release his first CD. We caught up with the budding star recently to learn more.

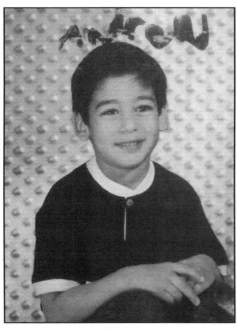

Andrew De Leon circa 1999
Photo: Courtesy (Andrew De Leon)

Is it true your family never heard you sing before your audition?

They heard me sing around the house, in a joking manner. I come from theater, so I'm always making strange noises and stuff. But I never actually *performed*. They knew I listened to opera but they had never heard me sing to it. They didn't even know I could do that. I know a lot of people who watched the show were very skeptical about how true that story was, but it was very true. I would only practice when my family was out or at work. I'm at home alone a lot. I would pull up instrumentals on *YouTube* and practice and look out the window to make sure no one was coming home. There had been moments when my dad would be getting home early and hear me and ask me what that sound was and I would blame the TV.

What was their reaction when they heard you sing on the *AGT* stage?

They had been in the audience biting their nails because they had no idea what I was going to do. They knew I was going to sing, but never thought it would be opera. My dad thought I was going to sing Metallica or Iron Maiden. When we got home we could not get over the reaction that I got from the audience. We invited some family over. My parents were doing most of the bragging.

Had you ever thought of auditioning before?

I never followed the show but I would watch the most popular auditions on *YouTube* and stuff. I'm not going to lie. Sometimes I would close my eyes and pretend that it was me and I'd imagine myself auditioning and getting a standing ovation. When it ended up happening, it was surreal.

What surprised you most about being on the show?

The way they edited everything. In my audition interview, they made me seem very gentle and sensitive. They weren't telling me to do that, and we talked about everything but they decided to edit out everything else. I'm not against it. Everything I said was true. They didn't tell me what to say. I answered questions and they edited it how they wanted it to seem. Nothing's fake on the show, it's a matter of editing.

What don't we see that goes on behind the scenes?

The taping process was very long. A lot of people backstage were stressed out. Everyone else that was there was a pro in their field and I wasn't. I had nothing to complain about. I was in Vegas, on television, and they were giving me free food. A lot of [other] people were not very thrilled. They didn't seem very happy to be there. There were contestants that didn't like not knowing if they made it through because they had jobs back home. It angered lots people and saddened others.

What happened after you were eliminated?

They sent me to the show counselor to make sure I was OK and everything. There's one on the set. I guess because of the way I looked, they thought I would kill myself or something. Then they sent me to the hotel room and I stopped at the store and bought a bunch of junk food. I hadn't been eating anything bad before the audition because of my voice, but after I got eliminated I was like 'Fuck this!' and bought candy and Fritos and soda and went to my hotel room and watched a Kevin Hart special to cheer up. It was very depressing. I was used to rejection, but not rejection in something that was important to me. Luckily, I had made some good friends. The Aurora Light Painters treated me to a night out to eat and to see *Phantom of the Opera*. It was very sweet of them. It took them about an hour to persuade me. They had already bought the tickets. I was in the third row. It was one of the nicest things anyone could have done for me and I was excited to see it, but in a way it kind of made me more sad, it made me think that it should be me up on that stage. The flight home was so depressing. I tried blasting my iPod listening to music, but nothing cheered me up. I think I needed to experience this sadness. I told myself, 'Just allow yourself to wallow. Eventually you'll be over it.' Of course it didn't work that way. I got home and got to see everyone else on the live shows and had this extreme feeling of jealousy. It had been about a month, watching and wallowing, of course my parents being a loving family, would say "Oh, they suck. You should be on there."

"After I was eliminated, they sent me to the show counselor to make sure I was OK and everything. There's one on the set. I guess because of the way I looked, they thought I would kill myself or something.

- Andrew DeLeon

Then they invited you back as a wild card. How did that happen?

I got an email from a producer, and at that time, it wasn't "You're coming back for sure." It was more like, "You might be coming back." I told myself, "Don't get excited." But I did make sure to practice every day. I wasn't ready to give up singing. I think the only time I said [that I was over singing] was right after I was eliminated and Nick asked me if I'd continue and I said 'No.' But it wasn't aired. Once I got back home I said, "I still want to do this and I'm not going to let this stop me."

It's a big platform, but it's not the only one. Some of the other contestants that they emailed to come back said no. I didn't say no because I missed the whole hectic part of it. I knew it would still be stressful, but I come from theater so I'm used to that and I loved that and I missed it so much. I missed being on a stage with an audience. They asked what songs I wanted to perform. I had about 10 songs to choose from. Then the costume department called. On my flight to New York, I was determined to prove everyone wrong. Little did I know that upon arrival I would immediately have to start rehearsing. I thought I'd get to sleep first and rest. Even before I went to my hotel, I had to go to the rehearsal room. There were about eight to 10 producers in a room and they wanted me to sing and I sounded awful. I was freaking out. I thought they'd think they brought me out for nothing. Luckily the vocal coach knew what he was talking about, and said, "We need to let him rest and have a good meal. He's jet-lagged and it effects the voice." So they rolled their eyes and said "Whatever." The next day I went to rehearsal and it was phenomenal. I wouldn't have been surprised if they had shipped me back to Texas though after that first performance. That's what their faces were saying.

What was your favorite part of being on the show?
As I walked into that lobby I heard nothing but screaming. Mostly girls, up against the glass. I asked someone who was standing there, High Pitched Mike from the *Howard Stern Show*, why they were screaming and he said "They're screaming for you, dumb ass!" I didn't know what to do so he opened the door and acted like a security guard. I didn't leave there for about an hour, signing and taking pictures and shaking hands. It was nice. I went up to my room and I was emotionally drained. Almost to the point of sadness. That night to celebrate all the contestants went up to the roof of the hotel and played music and hung out. Of course everyone was nice, which was great.

Another great moment was the night I got eliminated. I kind of knew that my moment of glory was over with the show. What was awesome is that I kind of didn't care this time. The reason is I was in my makeup chair and someone mentioned that Dee Snyder was in the building and I flipped out. I put my camera in my pocket, and I didn't care if the producers got angry with me. I'm in the waiting room, the red room, and one of the producers called me over and said [Dee] was standing right there. I look around the corner and there he is. Before I could even say anything, he just said, "You are awesome, and I dig the look, man." After that I had to perform and I think that was why I was so calm when I was performing. While I was singing, I was just enjoying the moment.

Do you get recognized a lot on the streets?
What's funny is people always say, "Are you that guy from *American Idol* or *X Factor*?" They never get the shows right. I remember at an airport someone came up to me and asked if I was from TV and I thought they knew who I was and they wanted a picture and they asked me to do a magic trick for them. I said, "What are you talking about? I don't know how to do magic." They thought I was Criss Angel! There have also been

times when my friends and I will go to a party and someone asks me to sing, which I refuse to do. I don't sing for drunk people.

Are you still performing today?

Since the show ended I have performed a few places: San Francisco, Nebraska, Kansas. Right now I'm working on an album. We started working on it in January and are now one song away from being finished. The album is called *Black Lights* and it has music ranging from classical opera to dance to rock music. I wrote all the songs except for one. Basically, I'm just devoting all of my time to recording, writing, and doing interviews about it. It's really strange how many people in the industry know who I am. Underground bands like Blood on the Dance Floor have contacted me and said nice things. That's pretty cool. It's being done independently so wish me luck on that. The great thing is that no one says no to you on what the music is about.

Has your *AGT* success helped your dating prospects?

I recently went to the Reality Wanted Awards in Los Angeles. They told me I could bring a date but I didn't. I wanted to take my mom because she deserves it. She got to walk the red carpet and be around the stars. She was very excited. But, no, I'm not really dating anyone right now.

Are you working any jobs on the side or going to school?

The album is full-time for me right now. We're planning to album release party and get together a tour dates. I'm pretty excited.

Andrew's album will be released September 21, 2103.

Bianca Ryan was just 11 years old when she won *America's Got Talent* in 2006.

Photo: Courtesy (Bianca Ryan)

BIANCA RYAN

(Season 1)

ALL GROWN UP, FIRST *AGT* WINNER HAS NEW MOVIE, CD IN THE WORKS

LONG BEFORE *AMERICA'S GOT TALENT*, an even younger Bianca Ryan already had her eye on Hollywood. "I had tried out for a lot of Disney and Nickelodeon things," she remembers. "I tried out for *Camp Rock* and *Hannah Montana*. I have always wanted to become an actress." And now she has.

The talented teen (and incoming freshman at Philadelphia's University of the Arts) recently completed her first independent movie, *We Be Kings*. "It's about a blues singer," she says. "His wife is dying and he is out on the road trying to make some money to help her while she is in the hospital. Along the way he finds me and this other guy (John Long) and together we play music and go on tour and get fans."

Bianca already knows a thing or two about admirers. She earned millions of them performing on *AGT*. Even when the judges weren't impressed with her semi-final song choice (Janis Joplin's "Piece of My Heart"), America voted the tween-age singing sensation through. The experience, she remembers, was "amazing and surreal. I just couldn't believe it was happening. When I look at it now it seems more like 'Wow, it is crazy that this happened.' Even more so than when I was 11 and 12. Looking back and thinking I was on *Oprah* and *Ellen* and I got to go on tour to Japan and Italy. It was crazy!" We caught up with Bianca recently to learn more about her *AGT* journey and life after the show.

What if you had become Hannah Montana? Think how different your life would be...

I am really grounded. I have a very good family and good roots. So I think I could definitely handle that. It would probably have to be little by little, not overnight. But I am pretty sure I could handle it.

What were your dreams and expectations after *AGT*? Did you think the business was going to be a little easier than it has been?

I did think it was going to be easier. For me, being 11, I thought, "Oh, I am going to get to have so much fun everywhere." But it was actually a lot of work. You travel to all these places, but you don't get to see much of what is there. I have been to Vienna and Japan, but I have never actually *been* there. You only see airports and hotels.

Has it been challenging for you since the show?

I guess when I was younger I didn't see it as hard as I do now. I took a couple of years off the whole career and singing thing just to be a normal kid and go through high school. Now that I am looking at it, I am like "Wow! That is my passion. I don't know what I was thinking. I have to get back out there." That is what I am doing now.

Had you performed professionally before *AGT*?

I had only been singing for two or three years. And that is including the first year where I am just singing to the radio and practicing by myself. Eventually my parents sent me to some lessons to make sure I was doing everything the right way. This is when I was doing dance lessons and just being a little dancer. I was also on *Star Search* when I was 9 years old and I did *Showtime at the Apollo*.

Your *Twitter* profile says, "I *WAS* that girl from *America's Got Talent*." Not "I AM." Are you trying to put some distance between yourself and the show?

Not really. It was more of a joke because when I am out with my friends, people will come up to me and be like "Hey, are you that girl from *America's Got Talent?*" I don't know. Maybe it is just because I feel older now.

Since you won, you probably can't go on any other competition shows...

So many people have asked me "Do you ever think of going on *American Idol* or *The Voice*? You could definitely win that!" But I am pretty sure I am not allowed to. Also Simon Cowell was my manager after *AGT*. But I would love to become a judge or a guest judge or be a guest where they come and perform on the finale! Just to get the whole experience now that I am 18 and understand everything that is going on would be cool.

How has your music evolved over the last seven years?

It has evolved in a lot of ways. On the show, I sang a lot of soulful music, with that old soul. And I still sing those kind of songs. But I also have expanded in so many ways. I sing pop, R&B, rock... I play the piano now and play the guitar. I have taken up the ukulele. I am always trying to find something new. I like messing around with all different instruments. You give me anything and I will learn it. And I write songs now.

You took some time off to go to school. What was that like?

I (went) to a creative and performing arts high school. So I always had music around me. We didn't have cheerleading or sports. We were just choir kids and band kids. Artists and dancers. It is definitely not a traditional high school experience. Our school – and you can ask anyone there – we would pretty much be the outcasts at any other "normal" high school. We were just the geeks that love the arts.

Were there cliques at school? Or did all the geeks stick together?

I am not really sure. I was not really trying to be popular in school. I know there are some cliques. But I was usually involved with every single one. I am friends with everyone.

Did you ever run into problems outside of school once you became famous?

No not really. Everybody in Philly and especially in my neighborhood has been so supportive of me and my career.

What happened to the $1 million?

That was put away for when I turn 21. Some of it was used to run some of my businesses that I have. Some was used for traveling.

Did you ever work in high school?

No. No jobs. Just music all the time. It is hard to keep a job when I am traveling. Even in high school though, I wasn't really trying to be in the spotlight or doing anything with social media. But I was still traveling and writing songs. At the beginning of my freshman year I was introduced to Quincy Jones which was an amazing opportunity for me. I flew out to California and I met him. He told me to really work on my songwriting and said he wants to produce my next album, which is still in the process because I took two years off. But he had me work with a lot of incredible songwriters like Diane Warren, Kara Dioguardi and Glen Ballard.

Ok, we have to ask – do you have a boyfriend?

No, I do not have a boyfriend and I am staying away from that for a long time. I had a boyfriend all through high school, but it just isn't worth it. Music is so much better. And music will never break up with me.

What else would people be surprised to know about your life today?

A while back I ran into a few vocal issues. I found out that I had extremely bad acid reflux and I had a slight scar on one of my vocal folds. I don't think it was really that that discouraged me, but it was just my mindset of "Oh my gosh, I have all these problems" that kind of held me back. Not only the physical issues, but the mental issues that go along with it. So that was part of taking the two years off to let that heal. And I was on medication for my acid reflux, which had been getting better. I continuously go to the doctors. Things are pretty much healing up. I am getting my voice completely back and getting back to lessons and performing. It is good to have all this music that I have been writing throughout the years, and now being able to sing them and start recording them. I am really expecting something big to happen soon.

Where did the scar on your vocal fold come from?

I had bronchitis and the doctor said it might have been from coughing really hard. Or it could have been from going on a roller coaster and screaming too loud one time. [laughs]

That must be scary – especially since that is your instrument.

For sure! I want singing to be my life and my career, so it was really scary. Being 15 years old and finding that out was crazy.

Did you ever think, "If I can't do music, what would I do?"

I actually never thought of that because no matter what I was still going to be a songwriter. I have always wanted to be a songwriter for other artists too. Maybe I could write songs for Katy Perry.

Is that your style?

I guess my songs are going more toward... I write a lot of Joss Stone kind of songs, more bluesy songs, Christina Aguilera style songs, Demi Lovato, Taylor Swift.

What do you think of the new season of *AGT*?

I have actually not been watching. I don't really watch TV that often to be honest. I am not really a TV person. I feel like it is extremely addicting and I am not going to get any work done if I keep watching TV. I prefer not to be addicted to a TV series so I can practice more.

CAS HALEY

(Season 2)

SKIPPED TOWN TO AVOID CONTRACT OBLIGATIONS AFTER THE SHOW

SOMETIMES YOU JUST HAVE A CHANGE OF HEART. Reggae-rocker Benjamin 'Cas' Haley did, not long after placing second behind ventriloquist Terry Fator during season 2. Cas, just 26, skipped town and went into hiding to avoid contractual obligations to the show and producers. "They were calling me, threatening me, of course, because I was under contract," he remembers. "It got really bad. At one point they would just show up at my shows and I would tell them, 'I don't want you here, I'm not answering your calls for a reason.' I just didn't want any part of it. Technically, I had signed the contract so they could sue me but I think they realized it just wasn't worth suing me. It wasn't worth the hassle so eventually they let me out of my contract."

Before signing on to compete, all contestants are required to sign a lengthy agreement which requires finalists to make themselves available to sign with show-appointed management and record labels. "It's really long and you don't have thousands of dollars to have a lawyer go through it so you sign it." Cas tells us. "Plus, I never ever thought I'd actually make it far enough to put it to use. So I finished second and they exercised their option and put me under contract."

The native Texan – who released his newest CD *La Si Dah* in 2013 – shared more memories from the show when we checked in with him.

What do you remember most about your time on *AGT*?

It was a lot of fun. I got pretty close with Terry Fator. I remember in the very beginning we had said, 'What if it came down to you and I at the end?' and ironically that's exactly what happened. I remember Terry – and he'll probably get mad at me for telling you this – but I love Terry. He would make me go on his weed runs for him. He's a family show type guy so he didn't want to be seen doing that so I'd go down while we were in Vegas and get him his weed.

Was it competitive between you and Terry?

In the beginning, not at all, because there are so many people and you never think you're going to make it to the end. But as the amount of acts started to get smaller, it did get tense sometimes. I love Terry so I say this in the nicest way, but sometimes he'd get on my nerves. I mean, he's a puppeteer. He's a nerd so sometimes he'd annoy me! But he's a good guy, with a good heart.

Do you think the producers gave you a fair edit?

Well, I don't know about edit. But I do think that sometimes Terry got advantages over me. For instance, when they let us sing with our idols, Terry got to perform with Kermit the Frog, and he was completely thrilled. That's a big thing for a puppeteer I guess. Beforehand, they had us fill out these forms of who we'd want to perform with, who our idols were, that kind of thing. I filled mine out, and of course, my answers were all these big guys — Paul McCartney, Sting, Stevie Wonder so I was pretty excited. And they put me with UV40. I mean, I like UV40, they're good, it's just they're not my idol at all. I guess it's a British thing, they are a lot bigger over there than they are here. But Terry got to perform with his first choice, so that was kind of a bummer for me. Another time, it was a 'Judges Choice' sort of thing where the judges got to pick the songs we were going to perform. They picked this Garth Brooks song for him, one that he'd been performing for ages and was really comfortable with — and they knew that.

But for me they picked a song I had never performed and wasn't comfortable with at all. I didn't want to sing it.

What do you remember from the finale night?

I remember just being over it. I wanted it over. The one thing that does stick out to me was Terry and I were standing on the stage and then they announced the winner and he leaned over to me and said, "I'll help you get your house, man." That was pretty nice. I mean, I didn't take him up on his offer, of course, I have too much pride but I thought that was a nice thing for him to say.

Would you ever do a reality show again?

I think with all these shows — and I've talked to a lot of people that have been on these types of shows – Casey Abrams from *American Idol*, Javier Colon from *The Voice* – I think they're not really made for people who enjoy the artistry of music. I tell people who ask me if they should audition, 'If you're looking to be a pop star, and you want to be famous for singing pop songs, then this kind of show will work for you.' I don't think it's meant for people like me or Casey or people that aren't looking to become pop stars.

How has your personal life changed since the show?

I'm still married to my high school sweetheart, Cassie. We had another child, I have a little girl now [Nolah] who's three and my son [Eben] is seven. After the show we moved back to northeast Texas and I took about a year off and me and my brother-in-law built my house from the ground up. We live out in the country and live a slow, country in-the-woods type life.

Do you regret going on *AGT*?

The show gave me the confidence that I could do almost anything. Like, 'I can go out and build a house.' It gave me a little bit of money to work with, and I've been able to turn that into something that we'll have forever. That alone was worth it. Besides all the BS the show brought, I was able to build a home for my family. I got what I needed and more, actually. I've been blessed and I've been really lucky to be able to stick with one thing. I think that's the hardest thing for people to do is stick with one thing. Most people don't know what the hell they want to do, first off. It's hard to stick with one thing if you're not sure about that thing. But I've always been lucky and I think that's helped me, even trying out with the show. I stuck with music through thick and thin. I always have this large bank of faith inside of me that the best is always ahead of me.

What would you be doing if you weren't a musician?

I do a lot of other things besides music. I'm a carpenter. I built my house and I've built other things. I enjoy that. I'd be doing something creative, which I do anyway, I just don't do it for my career. I might be a teacher. I love being a mentor and talking to people and helping young kids map out what they want to do, so probably something like that.

When did you decide to become a musician?

For me, it's always been so obvious what I wanted to do. Since I was 12 years old I knew that I was going to play music, and I've been lucky in that regard to be able to do it.

Do you stay in touch with anyone from *AGT* or your season?

I stay in touch with Butterscotch, she got third place in my season. She's badass, by the way. She got involved with all these cool jazz music people. We've done a lot together since the show, played shows together and stuff. Online, I still talk to Robert Hatcher who made the Top 10. He's a cool guy. The last time I spoke to Terry Fator was probably a year and a half, two years ago. He's doing good. He's definitely rich! I'm not really that interested in going out and seeing his show, to be honest. Maybe I'll go out there and take my kids there one day, who knows?

DANI SHAY

(Season 2)

BIEBER LOOK-ALIKE FINDS LOVE ON REALITY TV

DANI SHAY DIDN'T KNOW IT AT THE TIME, but getting bounced in the semi-finals of *America's Got Talent* was the best thing that ever happened to her. After nailing her audition with a parody of Justin Bieber's "Baby" – ("You're funny, you have a sense of humor and a talent," Howie Mandel said) – the 22 year-old singer took a chance by performing an original song and got bounced from the competition. No biggie. "If I had gone on any further, I wouldn't have been able to do *The Glee Project* [the following year] and I wouldn't have met Ali. So it all worked out."

She's talking, of course, about girlfriend (and *The Glee Project* runner-up) Ali Stroker, who was

Dani Shay in 2011
Photo: Courtesy (Dani Shay)

left confined to a wheelchair after a car accident at age two. The pair met – and secretly began their red-hot romance – while filming the Oxygen network series in 2012. On their first official date, the reality starlets rode a Ferris wheel together at the Santa Monica Pier. They went public with the relationship (Ali's first with another woman) by releasing a music video to Dani's original song "One." During the summer of 2013, the couple spent two and a half weeks together teaching music to children, teens and mothers with H.I.V. and A.I.D.S. in Johannesburg, South Africa. The following month, Dani was an Artist in Residence at a Georgia hostel made entirely of tree houses!

We checked in with Dani to learn more about her trips, music and high profile relationship.

Do you see yourself settling down with Ali and starting a family?

Yes, but not yet. I think Ali and I are pretty much on the same page. We foresee a lot of traveling and adventures and shows and albums and touring before we do anything like that. But we are talking about moving to California and getting settled in a house. Apartment life in New York is a little too tight for us right now.

Dani Shay and Ali Stroker
Photo: Courtesy (Dani Shay)

You announced your relationship in a music video. Why?

Because everything I do I try to make into a creative and interesting statement. When she and I got together, the song just kind of dropped out of the sky for me. I just wrote it. It wasn't long after that she was in New York and I was in Florida and the idea just struck me to make a music video. At first she was a bit nervous. She had only been off of *The Glee Project* for like a month so we didn't know if we had any time outside of the house to be together. And I was like 'Nope. I know I want to say this. And I know I want to say it with you.' I reassured her by saying "Let's just make the video and if you are not comfortable releasing it, we won't release it." And she loved it, of course.

Is it weird for you that so many people are interested in your personal life?

Yeah, I guess in a way. I don't think of it as a lot. Compared to big time celebrities, it is not a lot at all. It's not like I am plastered all over every magazine. It doesn't feel too bad or anything.

What kind of a challenge does Ali's disability pose to your everyday lives?

It's not really much of a challenge these days. After I got eliminated from the show, I knew that I wanted to be with Ali. I work out a lot. I did P90X the whole time I was gone until I went back on the show so that I could be physically strong enough to help her and carry her up stairs and all that kind of thing. Other than that, it is not really a challenge at all. And the pros way outweigh any challenge. There are no cons. I think literally the only thing is that when we travel it is a little more complicated because we have to bring more bags and she has to be able to move around on the airplane and things like that.

This is the first time Ali has had a relationship with a woman, right?

Yes. And if people were to say to her, "Is it a challenge for you not being with a guy?" I think her answer would be "No." She is a real gift.

Some people say the music business is still very homophobic. Do you find that to be true?

I don't really know. I haven't experienced people wanting to shut me out. I have experienced people wanting my personal life be a little more ambiguous and thinking that would be a better route for me to go so that I wouldn't be closing off the opportunity to make straight male fans. But I really feel the straight males that I want as fans will think I am awesome regardless of if they know I am dating Ali or not.

You can't put the genie back in the bottle now.

No, you can't. [laughs]

How was the experience of doing *The Glee Project* compared to *AGT*?

The Glee Project is a different type of competition. It's one of those things where you live together, so it just feels smaller. It's not a huge production like *AGT*. And we didn't do anything in front of a live audience. I feed a lot off of a live audience. In fact, that was a big difference from round one to Vegas. The live audition in Houston for *America's Got Talent* had that live audience and the energy was just so great and then during the Vegas round I started really getting in my head. There was no audience, just me and the judges and it felt a lot more pressurized. That is why I started to slip up. In *The Glee Project*, something similar happened. I got cast on the show and I got a little in my head about it. I think once I get past a certain point and I realize there is a chance I can go far, I start trying to control what is going on and I'm not as authentic and then it shows...

You did an original song that didn't go over with the judges. Was that your idea?

It was. I really did push hard for that. I was dead set on doing that song, despite other people's advice and the judges' opinions. For me it was about making a statement. The show is called *America's Got Talent* and I felt like that was part of my talent. Within the indie music scene, a lot people have an opinion about performers who "sell out" and become too mainstream. And I was afraid of being viewed that way. I wanted my music to be taken seriously. But it's funny because why wouldn't you want a mainstream audience? Why wouldn't you want more people to hear your songs and be impacted by them? I think I was just trying to maintain some kind of reputation. But I have learned a lot since then. I am open to a lot more now.

Would you do it all differently?

No. I feel like that is where I needed to be and what I needed to say at the time. Plus, I

Dani Shay, teaching partner David Goldsmith, and students from their music focus class in South Africa (Summer 2013). "We helped them write their own rap song, which they loved," she tells us. "They performed it during the big show at the end of the program."

Photo: Courtesy (Dani Shay)

definitely wouldn't take it back because if I had gone any further on *AGT*, I wouldn't have been able to do *The Glee Project* and I wouldn't have met Ali. So it all worked out.

The thing people remember most about you is your Justin Bieber routine.
I decided to do the Justin Bieber parody as the first statement that I made because there was no doubt in my mind that when people saw me they were going to think it. So I felt like the best thing for me would be to just address it right off the bat. Rather than try to sing something else and have everybody wondering, "Why does this person look like Justin Bieber?" So I just figured I would address that first off and then showcase what else I can do later.

Was that a stroke of genius or a tactical mistake?
Well, a lot more people know who I am now and they really loved what I did on *America's Got Talent*. But a lot of times they will come up and go "Oh, yeah, you were the one that did the Bieber thing." And I get it. They just link the two things because it is too obvious.

Do you still sing the Bieber song?
The "What The Hell?" parody? I definitely still do it at my live shows. I have fun playing that song. It doesn't happen as often, but for example, I was in an airport not long ago and this security guy asked the guy next to me "Is this your guitar?" And the guy responds, "Oh, no, that's Justin's."

You sure did look like him when you came out. Who did your hair and makeup?
I put myself together for that. And it was my outfit that I already owned. That is really how I liked to dress.

Are you still in touch with anybody from the show?
I keep in touch with Landau a little bit. We ran into each other at the airport a few months ago.

What do you think when you look back at your performances on *AGT*?

I watch the audition tape sometimes – especially if I am introducing myself to management or to producers. But I don't really go back and watch the following rounds very often. Because I can just tell that I was in my head. My performance of "Babylon" I can tell that I wasn't really there and I was really nervous. And hopefully moving forward that kind of thing isn't going to make or break my career.

Are you done with reality TV?

I don't know. I never thought I would do two shows. But I am kind of considering a third one. I am not too sure.

ELI MATTSON

(Season 3)

NOW RETIRED, RUNNER-UP BECAME 'SUICIDAL' AFTER SPINAL INJURY

ONCE EVERY YEAR, ELI MATTSON will sit down with a bottle of tequila and watch old videos of his amazing performances from season three. It's a nostalgic reminder of the way his life used to be. Eli – who placed second to good friend and opera singer Neal E. Boyd – is now retired from music. But not by choice. In 2012, at age 31, Eli gave up what he calls "hard drinking" and quickly discovered that years of hitting the bottle had covered up a painful spinal condition.

"I lived on a Greyhound bus for a many, many years and my back has gone out," he says. "My whole spine is out of whack and it's honestly just become too painful to play.

I've been in constant physical pain for a few years now, so I went to a chiropractor and he found a nerve that was being crushed. I leave the house once every three months or so. I can't walk very well. I walk with a cane now and I don't want to hop into a wheelchair. It's getting worse, so I don't move much. The pain got so bad that I got really suicidal there for a while last year."

The father of two – who now hopes to attend medical school – opened up even more when we spoke in July 2013.

What is your life like today – without music?
It's been very strange letting go of that part of my life. I was pretty bummed out about the whole thing. Some day I'd like to get back on the piano. In the meantime, I read a lot. I study up on biology. I never finished high school, so I have to finish my G.E.D. If I'm sitting here anyway, I can study and when I can take the test physically I'll be ready for it.

Have you tried to medically treat your condition?
The chiropractor I found cut his rates down so I could almost afford him, at the end of one of our sessions, he came out with a Bible and told me I was possessed by Satan, so I just had to stop going to him. I can't deal with a doctor telling me I'm possessed by Satan and that the devil's in my back. My poor wife has been so patient, she takes care of me otherwise I'd be homeless on the street.

So you are still married?
Yes, and we have a little apartment in Wisconsin. I have two daughters in two different states. I think my two kids from before our marriage is enough for us. If we ever had the means to, we might adopt or something like that. I'm trying to decide whether or not to go onto disability because of child support issues, it's all kind of a big mess with the bills that have mounted up, and people who saw me famous at one point don't want to help.

Why did you audition for *AGT*? What was your life like at the time?
I was living in Wisconsin and looking for a job. I had applied at a video store and had just found out that I hadn't gotten the job when I got a call from a friend who told me that *America's Got Talent* was having open auditions in Chicago. I remember it was

the morning after St. Patty's Day and I had gone out that night around Chicago so I was nursing a hangover. I remember scraping myself off the couch and pulling myself together, but I basically forget everything I was supposed to bring: a photo, etc. I got there about 5 in the morning and didn't leave until about 9:30 at night. I think I was the very last audition in Chicago. They almost didn't let me go through. It was kind of like a bad joke. There were three piano playing singers left and the other two didn't get through but I did. I remember they did a lot of interviews and took some photos of me that day.

"I was lucky enough to have a good lawyer and he got me out of my contract, much to the dismay of Simon [Cowell] and the other big cats. I called them up and was pretty angry with them. I may or may not have blacklisted myself from the music business after that."

– Eli Mattson

What do you remember most about auditioning for the judges?

I remember two things very clearly: the actual performance, and the feeling I got from actually just being there and performing in front of that many people. When I was backstage, you could hear the judges' X's going off and it just shakes the whole building. The buzzers going off seriously rattle the whole foundation. My bones were shaking in my body. I was trying not to over think the whole thing too much, not over think the song or you'll forget it.   The actual audition went better than I ever could have imagined it going. It was surreal and very cool, and one of those moments that will stick with me for a long time. After the audition, I remember going back to the holding room and being just so excited that I dropped down on the ground and just made, like, a snow angel on the ground in the holding room.

What happened next?

The production people took those of us that had made it through and put us into small groups in a conference room where you have to sign all the disclaimers. They take it all very seriously. They bring in a few suits to try to scare you into keeping quiet about what just happened at the audition. They tell you that they can sue you for $5 million if you break your confidentiality agreement. It's like the mob. It's just funny because all of the people there are looking for their big break and probably don't have $5 million combined. I also remember that day being a long day of hurry up and waiting.

This was your first competition show. Did you ever consider doing another?

It ran through my mind to do another one, but the third season of *AGT* happened in a real strange time in the music business. It was just before the writer's strike. It was a hard time in the music business. At one point after the show, things got pretty bad and I think I sent my producer Nigel Carro a desperate letter asking to let me audition for the show again. I figured since I didn't win the show, maybe I could try out again. I really need to apologize for that someday if I ever see him again.

So you would do it over again if you could?

I'd probably still give it a shot, I know who I am now, I was 26 back then, I'm coming up on 32 now, so whatever comes with that, I think everyone would like to take another crack at something in their life. I definitely wouldn't drink as much, I gave up that heavy drinking. I had only been clean off the hard stuff for about a year when I auditioned. I had been doing a lot of cocaine. After the show ended, people just give you the stuff. They just pour liquor down your throat at no cost. Then you get lonely, so you end up drinking.

Did the contestants hang out after tapings? What did you guys do for fun?

I was in the 'go out and get plastered' group. But we'd go to Universal City Walk and it's expensive there! We lived off our per diem for what we could. It would get pretty stressful, so me and Neal [E. Boyd] went to the bar at the hotel a lot. That was kind of our thing to do. But you'd be so tired and it would be so late by the time you go out that we'd just hope to catch last call.

How did you and the other contestants manage to keep your lives back home afloat during the taping of the show?

Before the show I had been on the road for seven years and the last normal job I had was Pizza Hut when I was 19. So this was cushy road life for me. Not a Greyhound bus like usual, we had a room at a Sheraton with a bed and shower! That was a nice thing for me. A lot of people who had normal jobs had their bosses and jobs supporting them to be on the show. Neal worked for Geico and his job would have been waiting for him had he not won.

What is it like behind the scenes of the taping of the show?

Backstage was always a mess of nerves, makeup and a lot of pacing. Everyone had their little mini panic attacks. During the show you're segregated for the judges, it's a lot like summer camp. It was a ginormous long summer camp, you make dear friends and I remember a lot of cliques. People who didn't get through Vegas week didn't get along with people that did. After a few months, the friendships fade away, that's how it was on my end. You get really close to these people because you spend so much time together, but when you leave the show, you go back to your normal life. I still talk to Donald and Neal from time to time. The friendships will always be there.

What were the work schedules like?

I was so simple; I sang and played the piano. With the dancers, they had so many rehearsals during the week, so I got lucky and didn't really have to deal with all that. For me, it was just like mentally preparing to not come across too needy on stage and make it more of a gig than a talent show. I tried to make it a true performance instead. I mostly just waited. I remember lots of waiting and downtime during the show. We'd get a call and go to the studio and just wait, for wardrobe, do your blocking, sound checks, and just long hours of sitting in the waiting room to go over your act. If it taught me anything it taught me how to handle waiting.

What do you remember most about finale night?

I remember being really happy Neal won it. I remember after Nuttin' But Stringz got cut, I was positive I was going to be third, if anything. When it came down to Neal and me, I had a flash of winning and I don't even know if I'd be able to play my song. I soaked up the long drawn out moment before they announced the winner and I remember being thankful that 1) it was over and 2) I could go outside and have a cigarette! It meant so much to Neal to win, and he really invested everything into it. I had my first child during the show so I had my own thing going on. I didn't want to get cut, voted off, though. And I wasn't, so I was happy.

What is the one memory from the show that really stands out?

The coolest night of the entire experience was the wrap party. The tension of having to leave next week was over, it was on the New York Street set which they built for *Seinfeld* so that was pretty cool. It was like that party at the end of *Return of the Jedi* where they all celebrate after blowing up the Death Star. Everyone was dancing, the producers, executives could talk to you, it was awesome.

What happened after the show?

After the finale, they send you to a psychologist for an hour so that they know that you can deal with the stress that comes with being on a reality show for an extended period of time. It's kind of a shock to go back to normal life after all of this stuff, so it's really hard for a while. They shipped us to a shrink for legal reasons, I suppose. But I wasn't bummed out about losing, honestly, I was just happy to be a part of it. It was hard though. We sat in a hotel for 2-3 months, and I remember the first time I woke up in my own house when I got home from the show, I didn't remember where I was. I didn't know what city I was in.

You signed a contract with the show's management after the show?

I didn't handle the management I got from the show as well as I could have and they didn't handle me well either. I took the trip to New York and had a table meeting with an exec at a record label and there's an identity crisis you make for yourself. They really just scare the shit out of you, with their 100-page long contracts. I remember them giving me this look like, 'We're not sure how to make this work.' They didn't do me any favors finding me any work really. I was in a real niche. You know the movie, *Almost Famous?* It was kind of like that. I wanted to do the rock-n-roll trip the way I was going; I kind of flipped out when it became all corporate. I was lucky enough to have a good lawyer and he got me out of my contract, much to the dismay of Simon [Cowell] and the other big cats. I called them up and was pretty angry with them. I may or may not have blacklisted myself from the music business after that.

What goals do you have for the future?

I'm going back to the school and trying to get fit enough to sit in a classroom again. I want to do biology-medical that sort of thing. I figure if I really focus maybe I can be a doctor or something by the time I'm 45.

HORSE

(Season 7)

'GLAD TO BE ALIVE' AFTER HORRIFIC CAR WRECK

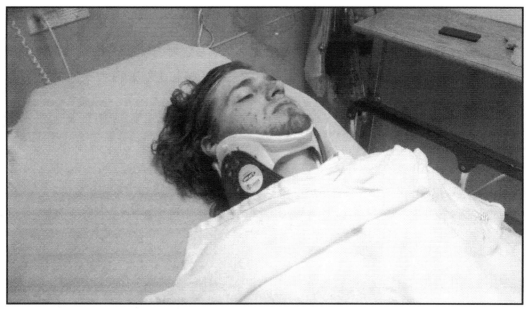

Zac "Horse" Gordon landed in a Pennsylvania hospital after a May 2013 car crash

Photo: Courtesy (Zac Gordon)

ZAC GORDON KNOWS HE'S LUCKY to be alive! After surviving dozens of direct blows to the groin on live television, the stuntman who calls himself "Horse" cheated death in May 2013 when he totaled his 2011 Ford Escape in Harrisburg, Pennsylvania. "I actually dodged a deer and hit a tree," he tells us. "I rolled the car one or two times and completely totaled it. I was convinced that I had to be injured. I went to the hospital and got X-rays but I ended up literally just having a scratch from my seatbelt on my arm. I wasn't even really sore the next day."

It was the second time in less than a year that Horse, 26, landed in the E.R. Just weeks after the season 8 finale, he jumped off a roof in New Jersey and went groin first through some pieces of wood that were held up by buckets, like posts. The injury caused the father of two so much pain, he pooped his pants. "I overshot and actually landed on one of the buckets of cement from two stories up," he remembers. "I broke my ribs which was the most horrible injury I have ever had. But all things considered, I was actually pretty lucky."

Horse's popularity on *AGT* prompted MTV to finally air his reality series that had been shelved for several years. *numbNuts* was described by the network as "celebrating the great American pastime of haphazard bodily harm in the name of laughter – a hilarious, adrenaline-fueled stunt competition game show that pits internet-contestant's stunt mishaps against our three web-celebrity Stunt Masters to see who can better perform steroid-injected versions of the stunts."

"I think a lot of people take me more seriously now," Horse says.

The show brought you a lot of recognition. Where does your act go from here?

It kind of opened up a lot of doors for me because the closest I ever came to considering doing an act was kind of like an Evel Knievel kind of thing. Going to outside appearances and stuff like that. I never considered doing it on a stage. So when *America's Got Talent* hit me up, I pretty much made everything up from scratch. Right now I am working on and am close to getting a deal to have some shows in New York City, hopefully very soon.

What kind of a show could you develop?

As far as a theater show, the theme I am working with is just kind of telling my life story. Because I feel like I am the only guy out there that quit my normal life to pursue getting hit in the groin. And I have two daughters. So I have this whole story of where I came from. It is something I can kind of reenact and have fun with it, almost like a comedy thing. Do skits and tell my story.

Did *AGT* find you from *YouTube* videos?

Yes. I first got a message from *YouTube*, I am pretty sure.

Zac "Horse" Gordon at home in Pennsylvania with daughters Raiden, 5, and Eevie, 1.
Photo: Courtesy (Zac Gordon)

Are you still making these videos?

Absolutely. Social media in general and *YouTube* have been what has gotten me this far. I still live in Central Pennsylvania, so nobody would have ever seen me without social media. I built up a big fan base even before I was on the show and I am able to make a little bit of income off of it. So it enables me to just stick to my roots and go out and try to entertain people.

Are you still working as a bouncer?

No. That was just a brief thing. I only did it for about six months or so. I have mainly just been a stay at home dad for about five years. I make my income off of selling my clips to TV shows, *YouTube* and other websites. All my income comes from getting hit in the groin. I don't work because I take care of the kids all day and I would have to pay a ton of money for a babysitter. So it doesn't seem to make sense.

Did you hold any other jobs before the bouncing gigs?

The only other part-time job I had since is I worked at an airport. I was the guy bringing the plane in and pushing back the plane and handling the luggage and stuff like that. The great part of that job is that I got to fly standby for free. So I used it when I got the MTV show. I flew out there for free to do the audition.

Are you married?

No. We are separated now. Very shortly ago, we separated. After the show.

She couldn't handle the fame?

That is one thing I always commended her on. I was doing a lot of this stuff – though not to that level – before we met each other and she never gave me any problems ever about it.

Did your wife ever kick you in the nuts?

Only for some background footage for *America's Got Talent*.

Tell us more about your background. How did you discover your "talent"?

I was just like a normal skateboard kid when I was little. I kind of discovered the ability to get hit in the groin from my little brother. He is two years younger and we used to have fights and he would kick me and that is kind of how I discovered how I could take a hit like nobody else would. I kind of used that to make my buddies laugh and get a rise out of them and then I started videotaping it.

How did you get the name "Horse?"

When I was younger, we had a horse at the house. It actually kicked me in the face when I was in kindergarten. So I kind of developed this fear of horses. And it kind of turned into this Batman kind of thing where I became 'The Horse' and instead of fighting crime, I got kicked in the nuts.

Did you go to college?

Yes. I got my Associates degree from ITT Tech. I finished school and got a job at a magazine company and I was there for about three weeks before I started to panic. I was doing advertisements and coupons and stuff like that. I went to school for multimedia, so I knew design and video editing. But I couldn't take the idea of being in an office for the rest of my life, so with a kid on the way I just flat out quit and the next day I recorded a really gnarly, dangerous stunt and made some money off of it and I have been doing that ever since. That was six years ago.

What did your parents want you to do as a kid?
I don't remember ever specifically knowing what I was going to do until later in high school when I got into video editing. But they never pushed anything on me.

What did they think of your act?
I never really showed them my stunts at all. They didn't know what I did until I started getting on TV for it. I started getting on smaller clip shows about six years ago when I quit my job. I think they were shocked at first and really scared I would get hurt. But after a little while when they saw me on TV and saw me making some money and kind of living the dream a little bit, they have been extremely supportive.

Is it a medical condition that causes you to not feel pain?
Well, I do feel pain. And sometimes it hurts very bad. I got it checked out a few times now. And literally the doctors said "If we didn't know that you did this stuff, we would have no idea. [Your private parts] are in just fine condition. There is no wear and tear at all." The last doctor I went to, it was on [Howard Stern's satellite radio] network. It literally blew his mind. He literally thought I had prosthetics or wore a cup. I literally did a groin shot in front of him and he did his doctor thing and inspected and was speechless. He had no idea how it was possible. It used to freak me out a lot. It doesn't make sense to me.

Aren't you concerned that one bad shot could cause all sorts of problems for you?
Slightly, I am. But I have done so much stuff that it has kind of faded that out a little bit. I have done things that shouldn't be humanly possible.

Do you have health insurance?
Right now I do not.

Isn't that a bit frightening?

It is. I lost it when I turned 26. I almost feel like if I get it that is when I am going to get hurt. It is something that I am going to get, especially now. The main reason is for the kids. It is very high on my list.

Do you still have a relationship with Howard?

I went on his show after *America's Got Talent*, a few months later. He told me to keep in touch with him. He has genuinely made me feel like he was really interested and rooting for me. Hopefully when I get some solid dates for the show I am going to be doing I will talk to him again and go on the show. He was great and not that I feel the pressure, but because he was so supportive, I really want to be successful and prove myself to him.

A lot of people didn't take you seriously, but he did.

He definitely took value in it. Obviously it is a joke and it is crazy. It is meant to be insane. But that doesn't mean that people can't find it funny or entertaining.

Were you surprised when you were eliminated?

I feel like I had the most unique act out of anybody. I didn't expect to win, but I felt like there was a chance I could have. I don't think it was really the audience for me. I think the people that watch it – or the people who vote – are not the kind of people who would be voting for me.

Now that you are available, are you finding that this is a turn on for women?

It is not a... It is more of an intriguing thing for women than a weird thing. It is not a boring job.

Do you tell them what you do right away?

The girl I am seeing right now actually knew me from the show. It is a lot less awkward when I don't have to explain.

What happened? You met her in a bar and she recognized you?

Yeah, she recognized me and came up and talked and we just hit it off.

How long has that been going on?

Not that long.

Do you have any desire to get out of Harrisburg?

Not really. I have become a real admirer of the simple life. My goal would be to hit it big for a couple of years, make some cash and just lay back on a farm somewhere with my kids and just live a simple life.

Is that where you lived your whole life?

Yeah. I lived in LA for a few months to shoot a TV show, but otherwise...

Were you a good student in high school?

I was alright. I never really tried. I tried my senior year and got decent grades. And I did alright at ITT Tech. I got like a 3.97 GPA. So when I applied myself, I did well.

Were you in trouble a lot?

I had my fair share of entertaining my friends, but if we met somewhere for the first time, you would have no idea what I did. I am pretty reserved, low key. I like to have my time to shine on camera.

Do you have any other talents that don't involve getting kicked between the legs?

I like to say I have some pretty intense dance moves. I used to be a gymnast growing up, so on the show I would do some flips. I am into like parkour and free running, so I can backflip off a roof.

Is there anyone you would like to kick in the nuts?

I don't think there is anyone I would like to kick in the nuts. I have only kicked a few people. But I have this thing called "Celebrity Nut Shots," where any celebrity that wants to kick me in the nuts can. Bam (Margera) has kicked me in the nuts. Sarah Underwood, the 2007 Playmate of the Year, Fabricio Werdum, the MMA fighter... And I got to add Nick Cannon and Howard while I was on the show.

So you are just eating in a restaurant and people will come up and ask to kick you?

It happens! Even before *America's Got Talent*, a lot of people knew me from the Internet and it would be like midnight at a gas station and somebody would come up to me. I would be like "alright" just so they didn't think I was faking it. And I would take the kick and drive home and be with my kids. I don't really do that anymore. I try to save it for videos.

A set of CDs autographed by Jackie sold for $6,200 on eBay in December 2012.

Photo: Courtesy (Jackie Evancho)

JACKIE EVANCHO

(Season 5)

BULLIED, PUNCHED AND CHOKED BY JEALOUS PEERS

JACKIE EVANCHO SEEMS TO HAVE IT ALL: a loving family, a red-hot career and the voice of a young angel. Still, the pint-sized soprano points out, fame comes at a price – especially for children. Despite selling millions of CDs, selling out concerts all over the world and starring in a major studio movie with Robert Redford, Jackie says she has lost almost all of her friends in the past few years. Even worse, the talented teen admits she was often tormented by other kids while attending public school in Richland Township, Pennsylvania.

"I've gotten bullied," she tells us. "I've gotten punched. I was choked once. Even my siblings have problems with getting bullied. It's like the thing to do to make fun of the Evancho kids. My brother got a rock thrown at his head... Kids are mean!"

Jackie says once she became an overnight sensation on *America's Got Talent*, her classmates "kind of started saying things behind my back and just left me there. I only have two friends, really. And I am really happy I have them because they are really great friends."

The teen's father, Mike – who operated a video security business until 2010 – says he, too, has encountered many people who are not very supportive of his daughter and family. "Sometimes along the way you run into jealous people," he revealed in an interview with Pittsburgh TV station WQED. "People will attack me and my wife on blogs, thinking that we are pushing her into this." That, Jackie insists, couldn't be further from the truth.

Singing has been a passion for the blue-eyed wunderkind since she was first introduced to *Phantom of The Opera* at age 8. Her newest CD, *Songs From The Big*

Screen, includes the *Phantom* favorite "The Music of the Night" along with a special duet ("I See the Light" from Disney's *Tangled*) with her older brother Jacob.

Jackie – who received a dirt bike from her family as a 13th birthday present in March 2013 – says she is closest with Jacob and her younger siblings: brother Zachary and sister, Rachel. But she always makes time for her fans. "When I am on tour or at the airport, a lot of little kids come and say hello," she revealed in 2012. "They ask for pictures and autographs. That makes me feel really good." When we caught up in July 2013, Jackie talked about auditioning for *AGT*, staying grounded and making her acting debut in *The Company You Keep*.

You are no longer just a singer. What is it like to be in a movie with Robert Redford?

It was a major honor because not only was it my first movie, but it was a major task. Before I did the movie I didn't really know who Robert Redford was. My dad told me about him and I found out how big of a legend he was and it made me really nervous. You don't want to make a fool out of yourself in front of a big legend like that!

How did you get the part?

Robert Redford was looking for a person to play his daughter, Isabelle. She is kind of sad because she lost her mom about a year ago. And so her character is very upset and confused. Anyway, he was in his hotel room, watching TV and he came across my PBS special. He saw me singing and thought, "Maybe I could direct this girl." So he contacted me and asked me to send in an audition tape. I got the script and sent in the tape as soon as I could and within a few weeks I was on a soundstage shooting!

Did you ever expect you would become an actress?

I always hoped, but I never thought it would happen. I am hoping to do more in the future, but my main concentration is always going to be on singing.

Could you have imagined when you started out on *AGT* that you would have all these amazing opportunities?

No. But then again, when I sing, I don't really think about the future. I think about the present and what is going on now. So I can get my full frame of mind into it and do the best that I can. When I was on *America's Got Talent*, I was kind of thinking that I was going to go on there and have fun and go back to doing what I was doing before which is traveling around the United States singing at little places. And I ended up doing a lot more than that.

How long did it take for you to get used to life on the road and all the commitments that come along with your success?

I think it was kind of something that I didn't really have to get used to because I was already used to it. I don't travel much more now than I did before *America's Got Talent*. Before the show I was always with my mother, we'd get into a car and drive across the United States to this little place where I would sing or audition and then we would drive back home and wait for an answer.

Do you ever get nervous being up on stage singing in front of all these people and television cameras?

Well, I am always nervous. Even now I am nervous. But in that moment, once I get on stage and start singing, the nerves go away and I am not nervous anymore.

Now you are traveling around the world to countries that don't speak English – and yet people know who you are. What is that like?

I think it is really cool. I never expected that people who didn't even understand what I was saying would take an interest in me.

What about kids your age? Do they appreciate your music or does it go over their heads?

They do, actually. They are very supportive of me when they need to be. But a lot of times they kind of don't mention it because when I am home I am just normal Jackie Evancho – the kid who loves animals and plays all day.

Tell us about normal Jackie. How do you manage to have a "normal" childhood?

Obviously I don't go to public school. But not all people need that to have a happy childhood. My brothers and sister and I all have fun together jumping on the trampoline and taking care of the pets. And I still have a lot of chores. And since I am not home as often, my parent let me have sleepovers more than the usual person would.

You still live in the same house you have for years?
Yes.

Do you think you would ever move to Hollywood?
No. I don't think so. [laughs]

Do you still take singing lessons?
I don't really take singing lessons. But every once in a while I will go to a professional singer and kind of sing a little bit for them so they can test my vocal health and make sure I am doing everything correctly. It is not singing lessons every week.

What happens as you get older and your voice starts to change? Could that impact your singing?
Yeah. Actually it has. And it worries me because sometimes I am singing or practicing and my voice gives out and I don't want that to happen on stage. Luckily it doesn't because for some reason my voice kind of flips into the right place and everything flows out naturally.

Would you ever like to sing more pop songs?
It is fun to sing those kinds of songs because you kind of feel like a pop star. And they have bigger careers than we usually do. [laughs] But I am hoping I can get to that point where I can be that big. But it is really fun to kind of just let yourself loose in one of those songs.

Do you ever sing karaoke?
I used to. When I was traveling, I would sing karaoke in bars.

What do you like to take with you when you travel?
I have to bring my phone. And it depends on my trip, but usually, my iPad, my phone and my computer. Really, it is just electronics.

What music is on your phone right now?
It is mainly stuff that has been on the radio lately. But I have some old songs too. I have "Moonlight Sonata" by Beethoven. And I have some of Muses' music.

You tried out for *AGT* a couple of times and didn't get on. What happened?
I tried out for *America's Got Talent* two times before. I don't remember where the first place was. The second place was auditions in New Jersey. Both times I gave it my all.

Photo: Courtesy (Jackie Evancho)

But for the second time in New Jersey, the night before I had performed with David Foster at one of his Talent Quest competitions. Right after that we had to drive to New Jersey. I gave it my all, but I was really tired.

Do you think you weren't ready yet?
No. I thought I was ready or else I wouldn't have tried twice! But looking back I think when I started off in 2010, that was a better time to start off. If I had started off any earlier, I might not have made it as far.

What do you think of Howard Stern and the new judges?
I love the new judges actually. I think they are awesome. They are really funny together.

You won an award for being one of the best mannered people in America? Are you really that nice?
Yes! When I am in a fight sometimes with my siblings and I think of something really mean to say, I can't even say it. I get a stomachache before I say it because it is too mean. And if we are out to dinner or something, my dad doesn't usually say please or

thank you too often, so I always tell him "Dad, come on, say please for once!" I am always saying please and thank you. On planes, in restaurants... My siblings and I are always getting compliments for our manners. My parents did teach us to be thankful for the things we have, but they didn't really push (manners) on us. I think it was mainly our own choices. Most of my siblings are like me, so I don't think I am the only well-mannered person out there.

Do you ever get in trouble?
I get in trouble every once in a while, but not as much as most of my siblings do. [laughs] Usually it is for talking back.

Do you have a more trusting, grown up relationship with your parents now?
It is a dangerous world out there, so it kind of limits my freedom. But they do trust me and they do believe in me. They are actually very trusting of me and I find that to be a compliment that they can trust me so much.

Do they have any crazy rules for you?
My Mom and Dad are really strict about saying "You have to be who you are." But they raised us well enough to know that I shouldn't get a tattoo or anything like that. At least not for a few more years. [laughs]

Kevin Skinner spent more than 10 years working as a chicken catcher.
Photo: Splash News

KEVIN SKINNER

(Season 4)

FORMER CHICKEN CATCHER – AND GRANDPA TO BE – FORGOT TO CLAIM HIS $1 MILLION CASH PRIZE!

HE MAY BE THE ONLY reality show winner to disappear without claiming his $1 million cash prize! Several weeks after returning home to Mayfield, Kentucky, "the lawyer for the show called one of my attorneys and said 'Where is this boy at?'" Kevin remembers. "'He is the only one in four years that we have had to track down to find out how he wants his money!' That's a true story. My lawyer called me up laughin' about it."

Kevin – an unemployed farm worker when he arrived for his audition in Chicago – says he didn't go on the show to become rich. When *AGT* staffers finally did track him down, he declined the quick lump sum payout. "I took the whole $1 million over 40 years," he tells us. "You are lookin' at something like $2,500 a month for 40 years. My last payout was $2,049 [after taxes]. But the way I see it, the world may not even be here in 2049. If I had taken the whole payout, it would have been about $250,000 [after pre-payment penalties and taxes], so I figured it would be smart to take the whole $1 million. Taxes was going to take most all of it anyways. But who knows, I might make another $1 million right fast. I have been opening for big names makin' $20,000 for 45 minutes! You can make money real quick." Kevin, who split with his wife shortly after the show – will become a grandfather in September 2013. He told us more about his life before and after *AGT*, when we tracked him down at home.

Before we begin…. Your mom was in a car wreck in May 2013. How is she doing?

She is doing pretty good. They put a pacemaker in. She had been having a problem with her blood pressure. So I have been stickin' pretty close to her until I see how that is going to turn out.

Glad to hear… Now on to *AGT*. When you won, did you think you were going to become the next Garth Brooks?

No, not really. That wasn't even really why I went on the show.

So why did you decide to audition?

My grandmother passed away and I wrote a song for her called "Her Song." That is actually the song I sang at the very first auditions in Chicago.

What do you remember about that day?

Everybody was comin' in singin' cover songs – songs the judges had already heard a hundred times. So I sit down in front of a table of about 12 people and auditioned with a song I wrote and they had never heard before. When I finished I looked up, and they was all really shocked and didn't really know what to say. The guy in the middle just kind of said "What do you do for a living?" And I said "I am a chicken catcher." These people are from LA and they are looking at me like I am an alien that just landed in a UFO. [laughs] That was kind of funny.

Do you feel like the show tried to change you?

Yeah, kinda in a way they did. I am sure you heard David, Sharon and Piers always said "Never change who you really are." Well everything was about the hat. My hat is just like my shirt or my pants to me. That is the truth. I walk out on stage and my hat is just part of who I am. When I got out in Vegas I started wearing my cowboy hat. People seen me with my backwards ball cap. But [the producers] had their idea of how they wanted me to appear. It kind of wasn't really who I was. I kind of feel uncomfortable with people seeing me that way.

But it worked and you got the votes!

That is true. I tried to stay true to who I was. I tried to take their advice. But I don't have any regrets. I just take it day by day and whatever God has in store for me is going to happen regardless. He put me out there to win the show and for everybody to enjoy the songs I have written. It's not just what you can do. You gotta have God in there somewhere to help guide you.

So how did you become a chicken catcher?

That was one of the better paying jobs in my area. You had health benefits. And it was good money. I would bring home about $600 a week. My dad was a mechanic and he'd say "Damn, you're makin' more than I am!" To me, I always liked to hunt and be outdoors, so I kind of had a rough edge anyways. It wasn't really no big thing to me. I just went in, caught 'em, and went back home.

"I was a catcher for 10 years. I would see guys that would come in that had been in the Marine Corps and they'd say, 'Man, our basic training wasn't this hard! We don't need money this bad.' And they'd just leave."

- Kevin Skinner

Silly question, but…what exactly does a chicken catcher do?

A semi would bring out these cages. Each trailer had like 20 cages. Each tractor-trailer would hold 7,134 birds. The forklift would take the cage off the trailer, run it in the barn, drop it, and the catchers would fill it up with chickens. Then they take them from the farm to the processing plant. That's where the cut them up and do whatever they do to them there. Five of us guys would catch 60,000 birds in 5 1/2 hours. This job separated the boys from the men real quick.

How long did you do it?

I was a catcher for 10 years and an assistant supervisor for four of that. I would see guys that would come in that had been in the Marine Corps and they'd say, "Man, our basic training wasn't this hard! We don't need money this bad." And they'd just leave. It is a rough job. It is hard work. It is not for everybody.

Did the chickens ever fight back?

No. [laughs] They have breeder barns with actual roosters that weigh up to 8 pounds. And they got the spurs. When you got roosters breedin' hens, if a person walks [too close] they'll try to flog you. The ones we caught were incubated at the hatchery. I guess [being a chicken catcher] kind of showed who I was. I don't beat myself up that I am not always winning an award at the CMA. The way I look at it is if that is what God has planned for me later on down the road it will happen.

How are your kids?

My son Reed is grown. He is 19. He is having a son. My grand boy, Braxton, will be here the last week of [August] or first week of September. I gotta get used to that name...'Grandpa.' [laughs] My daughter Sydney thinks she is grown. She will be 16. It was kind of tough for them adjusting at first after I won. My daughter would tell me "Dad, my friends treat me different now." I had to kind of sit down and talk to her and explain to her how people are and how friends will come and go with the good times. And sometimes when the good times aren't really rolling, you look up and your fair weather friends aren't around anymore. But I think for the most part they have realized what their dad has done and what I can still do.

Do they want to be in the music business?

My daughter, she could definitely be if she wanted to. But she's not really after that. And I don't push her. A lot of people would be pushing their kids, but I have never been that way with my kids. I taught them right from wrong. I never had to go pick my son up from jail. He's never been to court. He's never been in any trouble. I like to hunt and I taught both of them how to hunt. You know the old saying goes, "You teach your kids how to hunt and you don't gotta hunt for them later." I just try to guide them the best they can and hope they make the right decisions later on.

Did you and your wife split up?

That is something that happened real quick right after I won and I think that kind of speaks for itself. That happened right after I won the show. There is a lot of things that happened that I would rather not say. There were things that were found out. But when you go through something like that, you have to take whatever happens and try to deal with it the best you can. You know what I mean? I don't have any contact with her and haven't since she called and wanted me to file for divorce. I haven't had any contact with her since then. She is doing her own thing and I wish her the best.

A lot of people say when they become successful, it is the people around them who change.
Exactly. That is true.

Is she the mother of your kids?
No.

Were you married before?
I was. I have got two great kids and wouldn't trade them for anything. They are good kids, so I don't have any regrets at all. But yeah...

Are you still close with Grandma Lee?
Yeah. I talk to her pretty often. I know she quit smoking and she tripped backstage and hurt her shoulder. But now she is better. She is doing shows. She is somebody I always hung out with. We would go gamble. She loves to gamble on slot machines. I never put a dime in a slot machine my whole life.

Las Vegas must have been the craziest place you have ever seen.
Yeah. I have seen some pretty crazy stuff. But most of the people there are pretty nice. If I had to go on vacation, that would be one of the places that would be at the top of my list.

A CONVERSATION WITH...

KINETIC KING

(Season 3)

I 'STILL CAN'T WATCH' VIDEO OF FAILED CHAIN REACTION TRICK

THE KINETIC KING IS STILL SEARCHING for his queen. "[She's] someone who has red hair, maybe, loves scuba diving, Buster Keaton comedies and wants to go to Hawaii with me," Minnesota artist Tim Fort told *AGTNews.com* moments after being eliminated from season 6. "There have got to be plenty of women out there like that." Tim – who uses his degree in rocket science to design unique chain reaction art – tells us he has dated "quite a few women" since appearing on *AGT*. "But I'm holding out for someone who has a passion for diving," the divorced St. Paul native says. "Kinetic art is

The Kinetic King
Photo: Courtesy (Tim Fort)

optional. I've had a long-term platonic friend named Kim who came to my audition with me. She's an artist as well; she does crop art, which is making art out of plant kernels. I don't know if that will turn romantic."

Tim – who will turn 50 in 2014 – decided to become an artist at 35. He has created countless card pyramids, stick bombs and domino-like gadgets, but may be best remembered for the one that didn't work. During his semifinal performance on *AGT*, hundreds of painted popsicle sticks simply refused to fall – on live television! "I've never had anything like that happen to me in the career," he admitted when we caught up with him recently. "It was the worst possible place for a gadget to fail."

First, what made you try out for *AGT*?

I was trying to get the networks interested in my kinetic arts. I was hoping they'd put me on a show or make me part of another show. That's the reason I contacted them. It was the only ad I ever responded to on Craigslist that ended up working out! I contacted them and I went to the audition in Minneapolis just to talk to someone from the network. Someone from the production had looked at my kinetic art videos and I was amazed that they knew who I was. That was really gratifying. The first preliminary went very well. They started shooting B-roll footage of me there. I was amazed that they took my act seriously.

Performing in front of millions of people can be scary. Were you nervous how people would react?

I was, but they were surprisingly receptive. I had spent eight hours setting up that first stick bomb. It was the first time I demonstrated the cobra wave before a big audience. When they interviewed me, they asked me what I'd do with the million dollars and I think I said I wanted to go to Hawaii and get a mansion and go scuba diving with Playmates. I was being candid and quirky and I think that helped me get on the show. Piers said he was going to vote me down but he liked my answer so much he put me through.

On the show you said that you'd be remembered as the biggest loser after your trick failed. What were you thinking when it didn't work?

It was extreme shock. I found out later what had happened. It wasn't the humidity like I originally thought. About a week before I was on the show, I had painted all of my sticks. I wanted the colors to blend so I painted them and they were thoroughly saturated. They underwent plastic deformation and lost their elasticity. I had spent 36 hours setting it up and was extremely tired and cranky and wanted to get it over with. I pulled the stick and they just sat there like they were bolted to the stage. I've never had anything like that happen to me in the career. It was the worst possible place for a gadget to fail. I had to stand up there and not act stupid for a few minutes.

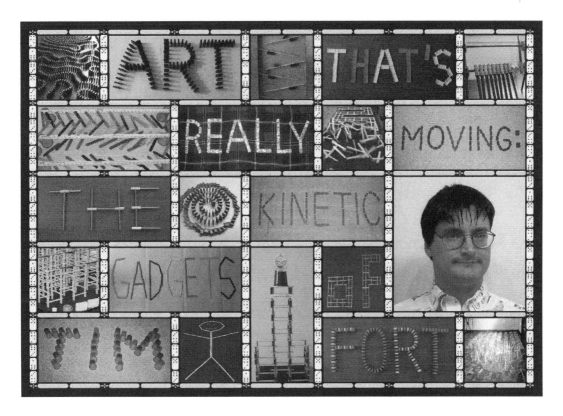

Photo: Courtesy (Tim Fort)

You had a great attitude about the whole thing though...

I'm kind of borderline autistic. I have Asperger's Syndrome so I tend to be more objective in my thinking than a lot of people. Instead of ranting on and on about how I was victimized, I just admitted that I goofed. I didn't test the sticks thoroughly before setting up my gadget. The next day I went to LACMA (Los Angeles County Museum of Art) and it was hard to not be mad at the world and Piers Morgan for being really critical of me. It was kind of hard to deal with. Later on that week I found out that I was called back as a wild card act. It was a mixture of elation of being able to correct my mistake but a little frustration going, "Here I go again." But when I did go on the wild card round, it was amazing how the audience was cheering me on. It was extremely gratifying when Piers went up on stage and proclaimed that I was the King and compared me to Rocky Balboa. That really made up for the disaster.

Are you able to watch that footage today?

I can't really sit through the clip. I cringe when I see it. I've only seen it once or twice since it happened.

Were you surprised when you were eliminated?

No. There was the consensus among the oddball, novelty acts that [a singer] would win. I think that's what helps *AGT* get high ratings. *American Idol* and all those are just about singers and dancers. But I think *AGT* is popular because they have novelty acts too. I am surprised that a dog act won last year though.

What's something people would be surprised to know about you?

I haven't had a functioning TV in years. I never did get a converter box. I just didn't want to deal with that, so when I was on the show I had to go to my dad's house to watch. I'm not totally out of touch with popular culture. I get so much video off the Internet. I watch the *AGT* acts on *YouTube*. Eventually I think broadcast TV will become obsolete. I think everything will be streaming video.

Where are you living these days?

I still live in Minnesota in an artist cooperative, which is low-cost housing for artists. We all look out for each other.

What have you been up to since the show?

I've been getting a lot of gigs since *AGT,* mostly at museums and trade shows. I'm coming out with a line of stick bomb kits called *Stick Storm* with Goliath Games. [Editor's note: Tim's stick bomb kits were released in August 2013]. I also finished work on a music video called "Tuna Melt" for Canadian scratch artist A-trak. Basically I made one of my gadgets run through an entire house for the music video. It was a stunning video, I'm very proud of the results. [In May 2013], I participated in a Ted X Talk. The video was me talking about my kinetic art career.

Any regrets about going on the show?

Not at all. It helped my career immensely. Before *AGT* I had to work a boring clerical day job and now I think I've crossed over to being a full-time artist.

Would you consider doing reality TV again?

I would consider it. It would be nice to do one that was taped beforehand, though. Live TV is scary.

LANDAU EUGENE MURPHY, JR.

(Season 6)

'I TRIED TO KEEP MY STRUGGLES PRIVATE'

Photo: Keith Albee

LANDAU EUGENE MURPHY, JR. didn't want the sympathy vote. "They had to pry the fact that I washed cars out of me," he insists. "I wasn't going to tell the world that. I wasn't going to tell them anything about me being homeless. That's why it was so real. Once they got it out of me, I couldn't do nothin' but cry, you know?"

Landau – a coal miner's son and father of five from Logan, West Virginia – says his story of struggle and survival even brought the *America's Got Talent* camera crew to tears. "They started pokin' and proddin' at me, like 'Tell us your struggles...' I was like

'You really don't want to know this,'" he remembers. "So I told them and the camera crew started cryin' and I started cryin'. But I kept tellin' them 'It's okay. I made it through.'

Landau plans to share more about his journey from rags to riches in a new book due out in late 2013. He calls it "a rough draft of my life story – the struggles I went through to get where I am at. People telling me I couldn't do this or that. All the different things that stop people from trying to follow their dreams."

The singer – who married his wife, Jennifer, in 2005 – admits it would have been easier for him to conform to expectations: cut his hair or perform a more contemporary style of music. "But I don't think I would have been as happy," he says. "God was telling me 'You can do it.' My life hadn't been easy up to that point. When I went on *America's Got Talent,* it was basically God telling me that I was ready. I never thought I would go on *America's Got Talent* or *American Idol* or any of that stuff. People had been trying to get me to do it for years, but I just didn't think I had the look. Or a shot. But things happen in your life..."

What prompted you to go on the show?

My father-in-law died and my mother-in-law was in her house by herself. She was 72 or 73 at the time so my wife and I would go and spend the night with her. One weekend when we came home, someone had broken into our house and taken everything that we owned – all our clothes, all our furniture, the copper out of the walls... Everything! That put me in a position where I had absolutely nothing. I was 35-years-old with absolutely nothing. I went back to my mother-in-law's house and I remember being real angry. And right at that moment, it was like God was telling me, 'I've given you all the talents you need.' I have been entertaining my family and friends since I was three years old. I felt like I was ready at the time. I figured I had nothing to lose. If they make a fool out of me, I still win. I got to be on television.

So you went and stood in line?

I went and stood in line at the Jacob Javitz Center in New York. It was weird because a lot of the people in line were trained to do what they were doing. They went to school for dance or had vocal lessons.

How long did it take?

We got there at like 6:30 in the morning and I didn't get back in the building until 6:30 at night. When we finally got in the door there were more lines. Once they heard me sing, they were like "Okay, we're gonna give you guys a call around May." Then as I was walking out of the room I was like "Damn, I can't believe I stood in line this entire time and that is all they are going to say. I should have sung 'Wet Willie!'" So I started singing "Country Side of Life" on the way out the door and the guy that was running the auditions called me back in the room. He said "Mr. Murphy, what all do you sing?" I said, "I sing anything, just give me a chance. I guarantee I won't let you down." He said, "I bet you can win this."

Did you take the quick cash payout?

Yes. It ended up being like $447,000. I paid Uncle Sam right away. And then I paid up my child support that I was in arrears for. I got in arrear with child support by trying to put a band together. I had a blues/soul band. I was the lead singer and we traveled all around Kentucky, Ohio and West Virginia. We were doin' really good, but then the band fell apart. That is when I went back to doing the charity stuff on my own. I was doing that before we put the band together. That is how they found me. They saw me in the newspaper, on the front page, every week in my hometown, doing charity things.

Did you treat yourself to anything with the extra money?

Yes. But the first thing I did was I paid my child support up and paid Uncle Sam. Then I hit the road. I didn't have time to do anything. I have been on tour for two years. Ever since the show. I hit the road and made probably another $475,000. Then Uncle Sam came and got $247,000 of that. [laughs] After that I bought my wife a car.

She didn't have a car?

When we got together I ended up tearin' up her car. Someone was pullin' on and off the road in front of me one night. I was trying to pull ahead and I hit a puddle of water and spun out and hit a telephone pole. I was almost killed. I was fortunate enough to walk away. I always said to myself, "As soon as I get some money, I am gonna buy her a brand new car." So as soon as I paid up my child support, I bought her a new 2012 [Mercedes] M300. I tried to get her a Toyota, but she didn't want it.

You once said you wanted to buy your own car wash...
I was so busy that I didn't have time. So I gave the idea to my older brother and he bought it.

"When I went on the show, I went as Doonie Tunes. But they didn't want me to use Doonie Tunes because it sounded too much like Looney Tunes. That's what the judges said to me that night at the Hammerstein Theatre. Sharon said "What is your real name?" And I said "Landau Eugene Murphy, Jr." And she was like "That's brilliant!"

— Landau Eugene Murphy, Jr.

Is your wife, Jennifer, still singing with you?
Yeah, we are still on tour together. She still does duets with me and background vocals.

Do you think you two would want to have children together?
Oh yeah! I want to but right now I am so busy I just don't have time for it. My son is grown and in college. That reminds me, I gotta go buy him a car now!

Some people refer to you as Landau Murphy. Did you drop the Eugene from your name?
No. Eugene is always there. A lot of times when I go out people still say my whole name. They are like "Landau Eugene Murphy Jr., how are you doing today?" Nick Cannon does that. When I went on the show, I went as Doonie Tunes. But they didn't want me to use Doonie Tunes because it sounded too much like Looney Tunes. That's what the judges said to me that night at the Hammerstein Theatre. Sharon said "What

is your real name?" And I said "Landau Eugene Murphy, Jr." And she was like "That's brilliant! Where did you get that name?" I was like "My daddy. That's why I'm junior." Everyone was laughing.

Is it weird to have fans?

It is, but I am getting used to it. The weirdest thing is that I am not just known in America. I got fans in Uganda and Dubai and Australia and Italy and China. I got fan mail from a town called Landau in Germany. After the show they sent me overseas to do some shows for the armed forces and this guy comes up to me and pulls out his ID and says "Where did you get your name from? Your name is special. This is the town I am from." And he pulled out his ID. "That's my name." It is amazing though. I really can't go anywhere without getting noticed. The airport or sittin' down at Red Lobster or trying to go to Walmart. It is the same anywhere I go.

Have you ever thought about leaving Logan, West Virginia?

No. Even when I am in New York or LA it is the same thing. At least here I know what it going on. I grew up half of my life in Detroit, so I hate the city. I was born and raised in West Virginia until I was 11 years old and my mom and dad split up and they moved me to Detroit. I had to change and adapt to a new lifestyle. I always wanted to come back home so when I had that opportunity, you know, at 25 I ended up coming right back here and fell right back into the life I left at 11 years old. I don't really want to go anywhere. I think I will always stay home.

Some people say when you win a million dollars it doesn't really change you, but it changes everyone around you.

It didn't change me, but it does change everyone else around – except for the ones that really, really care for you, I guess. I watched my family change. We all fell out for a long time because they expected me to do it all in a different way. They wanted me to take everybody on shopping sprees. I am like "It's just a million dollars and I didn't even get the whole million!" They actin' like I am a big time rich guy and I'm not. They were all mad because I bought my wife a nice car. People got mad that you just didn't take them out on a big shopping spree. You know, when you are broke, you always tell everybody "If I ever get a million dollars I am gonna buy everybody a car." You say that stuff, but as soon as you get that money you can't because Uncle Sam is standing right there. And your life is standing there. It took $250,000 just to fix my life!

Is it fixed now?

Oh, yeah. Everything is in order. I got a nice house for like $250,000. I got money in my bank account. All my bills are paid up. I am on a mountain all by myself right now, just me and my wife. We got a nice five bedroom home. But, yes, it changes the people around you.

Are you working on any new music?

I am working on a Christmas CD. I will probably self-release it. I don't think record companies are what they used to be. They don't really care about you no more. Plus with downloads, there are no record stores anymore.

Leonid Filitov is 'Leonid The Magnificent'

Photo: S_Buckley (Shutterstock)

LEONID THE MAGNIFICENT

(Seasons 1, 2, 6)

'I ASSUME THEY JUST DON'T WANT ME ANYMORE'

NO ACT HAS EVER BEEN more colorful, controversial and downright fun to watch than Leonid The Magnificent. He is the show's only three-time offender, appearing during seasons 1, 2 and 6. The towering Russian cabaret performer first appeared during season 1 auditions in New York in white spandex shorts, high-heeled boots and red and white angel wings. "You would be perfect for the top of my Christmas tree," Piers Morgan joked. "Otherwise you are totally useless." When David Hasselhoff also voted against him it looked as if Leonid's moment in the spotlight was over. Then Brandy brought the performer back out on stage, rallied the crowd to its feet and begged her fellow judges to change their minds.

Leonid dropped to his knees in a flood of tears. "For 33 years I was waiting to come on this stage and show who I am and what I can do," he pleaded. "Yes, for you I am Christmas tree. But for somebody [else] I can be God." Piers came around and Leonid survived to perform once more. He was eventually eliminated after a creepy, flirtatious exchange with the judges, where he invited himself to Christmas at Piers' house and tossed a wedding bouquet to David.

Leonid – who was working in Las Vegas prior to appearing on the show – returned the following season with a new act, catching the judges completely by surprise. "If he is put through, I quit," David threatened, igniting a fire in the outrageous performer. "I get so sick to beg people to accept me," he shot back. "I will never, ever give up my dreams. Go to Hell! I know who I am." Surprisingly, Piers and Sharon voted him through and Leonid was back on the radar – at least until the next round. He returned again in 2011 with a new "quick change" act, earning a trip to Las Vegas, where he was eventually eliminated. Leonid is currently living in Brooklyn, New York. That's where we tracked him down recently for an update:

What have you been doing since the show?

I still perform. I have my own show. I have my team. I travel to London and to L.A. and in New York. So those are my three most popular destinations. Usually I do nightclubs. I am a cabaret performer, so a small venue like nightclubs and a lot of private parties. I have different acts and different costumes. But the main deal is the same. It is very recognizable. People remember it from TV.

What kind of reaction do you get from people when they meet you?

Oh, a good one. People still like me. So no shame, no complaints.

"This year is going to be 20 years, how long I stay with my boyfriend, Taras. He is my manager. He is my lover. He is my assistant and costume designer. Why do we have to get married if we live together already? But maybe yes. He asked me. So maybe in October on my birthday. "

- Leonid The Magnificent

What is your best memory of being on the show?

Everything. It was fun. It was interesting experience. It helped me. It doesn't matter what [the judges] say. It is important what people think about me. So it helped to create my new act. I have to be more commercial. So I try to not only do what I want, but what people like.

The judges had very strong opinions about you. Do you think they were fair? Or was it just for TV?

I don't know, to be honest. I think ultimately people cannot like everything. But the show is not about "do I like it or do I not like it." It was about "do you have a talent? It didn't bother me that Piers Morgan didn't like me. That I don't care. But I would care

Photo: Taras Kardashov

when personal opinion would cross professional opinion. That was my biggest issue and why I came back so many times. Cause I know some people don't like gays. Some people don't like black people. So I understood that I cannot be perfect for everybody. But for a talent show, you have to judge by the talent, not by who is popular. It is not a modeling or fashion show. That was my problem.

You flirted a lot with David Hasselhoff. Did he appreciate the joke?

I assume yes. He is a nice guy. He is fun. A couple of times we met after the show and it was nice. He was nice to me. I was nice to him. There was no issue or fighting or screaming between us.

Do you think Howard Stern would like your act?

I think yes, of course.

Have you thought about auditioning again?

To be honest, last year [season 7] I sent in a videotape of my new act, but there was no response. So I assume they just don't want me anymore.

Your whole experience on the show started with drama. There was threat of legal action from your former employer, Jeff Beacher...

To be honest I am still angry with Jeff Beacher. There was no legal problem at all. He tried to use my name to get himself famous. He used the scandal and all that bullshit to get him attention. I used to work for him, but I never was his performer. I never signed any contracts. The only thing that he created is my name, Leonid The Magnificent. I was the closing act in his show and he said "You know, I think I need to lock up your real name. We need to make you a stage name." So he and Harry Morton, who was one of the producers of *Beacher's Madhouse,* they say "Hey, Leo, now you come on stage like Leonid The Magnificent." And I think he affects my appearance on *America's Got Talent.* Because nobody wants to have problems. So it upset me, of course. But everything is publicity. Everybody is using each other to get bigger name, to get attention and money. This is show business.

What kinds of clubs do you play in New York?

I am in a new off-Broadway show that is like the old TV show, *The Gong Show.* Kind of like *America's Got Talent.* Now it is an off-Broadway stage show. Some lady bought the rights to create stage show exactly like *The Gong Show.* So I perform there. I am a contestant. I come on stage as Leonid The Magnificent. I do it a few times a month. It is at a nightclub and they run the show... It is more of a freak show, like crazy people.

Do you know Prince Poppycock?

I never met him. I saw him on *America's Got Talent.* He wrote me a couple of letters. But I never met him or talked to him.

You paved the way for him to be on *AGT*.

Thank you very much.

Do you have kids or a partner?

This year is going to be 20 years, how long I stay with my boyfriend. Taras [Kardashov]. He is my manager. He is my boyfriend. He is my lover. He is my assistant and costume designer.

Do you see yourself being a dad one day?

A dad? I am a gay. I cannot have kids.

Of course you can. You can adopt.

I don't think so. It is too much responsibility. Then I have to change my style of life. I don't want my kid to get crazy like me.

Maybe you can start by getting a dog?

I don't need a dog. Dogs are for lonely people who don't have enough attention.

Will you and Taras ever get married?

We don't know yet. Maybe. He wants it, but after 20 years? Why do we have to get married if we live together already? But maybe yes. He asked me. So maybe in October [2013] on my birthday.

MELISSA VILLASENOR

(Season 6)

'SATURDAY NIGHT LIVE' IS STILL MY GOAL

BEFORE *AGT*, **MELISSA WAS RINGING THE REGISTER** at Forever 21. Now she makes a full-time living as a comic, hitting the road again in late 2013 for a tour of U.S. colleges. Her act has continued to evolve since she won over the judges with hilarious send-ups of **Celine Dion**, **Barbara Walters** and **Miley Cyrus**: "I don't want to just be someone that only does impressions and (my audience) knows nothing about me," she says. " I will do either character voices or impressions. But they will usually be in a story that is about me, not them. I think I am a funny person just being myself. So that is really what I have been working on a lot for the past year or so."

Melissa told us more when we met up in June 2013.

Are you still working the clubs in Hollywood every night, polishing up the act?

Yeah, but the road is where comics make their money. The colleges pay well. But it is nice that for the upcoming fall season I organized it in a way so that I am not burnt out, you know? I don't like to be on the road for a long time. Especially since I am alone. It gets very tiring. But I think twice a month is nice.

You go on the road by yourself?

It finally got to a point where being alone so much made me really love who I am. And understand the person I am. When you are hanging out with so many people all the time, you have no time to be alone. So now I actually love being alone. I love traveling alone. Sometimes during the day I don't like to be with anyone.

Does being a road comic get in the way of having relationships?

I did. I was dating a guy the first time I was on the road but he wasn't that nice and he wasn't committed to me or anything. So it was tough. I would think if I had a serious relationship he would want to travel with me sometimes. Right now I am not seeing anyone and that is probably why it is so nice. I can just enjoy myself and not worry about anything.

What is your goal for the next few years?

I am still figuring that out. *Saturday Night Live* was a big goal of mine – and it still is. But I feel like that is not in my control. Right now I am just trying to become a good comic. Once I really grasp who I am on stage and my persona, having a show wrapped around me would be fun.

Have you acted before?

I have never done acting. I have taken classes and gone on a couple of auditions. It is a whole other art. I feel like maybe one day I will feel excited about it. But right now that is not something that excites me.

What do you remember about your experience of being on *AGT*?

It was great. It was a really cool experience. I have to say it was one of the greatest times of my life. The Seattle audition was the best. I have never performed in front of a theater that big. And it surprised me. I went up there thinking, "They probably won't like it." And it ended up being really good.

Why did you think they wouldn't like you?

I never expect anything. I don't like raising my hopes. Even if I think it is going to be good, it scares me. I have done those impressions a lot. For many years. But I guess I was at a point where I felt like it wasn't something people would appreciate. I think that was my mentality at that time. So it was really beautiful.

After your audition, did you expect to win?

No. I didn't expect to win at all.

Is fame something you are comfortable with?

I don't really know. I haven't really reached anything massive. But I think because I am so close to my parents, I think I have a pretty good grasp on it.

Were there any issues with clearing material for your act?

Yes. Because I do some impressions. I remember I wanted to sing a few songs and they couldn't get the rights to them. For the Shakira song, I had to write my own version and I kind of messed it up. But I did my best.

What was growing up like for you?

I have three siblings. We were always hanging out with each other. I didn't really go out very much. Even in high school, I didn't go to parties or anything like that. I went to a few dances. I went to an all-girls school. I have always kind of been like a homebody.

So how did you decide to become a comic?

Simple – I realized I could do impressions when I was 12 and I decided then and there that I was going to do stand up. I would share my impressions with my friends and family. They would laugh. And I just loved making other people laugh. Including myself. I still really enjoy it.

Did you ever bomb on stage?

I bombed plenty of times. I still do. At some shows, crowds won't understand me. And that's fine. With impressions, you usually have to test it out on people beforehand. Then I will even try maybe at an open mic night. In this business, you just have to fail a lot.

Did you ever try out for other shows?

I did one audition for *Last Comic Standing*. But it didn't go well. This was way before *America's Got Talent*. This was four or five years ago. I honestly didn't have that good of jokes and bits.

What made you think *AGT* was a good idea then?

I didn't actually even want to do it. There was a lady that called me up and said, "I am working with *America's Got Talent*. I think it would be a really good idea if you auditioned and gave it a try." I said, "Alright, I'll go." What a stick in the mud I was! [laughs] I did the first audition at some hotel at Universal Studios [Hollywood]. I didn't even give it my all. I had such a negative mind that day. I never really watched the show. I don't know what was in my mind. I thought I would look silly on there. Then I remember getting the email saying "Congratulations. You get to go to the next round and perform in front of the judges." I was like "No way!" I ignored the email. I told my manager and he was like "Are you crazy?" So I did it and it slapped me in the face and turned out to be the best thing.

Michael Grimm and wife Luci on their wedding day in Hawaii.

Photo: Courtesy Michael Grimm

MICHAEL GRIMM

(Season 5)

'I GAVE ALL MY MONEY AWAY...AND PEOPLE STILL BUG ME!'

MONEY CHANGES EVERYTHING – just ask **Michael Grimm**. The season 5 champ says he gave away most of his "$1 million" cash prize, but the instant riches continue to bring him grief and unhappiness. "Winning that sort of money does no good," he tells us. "Everybody all of a sudden comes out of the woodwork on you. So I couldn't get it out of my hands quick enough."

Michael, who was so poor as a child that he was nearly taken away by the state of Mississippi – took the immediate payout, which was a little more than $400,000 after penalties and taxes. (To get the full $1 million, it must be paid out as a 40 year annuity.)

"I bought me a truck. I bought my grandparents a house and got married," he says. "The rest I just gave away. I gave $10,000 to someone that was needing help. I gave $40,000 to someone who was helping me through the years. I figured I had it, I can give it away and I can get it again. Why keep it and just let it be a burden in your life? People still think I have it and they still bug me. It is heartless the way they act about it. I am just glad it is out of my life, you know?"

Michael opened up more about the challenges of overnight fame and fortune when we spoke in June 2013.

What has your journey been like since the show?
Michael Grimm is one to never tell a lie. The last two years, the show has brought me a lot of fame.

Are you cool with that?

I am cool with it. I love my fans.

Your Grimmlins?

And Grimmettes! Most of them have been with me for years, even before I went on the show. The show just got the world to know who I am a little more. But with it comes all the negative stuff. I have lost a lot of friends, you know? People that I thought were friends in life. It kind of makes you question yourself. Makes you think "Am I a good friend?" I definitely have my faults, but I have always valued friendship. I think it is unfair for some people to hold [my success] over my head.

Why do you think that has happened?

I don't know why. I have no clue. But it hits you in the face when you least expect it to. Maybe at some point I will get used to it once all my friends have left my life. It's like… I don't know. I am reaching out to them, but they are not reaching out to me. It is very strange. You hear about these things with people who go and become famous and the people around them can't mold to that. You gotta have some tough skin to deal with it.

Did you get any fallout from Jackie Evancho's fans after you won?

Jackie has two types of fans: the ones that are devoted to her and the ones that are against Michael Grimm. I get those people who come to me all the time, but I stop them. I say, "Look, I am not the president. This wasn't supposed to be like this. We are artists. We aren't supposed to be competing with each other." It never was supposed to be a competition. There are people and players in this business who make it that. It is not the artists who do it. Of course Jackie is a wonderful talent. She is so wise for her age, too. She is going to be something really big.

Can you see why her fans might be upset?

Oh, I get it. When they come up to me and say "I think she should have won," I say "I think she should have won, too! I was really thinking she was going to win. I am sorry. I did not mean to win." I definitely was concerned about her when I won.

Do you think a lot of people voted for you because they like you and think you are a good person?

I guess my best friends at the time would disagree with that. I have been a good guy. I know I have. I give. I love people. All the success is just so I can share it with the ones I love. My grandparents. I have given all of my money away to my friends. You know? Like big chunks of it. It don't mean anything to me.

Who did you give $40,000 to?

Someone who was with me during the show and during some hard times before that. But you know, the way I am, I just figure, "I got the money, you were with me..." That's just the way I am.

"You want to talk about frustration? I win *America's Got Talent*, I get a show on the Strip, and it doesn't get promoted. The management I was assigned to at the time came to watch me and never helped once."

— Michael Grimm

Was this person a family member?

No. But there can be some ungrateful ones in the family believe it or not. This one is an ex-manager of mine. I would tell every artist out there that if any manager says they are not in it for the money, unless it is your parents or somebody that loves you, you need to get rid of that person. They are either lying to you or they are completely ignorant to the music business.

Do you plan to stay in Las Vegas?

I really don't know. I love Vegas. It has given me a lot of work through the years. But since winning *America's Got Talent*, playing in Vegas has not been easy. You would think it would be. I booked a show right after *AGT* at the Flamingo and we just couldn't get the people on board. You want to talk about frustration? There it is. I win *America's Got Talent*, I get a show on the Strip, and it doesn't get promoted. The management I was assigned to at the time came to watch me and never helped once. And I tell you I fired every single body that was signed on to work with me after I completed the Flamingo show. They all stood there in the end with their hands out. They wanted me to fail. They did not help. I begged for help. I was the only one doing a damn thing. Here I am headlining a show on the damn Strip, something they all talk about, and yet they all don't want to help me.

Photo: Courtesy Michael Grimm

Why is that?

It blows my mind. I can be doing a lot better than anybody on the Strip right now. There is just no originality on the Strip. And I can do this. The problem is that show I did back then sort of gave me a reputation in town, which it shouldn't have. Because nobody helped me. It was all me. That is what I am going around fighting for now. It was still a success in the end. We still packed them in during the second week. I know everybody wants to say it was a failure, but it was not. I won *America's Got Talent*. People flew from around the world to come and see me. So that part has been tough.

When you won, you were required to sign with a management company that is connected to the show, right?

And the management company did nothing! It was a horrible, horrible management company that they set you up with. That is not a good situation. The guy they assigned me to was a green-horned rookie. He had no experience in the music business at all. And I do. I was telling him how this business works. He was learning from me. That is not good.

So they had you locked in for a while?

They don't have their claws in me anymore. That is good.

Will there be more records?

Absolutely. Nobody is going to stop me. There are fans and there is money to be made from me. So if nobody wants to jump on it, I will make the money myself. They are waitin' for the album. It is going to be called *Fairy Tales*. Hopefully I can get it done soon. The last album I did was self-released. I did it all in-house.

You have been married for two years. How is it going?

It has gone by fast. It has been wonderful. We are having a wonderful time. The years are going to go by real fast. It's a bummer that when you are having a good time in life it goes by so fast.

Where did you meet Luci?

She used to come out and see me and she patiently waited for me. She wanted me and what she wants she gets. Patience is a virtue. She is a very patient person.

A musician's life can be difficult on relationships.

She gets it. She understands this business. She is an agent. She started herself as an artist and an actress. She comes from Czechoslovakia. She came to America to follow all her dreams. She has done a lot. She was actually in *Titanic*, the movie. She was in the recent *Hangover* movie. She is always into something.

MURRAY

(Season 5)

TROPICANA HEADLINER MARRIES SEXY ON-STAGE ASSISTANT

Photo: Courtesy (Murray Sawchuck)

BY THE TIME HE WAS 19, Canadian illusionist Murray Sawchuck had already held 21 different jobs. "I started working when I was 12 at a bakery after school making Scottish meat pie shells because I wanted to buy a car by the time I was 16." he remembers. "I would get something like 25 cents a tray. I also had a couple of paper routes and then I washed dishes for a restaurant in

Canada called The Keg. Any time somebody offered me more money for a job I would quit. I worked at a bike repair shop, pumped gas, cooked fish and chips..." And oh yeah, he still found time to perform magic. "I did my shows on the weekend and made about $100 a piece," he tells us. "My dad would have to drive me!"

Murray – who made a Ferrari appear out of thin air (and a steam train locomotive vanish) during his time on *AGT* – has finally found steady employment at the Tropicana Hotel and Casino in Las Vegas. The resident magic expert from TV's *Pawn Stars* is also a newlywed. In July 2012 he wed his onstage assistant, Chloe Louise Crawford, who also appears in the cabaret show *Fantasy* at the Luxor Hotel and Casino.

It could be his best trick ever...

How did you manage to land Chloe?

She lost a bet and I won. [laughs] How do you like that? We met five years ago when I was touring down in Puerto Vallarta. She was dancing and I had my show down there touring and needed an assistant. She actually liked magic. When I finished my show she wouldn't just run back to the room. She would hang out on stage and help put stuff away. So she had a real, true interest in magic. At that time we were both dating other people so we kept it platonic. And as time went on we broke up with the people we were dating at the time and we hit it off and dated for five years.

How long before you knew she was the one?

I knew she was the one right away because she got me. She didn't want me to change and she took me at face value. That was huge to me. She is very driven like I am. She likes challenges.

A lot of guys might be insecure about dating a beautiful dancer in a burlesque show.

I think a lot of people do have trust issues or they are worried about them running off with somebody else. But at the end of the day, you have to worry about that in any line of work. Doctors sleep with nurses. Lawyers sleep with secretaries. If you are dating an attractive person that is always going to be an issue. But you have to understand that if you found her attractive, every other guy may feel that way, too. She is a pretty woman. Like I tell people, when you drive a Ferrari, people are going to want to steal it. People always say is it weird being married to someone in a topless review? Not really. It is our business. If you have a body like that, show it off. Because one day you won't have it. If we were in the middle of Montana or Oklahoma it might be weird, but we are in Vegas.

Murray and Chloe were married in July 2012
Photo: Courtesy (Murray Sawchuck)

Why do so many magicians marry their assistants?

I think it is convenience. It is an interest. I think it also gives those girls who are dancers a featured role. If you are in [the Las Vegas show] *Jubilee*, there are 98 dancers. They are all pretty and you don't really stand out. But when you are a dancer with a magician, you are the assistant.

How did you propose?

We have two dogs (Chihuahuas) and sometimes at night we will take them for a walk at this park by our house. So I put the engagement ring on the little one's collar with a pink pipe cleaner. And Chloe sees it and says, "Isn't there something on her collar?" And she starts to freak out because it looked like she had something caught around her neck. She actually undid the whole pipe cleaner still not knowing what it was until I got down on one knee and asked her to marry me.

So you are turning 40 this year?

Yes. Except I never tell anybody my age. I always tell people six or seven years younger. I hate it. I wish I had the knowledge I have now when I was 20. But I also feel much more in tune with who I am now. I feel like I really paid my dues. At my age right now I feel like I have had a lot of great highlights so far. I wish somebody would have told me where I would be at this age, so I wouldn't have stressed so much in my thirties!

How did the Tropicana show come about?

Just as I was shooting *AGT* I was doing a kids TV series called *The Jadagrace Show* here in Vegas. It was a show kind of like *Hannah Montana*. They brought me in for four or five episodes. I was Murray the Magician. Kind of like the guy on *Home Improvement* looking over the fence. The kids always had issues and they would come into the workshop while I was building something... Then of course, every show there would be magic. So while I was doing those producers were in talks with bringing The Laugh Factory from Los Angeles to Las Vegas. Then *AGT* hit and I got some notoriety. And that really locked in who I was. They said 'You look like you have a real chance of selling some tickets here in Vegas. Would you like to be the new Mac King [a popular family-friendly comedian]?' So I reconstructed my show. The first month was weird, having people literally two feet in front of you. I have played comedy clubs here and there, but my venues were usually 1,000 to 2,000 seats. Cruise ships or resorts. So I changed that and we put the show together and they liked it and we celebrated our one-year anniversary on May 1 (2013).

Did that gig come about because of *AGT*?

It really did because it gave the power of the recognition. It gave me some notoriety and credibility. Although I wasn't doing tricks on the show, it gave me credibility and they saw that I could perform in front of large audiences. And now I was nationally recognized.

You were once on *Last Comic Standing*. Did you want to be a comedian?

Ten years ago I wanted to because I realized it was really hard to get on TV as a magician. There is always once massive magician out there at a given time and that is it. First it was Copperfield. Then David Blaine. Then Criss Angel. There are millions of singers with albums. But in magic it doesn't work that way. So I felt I really wanted to change my style and become a personality. Like a Johnny Carson or a Dean Martin. You knew Dean Martin sang. But he wasn't looked at just as a singer. And I wanted to be that way. I wanted to use magic as my vehicle, but I really wanted to be a personality because that will last longer than anything.

Did you ever play clubs?

Back in the early 2000s, while I was [doing magic] at the Frontier I would go in on my day off to do open mic night at the Laugh Factory. I stood on the street from 10 in the morning 'til 5:00 when they opened the door to put my name on the list (to perform) because they only took the first 15 people and if you didn't get there early enough, there would already be 20 people in line by noon. So driving from Las Vegas to LA, I wanted to make sure I did my three minutes that night. Then 10 year later, after *America's Got Talent*, The Laugh Factory is producing my show here in Las Vegas.

You have done a lot. You studied broadcast journalism.

I always wanted to be a magician, but I also wanted to be a personality. I liked the radio and mom and dad wanted me to get a real job as well. I thought, "It's close to entertainment. It would be kind of cool to be on a morning show." So I went to Columbia Academy of Broadcasting and got a degree in Broadcast Communications and Television. Then I realized I would have to go up north and make $800 a month and that didn't appeal to me too much.

Where did the spikey blonde hair come from?

I used to wear my hair like Brad Pitt back in the day. And for Halloween one year I decided to spike it up high. It was probably 6 or 7 inches high. I sprayed it half orange and half green and I put an upside down triangle on the back of my jacket and I went as Guess, 'cause that was the old Guess jeans logo. And people liked the hair up. They said, "You look like Max Headroom." Then I was camping around graduation time in high school and I woke up one morning and my hair was a mess and the girls were like, "Wow, that's really cute." So I figured "if it can be cute at 8 in the morning, it can be cute at 8 at night." Then I was looking for more great branding ideas and I came across Rod Stewart on some MTV thing. He was in his mid-40s and had a yellow jacket and black pants and his hair was all messed up. And I thought "wow, that works for him. There is no magician who has ever had hair like that." So I started doing it a little at a time. I just kept making it higher and higher and blonder and blonder.

Murray channels Brad Pitt in the mid-1990s.
Photo: Courtesy (Murray Sawchuck)

What was your worst gig ever?

I never got booed off stage, but I once performed in Canada at an Irish country bar. They wanted some magic at like 7:00 on a Friday. The last thing they wanted to see was a magician. I was underage, so I kind of snuck in, did the show and left. It was awful. The stage was crammed. The sports were still on TV and I was wearing a tuxedo with tails a red tie and cummerbund.

How did you end up with *AGT*? Did they scout you out?

Every year they scouted me out. And I just kept saying no. I was like "I don't want to be on a gong show. I worked too hard to win these awards." Then I saw William Hung on *American Idol* and I thought "Son of a gun. He has no talent and he is massively famous because of being on a TV show!"

NEAL E. BOYD

(Season 3)

SLIMMER BY 75 POUNDS, FORMER CHAMP EYES POLITICAL OFFICE

Photo: Courtesy (Neal E. Boyd)

THE THIRD WINNER OF *AMERICA'S GOT TALENT* now wants to be the show's biggest loser. Neal – who has struggled with weight issues all of his life – has lost more than 75 pounds since 2008! "I am trying to drop another 100," he says. "My target weight is 225."

Neal – who celebrated his 37th birthday in 2013 – credits his new, slimmer figure mostly to diet and exercise. "I have a trainer and a dietician teaching me what the best things are to eat," he says. "I love my fruits. I am learning to eat salads and vegetables and understanding what the whole diet pyramid is about. Before that, on the show, they were feeding us donuts and Doritos or whatever was on the craft service table. I couldn't wait to get back to the hotel to get a nourishing meal." Luckily, Neal says, he managed not to bulk up during the three months of production. "We did too much walking around Universal Studios. I would say I maintained my weight during the show. Plus you are not eating much and you are sweating so much under those hot lights."

We caught up with the "Voice of Missouri" to learn more about his life and career today:

First – when can we expect some new music?
We are in the studio now recording a Christmas album! We started it back in February [2013] and are looking for producers for it right now. I am hoping to have it out this Christmas.

Will you self-release it?
I currently don't have a record deal. I was with Universal Music. I am back and forth to Nashville right now trying to get a label for this next album. [Self-releasing it] is definitely an option. A lot of people I have been talking to are pushing me in that direction.

Has your style and sound evolved much?
Absolutely. It is more pop-classical now. Similar to artists like Josh Groban, Russell Watson. What I like to do is take contemporary songs and turn them into more classical. One of the biggest successes I have had was taking "God Bless the U.S.A." and making it into more of an orchestral anthem. That has got me tons of gigs at Major League [baseball] and NBA games, singing for the USO and things like that. I have traveled a lot on that one song.

How often are you on the road?

I am usually on the road about two weeks out of each month doing either concerts or speaking engagements. I have been doing a lot more speaking engagements recently.

Is the experience of being on *AGT* what lit the fire?

Absolutely it did. It gave me a ton of opportunities. I have sung for three presidents since the show! I have sung for both Bushs and given a private concert for President Obama. As they say I am an equal opportunity performer. [laughs] Any president. I remember the first time I ever performed for a president it was Bill Clinton in 1996. I was still in college. You don't pass opportunities like that up.

When did you sing for Obama?

Our U.S. senator was coming into St. Louis and they called me to headline the event. They said there was going to be a special guest, and it turned out to be the president. There were probably about 1,000 people at the hotel and I sang before he spoke – probably about a 40-minute concert. Afterwards he told me "Good job!" and I got my picture with him. It was fantastic.

You also want to go into politics.

I have always been involved politically in the state of Missouri. I did my time as an intern and one of my degrees is in political science. For years I worked for different congressional candidates, state representatives and senators. I have worked for both U.S. Senators Bond and Ashcroft and the time came about a year and a half ago that our state representative was coming up for term limits. A seat was opening up and I was approached to run. The incumbent [Steve Hodges] had one more term left and he won.

Will you run again?

I think so. I think I am probably going to give it a couple of years, because I want to work on this album and I still have some traveling to do with the music. Things just haven't settled down yet to where I think I can give the office 100 percent.

What platform were you running on?

We were running [to make Missouri] a 'right to work' state. We lost a lot of jobs to other states nearby, simply because we were not a right to work state. That was pretty much the platform I was running on. I was running as a Republican.

Sharon Osbourne said she wouldn't vote for you?

I saw her say that. Tell Sharon I love her. She has no idea of my political background, I am pretty sure. But I love her to death and I think I could change her mind.

Do you think some people didn't take you seriously as a candidate since you were on a reality show?

There is a lot of that. People forget who you were before the show sometimes. Luckily I was running in an area where people knew who I was. But at the same time, it is hard to get past the lights and the glitter and the TV. People sometimes just want to put you in the mix of just being a reality show star and that can be hard to overcome. That is when you have to go in and remind people that you have been singing for a long time. And doing these other things for a very long time, even before you got on the show. It is something you just have to work hard at every day to remind some people. I have fans stop by my home in Sikeston randomly all the time. I had some people stop by today. They find out where you live and you just have to be as nice as you can and say "thank you" and sign autographs.

You are a big star in your hometown. You are the "Voice of Missouri!"

I am definitely the Voice of Missouri in my state. [laughs] That was a title that took a long time to earn. I was given that title a long time ago. That in itself is an honor.

What happened to the "$1 million prize?"

I invested it.

You took the lump sum payout?

Yes.

Were you aware that it really wasn't a million dollars?
Yes. I was aware. They kind of made that apparent to you.

So you put it in the stock market?
I put it in the market. I bought my mother her house. I have taken care of her. I bought myself a nice car. To be honest with you, you live off what you make from the various gigs you do. You live within your means. I have a business degree and a Masters, so I was very realistic about what you can do with that kind of money. But the main thing is just keepin' your career moving because you only have momentum for a certain period of time. Hopefully no one has blown all their prize money.

How is your health? There were concerns at one time...
I had some moments of exhaustion for a bit when I was getting used to the road. I wasn't eating right. I wasn't sleeping enough. And I was living on planes. We had a tour with Paul Potts and once that ended, I went on the *Jerry Lewis Telethon*. By then I had been on the road for probably a month straight. I was dehydrated. When I got back, I just wasn't feeling good. It was time to take a break. They tell entertainers that you have to pace yourself on the road, but of course you think you are invincible at 32. Then you realize the hard way what an entertainer's life is really like and that you have to rest.

Do you ever go back and re-watch the old performances?
On occasion I do. When I give speeches sometimes we will show them and talk about them.

What do you remember about your audition?
I was so nervous that day, I can barely remember it! They do a lot of editing when the show comes on television. I can remember being there a lot longer. I was on that stage for what had to be 25 minutes and on television it was about five minutes. I do remember that when I started singing it was so loud, I couldn't even tell if I was on key. I was just blasting through this incredibly hard aria and the only thing I was thinking was "I have to nail that last note." I don't remember the judges standing. I just remember putting my head in my hands and saying "It's done." When David [Hasselhoff] told me I was the frontrunner, I kind of knew it was mine to lose. At that

point I had to keep myself motivated throughout the show, try not to make any bad musical choices and just stay at the top of the pack.

What would viewers of the show be interested to know about your life today?

Well, I am not married. No girlfriend. Pretty much just singing, traveling, mentoring a lot of younger performers around the state of Missouri. Still really active in politics and in performing and traveling to different cities. I spend a lot of time in Nashville with songwriting partners and I try to write new stuff. I am still in love with country music. Who knows maybe one of these days I may put out a country music album.

Wait – you sing country?

I can sing anything! Of course, I don't sound like Randy Travis or Keith Urban. [laughs]

Have you sung on stage?

I have sung country on stage everywhere. I was the karaoke king before *America's Got Talent*. My big songs were "New York State of Mind" and "Faithfully" by Journey.

Prince Poppycock spends up to three hours in hair and makeup before each show!

Photo: Courtesy (John Quale)

PRINCE POPPYCOCK

(Season 5)

LAUGHS OFF HATE MAIL, DEATH THREATS AFTER MAINSTREAM SUCCESS

NOT EVERYONE WAS A FAN of the roguish opera dandy. Poppycock – the flamboyant, powder-faced creation of L.A. nightclub performer John Quale – was a bit too overwhelming for some *AGT* viewers to watch. "Within that first year, I definitely got some hate mail," John reveals. "Physical pieces of hate mail. I have a P.O. box that is available to the public. It was mostly gay bashing. And there was a death threat. Nothing too unusual. I found it mostly amusing. I thought I had finally arrived." John – a metal shop worker by day – "arrived" on June 8, 2010, when 13 million *AGT* viewers witnessed his emotional – and somewhat hilarious – audition, taped at New York's Hammerstein Ballroom. "You are a true individual and a true artist," Sharon Osbourne lauded, beginning what would become a royal march to the top four.

We checked in with the colorful performer in June 2013.

How is life after *AGT*? Much different?

Yes, definitely. I am known all over the world. The show plays in syndication for years. It is very strange for the contestants because you start getting mail from each country where your season is played. I am sure other contestants have a similar experience. I think that is one of the things that is a surprise for the contestants after the show airs because it doesn't end there. It takes really, like two years for them to finish and move on to the next season.

Does that make it easy to tour all over the world?
This summer [2013] I am doing Dita Von Teese's tour. We are doing LA, San Francisco, Chicago. I am trying to negotiate a couple of offers from China. But that is hard. I did Italy last fall for this spectacular wedding. I didn't officiate it but I played at one of their parties. This very wealthy Saudi Arabian prince married a Lebanese starlet. That was crazy. It was by far the most extravagant wedding I had ever seen. It went on for like five days.

That is what your wedding will be like one day?
We'll see. My prince has yet to come.

Didn't you have a boyfriend during the show?
He was an addict and he was sober when we were seeing each other, but then he decided to start using again. Then he decided what he really wanted to do was date someone else for two years. I think the experience of being on the show had some negative attributes. I wouldn't call it fame, but the attention I got from being on the show does affect personal relationships and working relationships and it does put strain on them. Everything is good now and I have lots of love and support around me.

You talked a lot on the show about how difficult it was growing up. Do you find that people treat you differently now?
Not really. I am a pretty private person and people don't recognize me when I am not in costume, which I absolutely adore. That includes the cool kids. If I do end up going to the disco with my friends they don't know who I am. But I think the biggest outcome in that regard has been the discourse I have been able to create through social media with kids. It's a hard line to cross because I can't save anybody. I am not magic, as much as sometimes people want me to be. I do have my words and I can give support, but I can't be responsible for whether a 15-year-old takes their own life or not. So I encourage them to seek real help – not just from a birthday party clown – but through school counselors or The Trevor Project.

Do they reach out to you directly?

Yes. Mostly through *Facebook*. Sometimes through *Twitter* or through my website. I am not always perfect in getting back to everyone, but I do try.

Too bad there wasn't someone like that for you, right?

There was in terms of music and drama coaches I had in my youth that showed they believed in me. I never really struck up a pen pal relationship with Morrissey...but I would have liked to. [laughs]

What is the status of the Prince Poppycock movie you were hoping to make?

I would still absolutely love for it to happen, but my dealings with the juggernaut of the entertainment industry have been less than fruitful. Everybody looks at what I want to do and they just see dollar signs on the bottom line. So they say no. Now I am trying to focus on more streamlined, less production intensive things right now that hopefully can grow into something.

Do you think singers have an unfair advantage on *AGT*?

Singers do have an unfair advantage because it is very easy for a singer to come up with a new act. And you don't have to write the song. Everybody else pretty much has to write their whole act.

Overall are you happy you did the show?

Oh, absolutely. I think I had to recover a bit. There was a bit of P.T.S.D. kind of thing from the show as well as the subsequent reaction from the act. It was a little alarming because in less than a year it went to very large audiences. And because of social media... Even when they are just saying good things, it can be a little off-putting.

How much were you earning playing clubs before *AGT*?

My normal price was about $300 but I had started getting nights that were about $1,000. But there is no comparison [to after the show]. There have definitely been lean months since then. It ebbs and flows. The wave of *AGT* notoriety does kind of crest and crash. You have to continue to evolve and strive as an artist and find new ways to stay relevant and on the radar.

What is something most people would be surprised to learn about you?

I grew up on a farm shoveling shit and using power tools. I own a pig and I keep bugs. We have a manure pile in the backyard.

Prince Poppycock and Elroy
Photo: Courtesy (John Quale)

Where do you live?

I live in Los Angeles, Arlington Heights. It's kind of the hood. I have a house. It is a 1910 craftsman bungalow with a yard. The house is pretty big, actually. I have a roommate. I met him waiting tables at Morel's French Steakhouse and Bistro at The Grove [in Los Angeles] in 2006.

Where did you get the pig?

He was purchased by *Vogue Homme* for a photo shoot that a friend of mine worked for. They were going to get rid of him on Craigslist. She decided that she wanted to take him home. Didn't want to let him go to some stranger on *Craigslist*. He is a miniature Vietnamese potbelly pig. He is all black. He was published. He is a supermodel. He was in *Vogue Homme*. He is the top reigning supermodel pig in the world right now. She wasn't able to keep him and both my roommate and I have always wanted a pig so we said yes. He came over for a night. He is very cute and cuddly. You can rub his belly. He cuddles up in bed under his blanket. He will spoon with you on the couch. He comes when you call him and he uses the litter box inside – but we let him out every day. His name is Elroy.

Is he going to join your act?

We'll see. I have not been so good about training him. But I would like him to. Need to find a harness with a pinwheel on it. Then we can just have him run back and forth.

So you grew up on the farm. When in your life did you realize you were destined for life in the big city?

I did not enjoy being part of the horse culture very much. It was my sister's thing. And my mother's thing. I gained notoriety very early on for having a very beautiful voice as a child and I was encouraged by elementary music teachers to audition at the Kennedy Center for the Washington Opera Children's Choir. I was part of that for two years as a soprano – until my voice changed. It is something that I don't ever remember not doing. Had to fight a bit because it is definitely a world my parents weren't used to. They expected me to just grow up and go to the best school possible and make as much money as possible. When I chose to go into the arts, everybody was supportive, but they were just a bit confused.

When did you come out to them?

When I was 15. I was always kind of... I think everyone always knew.

Photo: Courtesy (Darren Taylor)

PROFESSOR SPLASH

(Season 6)

READY TO RETIRE: 'I AM GOING TO GET OUT OF THIS BUSINESS BEFORE I AM PULLED FROM THAT POOL!'

PROFESSOR SPLASH IS GETTING READY to hang up his wetsuit.

"I would say there will be no more high diving in 2014," he tells us, exclusively. "My nerves are shot with diving. I am scared. Every time I do a dive, whether it is 8 meters or a world record, I am shot for two or three days, where I can't eat. My face looks like hell. It is the worst best thing that has ever happened to me."

With 29 world records to his name – and a few more on the horizon – Professor Splash (a/k/a Darren Taylor) says years of leaping from 20 or 30 feet into mere inches of water has taken a toll on his 52 year-old body. "My skin used to turn colors Max Factor hasn't come up with yet," he jokes. "Now it just doesn't do that. My skin has just kind of gotten used to it. My girlfriend complains about it because she says it feels like a lizard! But my mind... My hands were shaking so bad when I got on to the platform in Istanbul to jump 11.40 meters this summer. My heart was beating like a hummingbird. It was really difficult."

When we spoke with the Denver-based daredevil recently, he said life after diving will include opening a restaurant, marketing his own line of inflatable splash pools and more.

So this is your last year of high diving?

Yes. That's it. I am going to get out of this business before I am pulled from that pool! Right now, it's right there at that level. I will be having a very busy September. I will be breaking four or five world records before I even head into October. The Professor Splash thing, the 15 minutes of fame... my freakin' watch broke on this trick! Right now I am really starting to bring in some big money. I have figured out, of course, that I am never going to make *a lot of money* at what I do. I have to get into branding myself. That is the only way I will be able to make real money and get off the platform. Then I won't even jump the curb anymore.

What would you do if you couldn't dive?

I just cut some new music. I am writing some real 21st century music. I am extremely excited about that. There are many things I can do: speaking engagements, motivational speaking. I can rouse people out of their freakin' seats! I can always do that. I could do that from a fucking wheelchair if I get toasted. It is not lucky. It is just skill and opportunity coming together. I am looking to open a restaurant as well. Wait 'til you taste Professor Splash's sizzling green chili sauce! I can get bought out by Kraft with my jarred or canned spaghetti sauce or my hot green chili sauce. It is going to knock people on their asses!

Are you already selling it?

I haven't started marketing it yet. It has got to be a 24-7 thing when I do a restaurant. And that is extremely difficult. I have done it before. I have cooked high volume, good food. Even catering. I have some ideas about catering. Some really good up to date modernistic catering. I can send sauces to your bar or restaurant in bulk, just like kegs of beer.

Have you considered creating your own line of swimsuits or kiddie pools?

I am thinking more like splash stations. Rather than just a boring little kiddie pool for kids under two, I will make a play station that is 12 x 12 x 12 that is inflatable and can entertain six young kids and splash water in their faces. Something that would cost about $350. I have got to get the Chinese on board. The only way for me to make this really work is through retail using my name. I don't want to be just a backyard stunt, which I am right now. I just have a little act. It is not a business yet. But with my popularity right now, I would think in three out of five households in America, someone in that household knows who I am. That is all thanks to *AGT*.

Do you get paid to set the world records or is it just an honor?
It was an honor with *AGT*. I did that one for nothing. Now I am making [in the] mid five figures [for each jump]. I am my own agent. Still, there is a fine line. There are a lot of people saying "I'm not going to give you $50,000 to do this thing for five seconds. There is not enough there." But in reality, once people see it they say "We have never seen anything F-ing like that. Ever!"

Is that how you make a living now?
Right now it is all about major TV. This is a million dollar dive. And people are able to capitalize on this extraordinary water spectacle. I got everything – splash, physical peril and showmanship! I got a good act. If I had done a couple of things different with *AGT* and had a couple more people on my side of the think tank, I would have won. Nothing against Landau Eugene Murphy Jr., but the thing is I have a great act that just keeps on going. I have looked up the other *AGT* performers and I see what they are doing nowadays. People are making millions off of my dives. I figure a half a billion people have seen me do this thing. It is staggering.

That is more people than saw Nick Walenda on the tightrope!
I know Nick. I have worked around Nick. I am just not too impressed [with what he does]. I am sorry. I will voice my opinion on that. I know an Italian guy who does the world record incline tightrope. Also some Chinese people I met who do rapid-fire tricks at the international tightrope championships. There was an Italian woman who went across Niagara Falls with baskets on her feet!

What does your girlfriend think about what you do?
She is okay with it. When I was on *AGT* I brought my ex-wife. And she had been around the world and done a lot of exhibitions with me and seen how I get and how to deal with Darren Taylor, Professor Splash. That guy is a son of a bitch. I don't eat for a couple of days, I am cranky. Things go wrong. If it can go wrong on a set it does for me.

Are you going to marry this girl?

Maybe. She is really cute. She reminds me of a girl that I broke up with back in the '80s. Her name was Jodi. She had dark hair and a beautiful face. It didn't work out. I see a lot of Jodi in her. This woman is prettier. But she is keeping me real young. We are having a good time. Her name is Sherri.

What does she do?

She is a real estate agent for the last 22 years. She is a great girl. I just got her into golf. My golf game is fabulous. I am down to a 9 handicap and I want to chop that down even further.

Do your jumps ever go wrong?

I did a world record in the Ukraine not long ago and really crashed. I had neck injuries. Upper and lower back injuries. Just severe brain shake. I got really jacked up bad on that one because there was some really bad construction of my platform. So that is in my rider now, too. I can't have someone throw a ladder together an hour before I am performing.

Are you able to get health insurance?

Absolutely. High pool insurance.

Did anything go wrong on *AGT*?

For one thing they brought me out there to do the world record for shallow [water diving] too fast. We could have really played that up. I did a tank show. This one producer there would not allow me to use gasoline. I spent 20 years on the fair circuit where I could really get some burns going. I could get burns going 10 or 15 feet off that pool. I would have had Piers and Howie and Sharon leaping out of their seats for cover. Right when they do that and I hit that water, I would have been able to come out with a blanket on me and hit the crash pad outside the tank, which means I am no longer inside the tank and they think I am. And I would be able to get the hell away from that and sneak up behind them and go, "Here I am!" So there are a lot of things I could have done to show some magic. I am Vegas. Star Attractions in Vegas has been asking me for a rider for years. Cirque du Soleil has sent me all kinds of things saying, "We want to work with you."

Was there any downside to appearing on the show?

The only downside was that I didn't really have any help from my family or friends. Everybody thought it was a joke until I went to semi-finals. Another problem was three of the acts were from Colorado. It split the Colorado vote. Everybody was talking about the Silhouettes. These kids had their phones and their friends. I was like, "Are you kidding me?" They are cute little tear-jerkers. Everybody had a bleeding heart about their act except for me.

Is there more to your act than just belly flops?

You betcha! I am not just a one hit wonder. It is a lot safer than me jumping into 12 inches of water, too. I was setting *AGT* up for another world record in that tank but no one wanted to see it.

Cjaiilon Andrade - a/k/a Snap Boogie - started his career with a Boston-based dance crew called the Floorlords.

Photo: Splash News

SNAP BOOGIE

(Season 6)

'I USED TO ROB PEOPLE'S HOUSES... JUST FOR FUN!'

SNAP BOOGIE WALKED ONTO THE *AGT* STAGE wearing his heart on his sleeve. "We were always poor when I was growing up," he shared with viewers in a pre-audition interview. "I got a lot of friends that are locked up. My brother is locked up. It's been really hard for me." What Snap – whose real name is Cjaiilon Andrade – didn't share was just how different his life was, growing up in a rough and tumble section of Boston.

"I used to rob people, Yo! I used to go in people's houses," he admits. "I don't do that shit no more, but I used to. I used to go in people's houses and take things and sell that stuff on the street. Not to survive. Sometimes it was just for fun, but mostly because of peer pressure. I had my friends around me and I didn't want them thinking I was a pussy or a bitch. That is what goes on in the hood nowadays. Most people in the hood can survive off of welfare and just chill. So it is more like peer pressure. I felt like I had to do it so I wasn't looked at like a pussy."

Snap – who later worked as a street performer to help pay his mom's bills – says it was dancing that eventually straightened him out. "Any time [my friends] went out to do something I would be like 'I'm gonna go dancing on the streets. I'm gonna make some money,'" he tells us. "Now some of them are in jail. I still keep in contact with a lot of my friends that have gone to jail. They were excited about watching me on TV. It was a really good thing. I hope I was able to kind of like inspire people. They can [change] too."

The rising dance star opened up even more when we connected in August 2013.

Is your brother still in jail?

He's in jail. I'll be real honest with you. My brother is in jail for a murder that he didn't do. Or I believe he didn't do. I am not sure of the whole situation, but I testified that I know he didn't do it, because he was in the house at the time of the murder. It was weird. I didn't want to talk about that on a TV show, because then I would get so many different opinions. I didn't want people talkin' trash about my family. I got a little sister. It's terrible. Things like this happen every day, but once it gets out in the media, people talk about it so much and that is what you have to live with for the rest of your life. That's why I didn't want to talk about it. But that's real. That's who I am. It has been fuckin' crazy.

Did you ever get arrested?

I've gotten arrested. I never got arrested for any of the crimes. I got arrested for street dancing! Not for doing crazy shit.

Because you didn't have a permit?

No. Most places you don't need a permit. They arrested me because the cops are crooked and they wanted to arrest me. They had this bullshit excuse. This was in New York City. They asked me for my ID. I am doin' my show and the cops came up. Like five cops going in my crowd. I had a massive crowd and the police just came inside of the crowd like I was some type of terrorist! They were ready to jump me. I was being very professional about it. They were yelling at me and pushing me to act on impulse by pushing my girlfriend away. But I am not stupid. My girlfriend is not stupid. She is a teacher. So she chilled out. So they asked me for my passport and they said my passport didn't have my address on it, so that is why they took me in. They said the passport was not a valid ID. That is one of the dumbest excuses I have ever heard in my life. I could have definitely gone to court and sued the shit out of the police officers.

This happened after you were on the show?

This was definitely after the show. After a while, though, people don't really recognize me unless I am on camera. I like that. At first I was drawn into the fame thing. All that craziness. It was kind of making me depressed because I wasn't makin' nothing. I asked myself what I wanted to do. I know I just wanted to be happy. I like to travel. I love to dance. I love to create atmosphere. That's why I am on the street.

Where are you living now?
Providence [Rhode Island]. But I spend a lot of time out of the country or out of state. I barely have time to rest.

How long have you had the girlfriend?
We have been together a little bit over a year. She has been helping me with my shows.

Are you able to make a living now as a dancer?
Yes. Some of that is from *America's Got Talent*. Some of it is just from people hittin' me up. They've heard good things about me. Street performing is how I survive. Part of street performing is psychology. I have mastered it. I can go out there any time I want and get a massive crowd.

Can you make a lot of money?
You can if you do it right. Some of them know what they are doing. But really, you only have a certain amount of time and a certain amount of the year to perform.

Have you thought about doing more TV?
I don't really want to put myself into another reality show. Unless it was a reality show about street performing. You know what I am saying? About the lifestyle. It is one of the coolest fucking lifestyles in the world. Look at the Naked Cowboy [in Times Square]. He is making millions.

How come a solo dancer has never made it to the finals of *AGT*?
Honestly, I think solo dancers...we all can make it and everything. I don't know. I think it is being saved for someone who really does deserve it. For someone with all the soul in the world, who has got that personality, that thing. That will probably take 20 years. We are still trying to find a new Alvin Ailey or Michael Jackson or James Brown. There are not really too many people like that out there.

Do you think having a good personal story helps get people to vote for you?

Personal stories definitely have a lot to do with voting for people. I think the personal stories are the most important thing. But at the same time, I was trying to explain to the producers at times, not to just put out everything about my brother being in jail and all that stuff. But I guess they really liked that story. I am a fun freakin' person. I like to have fun and chill no matter where I go.

So were you pleased with how they told your story?

They did a pretty good job. They didn't reveal too much. They didn't talk about everything that happened. They just talked about all the little things that'll get people to love me. I was hoping for people to love me. I wanted to get that little bit of fame at that time. I was fame chasing.

What were you hoping they would share?

That last round, I really wanted them to put out my fun personality and that I am a crazy kid. I wanted them to show me hangin' out with friends and relaxing. I do come off as a serious person a lot of the time when I was on the show, but at the same time, I want people to see that I am fun too. Entertainment is all about having fun, too. And dancing in general. If we are all serious, then nobody's gonna have fun. I try my best to have fun, even more than makin' money and fuckin' doing all this crazy, serious work. Because at the end of the day if you don't have fun, you have a terrible life. You gotta have great stories to tell your children and your grandchildren. I want to be the guy calling somebody "whippersnapper," you know? "Come here, you whippersnapper..."

What do you remember most about your audition for the judges?

I actually kind of snuck into the taping. They called me the day before and I was up in Boston. They said they might need me, so I waited, but they didn't call me. So I called a friend of mine and said, "Do you think I should go to New York even though they didn't call me or nothing?" And she was like, "Yeah." So I got to New York and just kind of talked my way in. I wasn't really supposed to be there. At first I was really scared. I thought I might get arrested or something. I went in there and said, "I'm so sorry I'm late. I am supposed to be inside right now." They were looking for my name and couldn't find it. Then about seven producers came down to talk to me. They knew

I was lying but they were like "It's okay. We might be able to fit you in as a standby anyway." At the end they still had extra time, so they were like "What the hell?" It was one of the best moments of my life.

What made you want to be on a show like *AGT*?

I wanted to be famous. I wanted to be famous and make some money so I could do something for my family. I have a really big family. Not many of us are successful. We are just a big family of nothing, you know what I'm saying? We are so big. Way too big to be where we are right now. I am still trying to do something for my family, a little bit.

You never talk about your dad. Is he in your life?

Yeah, my dad is around. But I don't really see him too much. I say "What's up?" or "Hi" here and there, but he is never really around too much. We just go about our business. He is a cool guy.

Was he a part of your life growing up?

Not completely. He wasn't there every day. I would see him once a month or something like that. He would take me out shopping. But he wasn't really always there. He was such a busy man. He works at the World Trade Center in Boston, cleaning and washing dishes in the restaurant.

If something happened that you couldn't dance anymore, what would you do?

I can play music. I play a lot of instruments. I can definitely play the bucket drums and the steel drums. I would keep working in music. I think I would be depressed like crazy. There was a time where I did say that I would kill myself if I couldn't dance. But that is not the case [anymore]. I think I would find an alternative. I am pretty talented and there is so much more to me than dancing. There is something about performing that is just in my energy.

Do you still want to be famous?

No. I don't care about it anymore. If it happens, it happens.

Special Head was one of the most memorable
acts of season 8.

Photo: Courtesy Danny Wolverton

SPECIAL HEAD

(Season 8)

'I WANTED TO QUIT BEFORE MY PERFORMANCE'

SPECIAL HEAD SAYS HE WAS READY TO QUIT the show in the days leading up to his live performance at Radio City Music Hall. The hairless street performer — who stunned America by levitating off the ground during his first audition — was unceremoniously cut after being criticized for what the judges considered to be a less-than-amazing follow-up to his audition.

So why the beef? Special Head (real name: Danny Wolverton) says the latest act wasn't his idea. "I had a completely different thing planned out," he told us. "I was going to burst electricity out of my body like in *The Empire Strikes Back*. There wasn't going to be any disappearing thing. I had my own act planned out. And for certain reasons what I wanted to do couldn't be done at Radio City Music Hall. It wouldn't be allowed. So then all these [ideas] kind of got sculpted into this other mance. The whole thing was rushed. I wanted to go in a later week. I felt as though I needed more time and they really wanted to see me in the first week."

The entertainer, 28, says he thought about simply walking out, but didn't want to leave producers in the lurch at the last minute. "I personally wish that when they said I wasn't able to do my act, the way I wanted it to be done, I would have just walked out," he says. "But I felt as though they were putting a lot into me and I had this duty to them to not let them down. It would completely mess up their production if I quit in the middle of a show. And it would have been bad for me because then it [would] make me look like a quitter."

He shared more two days after his elimination:

What were you doing before *AGT*?

I was a human statue at first. This seemed like a natural progression of a performance craft.

So you would stand on the street dressed like a character and not move?

Exactly. I was a silver musical statue. Whenever you would tip me I would play a little song on either the xylophone or the pan flute. At first I was a baseball player statue and I would have a friend who was like an assistant watching me – this is for when we were doing private parties as ambient performers. I would start out with a baseball bat and my assistant would switch the baseball bat out with other objects when people weren't looking. People would look up and I would have a plunger in my hands.

So you worked primarily for tips?

Yeah. I like street performing because it brings me down to the audience's level. There is no barrier like a stage that lifts a person up above an audience. But at the same time, I sometimes will get harassed by kids and that gets obnoxious. So I am kind of happy that the way opportunities are playing out for me, I probably won't have to do that anymore.

Can you make good money as a street performer?

Yeah, if you get good at it. It is definitely a skill. Half of it is knowing how to hustle people. Knowing how to get people to feel good about giving you money.

What is your life like outside of performing?

I certainly have led a very interesting life. I was a musician before I became a performance artist. I started performing at burlesque shows and vaudeville shows. Before that I did projects in musicology, traveling around Africa with portable recording equipment. I went to rural villages in several countries and recorded traditional African music. And then I remixed that to electronic music. While I was over there, I got caught in a civil war situation, where there was genocide taking place and we had to flee on the backs of motorcycles, past rebel road blocks where there would be a burning bus in the middle of the road and then on the side of the road there would be angry youths with rocks and machetes. There would be burning tires in the middle of the road. It was quite a scary experience. I basically had a near death experience and came close to dying. And then I went straight from there to an internship at a recording studio in Johannesburg, South Africa, where the producer puts me up in a crack house! The producer put me up with a star singer whose boyfriend is a crack dealer. He shot his girlfriend in the leg three months before I arrived and got his gun taken away, so the only gun in the house was owned by his 17 year-old son. It was a wild situation. People would bring stolen TVs to the door to get more crack.

How did you start going down this road?

I was raised by hippie parents. I was raised in the religions of Baha'i and Native American Peyote. My mother is a Buddhist now, so I have been influenced by three religions. I was raised by hippies, but my way of rebelling was to kind of try to become more straight-laced. I went to business school. After business school, I thought the thing to do was to get a job, so I became a life insurance salesman. I sold insurance for New York Life. And then I was like, "Now I can officially speak badly about large corporations, now that I have had this experience." But after that I decided I was going to pursue my dreams in performance. It was kind of a gradual process. After the bad experience working in insurance, I started a landscaping business, because it was more enjoyable to work with plants. And through having my own business, I was making more money. At this time I was involved in a burlesque show. And I also realized that if you play it right, you can make money as a street performer. And so about a year ago I sold my landscaping business and moved to Los Angeles to become a street performer.

So how did you end up on *AGT*?

The reason I went on the show is because people on the street, when I was street performing, would say 'Oh, you should go on *America's Got Talent.*' And, you know, people that were pros were like 'Oh, that show, it'll ruin your career.' And really the thing that changed my mind was the fact that my grandparents really like the show. It is a fun show to watch. So I thought, "Okay. It will make them happy to see me on the show. It will make them feel like I am successful."

How do they feel about the way it turned out?

They know that I did a good job and that certain things were out of my control.

How do you feel about the way it all went?

It's a learning experience. It basically has taught me that in life, you must rely on other people. And in doing that you have to be willing to accept that other people will let you down.

Where did the name Special Head come from?

Well initially it was a joke. It was a joke band that my friends and I have. There is this singing monsters app. It was a joke band where it was me and two other people who would beat box and make silly noises. All a capella beat boxing. And we thought it sounded special, so we called it Special Head. Then I kind of adopted the name. I guess the idea behind it is, and I said it as a quote on the show, I said "We all have special heads because we are human. Our intelligence allows us to embark on this grand journey of being able to have a spiritual experience.

TAYLOR WARE

(Season 1)

STILL YODELING AFTER ALL THESE YEARS

AMERICA'S YODELING SWEETHEART is all grown up and heading to college! The pigtailed tween – who yodeled her way all the way to the very first *AGT* finale – enrolled as a freshman at the University of Alabama in August 2013. "I'm studying marketing," she tells us. "Everybody is always asking why I don't study music, but a lot of things in the business can't be taught."

Taylor – once the yodeling voice of *Yahoo!* – was in fifth grade when a friend told her about a new TV talent show that was holding auditions four hours from her home in Franklin, Tennessee. "My mom and I drove to Atlanta and stood in line for like 12 hours," she remembers. "After I auditioned, they said 'Ok, if you made it we will call you back in three weeks.' But there was no call, so I figured I didn't make it. Then they finally called and said 'Simon Cowell wants you [in Hollywood] in four days.' It was just a whirlwind. We are just people from Tennessee. We didn't expect anything like that to ever happen." Nor did Taylor expect to tour Europe and Australia – or appear on the *Oprah Winfrey Show* – after the show ended. "*AGT* really opened up a lot of opportunities and it still does," she says.

She told us more in June 2013:

So, Alabama...are you a big football fan?
I am. I haven't always been an Alabama fan, but I have grown to love it.

What do you think you might do with a marketing degree?
To be honest with you, I haven't really thought that far down the road. I would probably enjoy something that has to do with music. But if I couldn't be in the spotlight, I would like to be behind the scenes. I really enjoy the whole village that it takes to make a star a star. It is the little things that can make somebody special. I pray that my marketing degree will only be there to help me. But if it doesn't work out, that is okay because I will always enjoy yodeling. I love to do it.

Are you still yodeling? We haven't heard from you in a while...
I haven't really taken time off, I have just been kind of going through high school so it kind of goes back and forth. But now that I have got some me time, I am really trying to get back into it.

You were performing professionally for a while after the show, right?
Oh, yeah. The show really opened up a lot of opportunities and it still does. Right after *AGT*, I got to be on the *Oprah Winfrey Show*, which was an incredible honor. Then I went on a tour in Europe and Australia, just yodeling different places. The show's publicity has really taken me places I never thought would be possible.

Do people still recognize you from the show?
It is not so much recognizing me, but if I tell someone I yodel they are like "Wait, I watched you!" It is really neat. I just recently did a voice over for Silk soy milk for one of their national TV commercials. It is things like that. The show made me known as the yodeler.

You have also done some other projects that didn't involve yodeling...

I did for a while. I love being the yodeler and I am very blessed to have the talent that I have. I am more in the writing perspective now. I have always loved it and I have loved performing. But there is a thrill about the yodeling that I just can't replace. It is corny and not a lot of people do it, but I shouldn't give it up just to sing like everybody else. Because nobody else can really do this.

Taylor Ware's 2013 senior picture
Photo: Courtesy (Taylor Ware)

You were in a group for a while called Taylor and Tennille...

That was a duo that I had with a friend of mine that I met over *YouTube*. I always thought it would be fun to be in a group. Anyway, we were signed to a label and then she decided she didn't want to do it anymore. So it didn't work out. That's one of those things I like to tuck away and forget it ever happened.

Who walks away from a record deal?

I don't know. It was a big letdown, but I would rather it happen then than later. Kara Dioguardi was our producer. We wrote with her a lot.

So then you started a new group, called Tay and Kate?

It was really kind of the same deal. We never really got anywhere. We are still best friends and we thought "Let's just try singing together." But she kind of decided she didn't want to sing anymore either. We are still friends, but she has kind of moved on.

You should probably stick to being a solo act!

It's less maintenance! As fun as it is to be in a group, I have always loved the yodeling and that is something you can't really do with someone else.

Can you bring yodeling to a different level? To the pop charts?

I am concentrating more on writing right now, but that is what I have been trying to work on. Just making it where it is not like "Hee Haw" yodeling. Just making it more enjoyable and fluid and trying to write it just to add to songs.

How did you start yodeling?

I actually taught myself to yodel when I was 7 from an instructional book and tape. We were at a music seminar here in Nashville and we were walking by and someone said, "There is a yodeling seminar going on." I was like "Dear Lord, not yodeling." So we went in and the lady told me "Oh, you are really good" – meaning, of course, that I was horrible. But I just really took to it.

Do you remember much of your *AGT* experience?

For the most part. A lot of it was just a rush. It was such a neat feeling, but also terrifying for an 11 year-old. But I loved being a part of it. I made so many great friends and the experience is something that you can't replicate. The exposure.

What is the best part of being 18?

Nothing really. I turned 18 and my parents were like "You still live in our house. You still go by our rules..." So nothing has changed. I went and voted and bought a lottery ticket. That was about it.

Do you still wear the ponytails?

I do occasionally. I don't perform with them anymore. My friends laugh at me. But it is okay.

Do you have a boyfriend?

I do have a boyfriend.

Do you have any siblings?

I have a little brother. He is 13. He is a mess. He is just an all around boy. Plays every sport imaginable. A real pain in the butt. [laughs]

Do you still watch the old videos? I do, every once in a while. It is neat to see myself. I mean, I don't go and stalk myself. [laughs] But it is neat to see how much I have changed and how much I have grown and what I can do and things I wish I did differently. And embarrassing moments.

Like what?

On *AGT* one time, on the round I was the audience choice to move on, I forgot I was supposed to lead off the song because I was just so excited and so nervous. And I just stood there on the stage for like two minutes until one of the producers screamed at me. It was just such a shock.

Are you friends with Bianca Ryan?

I have kept in contact with her a bit over the years. Everybody kind of grows apart, but every once in a while I will say hi to her. We stayed pretty close over the years.

Do you stay in touch with anyone else?

Actually one good friend I made on the show was Jessica Sanchez [season 12 runner-up on *American Idol*]. She got eliminated in one of the early rounds on *America's Got Talent*. The *American Idol* tour came to Nashville last year, so we got backstage passes. We ended up going shopping the next day. It was really neat to reconnect after all these years.

Have you tried out for any other shows?

I thought about it, but you can't really beat second place, unless you win. I figure I had my experience and it was incredible. Instead of being on another show, I would rather try to make more of a career out of this.

What other types of offers do you get?

Over the years I have gotten a lot of offers from shark-like people. After I was on the show different managers that I had never heard of would come up and offer me contracts until I was 25. I have had offers to do shows that were way far away. There was this one offer to do a New Year's Eve party in Oregon. They offered me $5000, but New Year's Eve is very special to my family, so I turned it down.

A CONVERSATION WITH...

TIM HOCKENBERRY
(Season 7)

PLANNING 2013 WEDDING AFTER YEAR-LONG BREAKUP
'I'VE NEVER BEEN MORE COMMITED TO ANYTHING IN MY LIFE!'

HE'S READY TO TIE THE KNOT. Again. Tim – a longtime veteran of the Bay Area music scene and former touring vocalist with the Trans-Siberian Orchestra – introduced the world to his girlfriend, Cuban model Bronwyn Chovel, and their three week-old daughter, Sonia, during season 7 auditions in San Francisco. Now, he tells us, they are officially becoming a family. "I proposed to Bronwyn," the Joe Cocker sound-alike revealed in early August 2013. "I got down on my knees in my apartment and I begged her. I put a way more expensive ring on her finger than I could afford... She said 'Most likely.' She gave me a soft 'Yes.' I gotta marry this girl!" Tim – who is divorced with three other children – says he hopes to have the wedding "probably in October or November."

"I don't mean to sound presumptuous, but she loves me as much as I love her," he says. "We have been inseparable since I proposed to her."

Tim – who shared his very personal story of drug and alcohol abuse with *AGT* viewers – admits the couple have had "a lot of problems" over the last year. Not long after he was eliminated from the competition, Tim says he walked away from the relationship altogether, leaving Bronwyn to care for their daughter on her own for almost a year. "But we sort of resolved it all," he says. "She is totally on board with me now. We are trying to figure it out. We know we gotta climb some of the wreckage here. We both said a lot of things that we are sorry for. Now I am just crazy in love with this chick. I can't shake it. The fact that she is a little bit crazy is what I am attracted to."

The wedding, Tim insists, "is totally going through. I have never been more committed to anything in my life. I really have to hunker down and sort of grow up for her a bit."

Tim continues to perform about 100 shows a year and is set to begin recording a new CD with the Nashville Symphony in late 2013.

Why did you audition for the show?
They came to town and I was a huge Howard Stern fan. My 10-year-old daughter told me to audition and I told her, "Sweetie, Daddy's going to be 50 years old next year, I don't think they're interested in hearing some old guy sing love songs." And she said, "No they take old people too, you'd fit right in!" I walked to the audition with her. I wasn't standing in line like a lot of the people, waiting for my big break. I was basically doing it on a dare. I've toured with other bands so I'm not like this rags-to-riches [story] that they're looking for. I was floored when they pushed me through.

What do you remember about that first audition for the judges?
To tell you the truth, I was going to do [my performance] a lot more like Joe Cocker than I actually did. I can actually impersonate him like crazy. But I decided that I didn't want to do it that way. I was actually planning to sing the lyrics, "I am so beautiful to me," and do the whole song from the first person narrative but I chickened

out. Then all of a sudden they took me seriously so I was like, 'I better figure out some other songs to sing because it looks like I'm going to compete with these little kids.'

What was it like backstage during the show? What was going on behind the scenes?

There were a lot of little kids with weird parents. So I was like, basically my job was to crush the hopes and dreams of small children. At first I thought it was kind of creepy but then I kind of got into it. There were a couple of kid acts that wouldn't shut up backstage

Tim and the future Mrs. Hockenberry

and were just running around, singing and trying to get attention all the time so I was taking great pleasure knowing that I was just going to completely destroy their lives. The irony of it all is those little, crying dancer kids crushed me. They kicked the shit out of the old man, in the end.

Did you think at any point that you might win?

I was eyes wide open; I knew how this whole thing works. I had a bunch of attorneys look at the contract that were like, 'Dude if you go into the finals, you realize that they own your ass!' For my last semi-final audition, I was working with a friend of mine and we said that we need to come up with a song that will not necessarily get me through to the finals but get Howard Stern to stand up. I said, "If I sing 'Imagine,' the first line is 'Imagine there's no heaven' and that drops out the Midwest voters really fast. So we kind of strategically did that last performance. They put me on as the last singer standing and the producers were really cool to me, I have to say. The people behind the scenes of that show are awesome, and they saw the writing on the wall. I'm too old to sign a contract with Simon Cowell anyway. Really, dude? What are you really going to do for me?

So you obviously weren't too upset that you didn't make the finals?

The reality of the situation is that it's not really a million dollars. It's $25,000 for 40 years, so basically I'll be getting my last check when I'm 90. Not only that, but they take all your publishing. They take everything! It's crazy. So I was sure glad to get off when I did. I would have only had one more episode for exposure if I had gone onto the finals. And basically, I wouldn't have won against those dogs. There's no way. The whole country was rooting for the dogs. I could see it on the Internet. I had to do something kind of lackluster, but good enough to get Howard to give me more love.

Have you thought about trying a different singing competition?

I actually plan to do *The Voice*, but they make you wait a year. I actually have other things going on right now so hopefully I won't have to do that. I was pleasantly surprised at how the audience jumped up for me.

How accurately did *AGT* convey your personal story?

I mentioned once that I was a recovering alcoholic and they kept saying, 'Keep saying that, keep saying that.' A lot of people that get clean, they basically wear it as who they are, a sober guy. I don't live my life like that. When it comes to drinking and using drugs, I just keep my mouth shut. But they definitely wanted that to be a big part of my story, and I was like, 'Whatever sells your show.' I didn't really care. They were really nice to me though. They didn't hoodwink me or anything.

How did your family feel about you sharing your personal story with the world?

My family was freaked out. My mom and dad were just like, 'What about the other kids?' I brought all my kids down to a couple of shows and they came to my town and interviewed me and my family, but they cut all that. All my kids were at my first audition, too. They filmed all my kids running and jumping in my arms after my audition but they edited all that out. They said they just wanted the hot chick and the baby. So all my other kids were cut out of it, which was a total bummer. My ex-wife didn't speak to me during the whole show because it looked like I chose the baby and the girlfriend over all of them.

Do you ever regret going on the show?

No. It was a good time. But when I realized what you don't actually win I was like, 'OK, this was a mistake, how do I get out of this now?' But I'd definitely do it again. You're on national TV. Not that many people knew who I was before the show. I fit the model perfectly. I have some people throwing money at me that probably wouldn't have done that had it not been for the show, so it was a good experience overall. Just the personal life stuff was kind of a nightmare.

Tim and Bronwyn have a one-year-old daughter, Sonia.
All photos: Courtesy (Tim Hockenberry)

Tone The Chiefrocca (L) and his 15 year-old brother Cody lost their father in 2012. The rapper is best known for his season 8 song "B-Double-O-T-Y."

Photo: Splash News

A CONVERSATION WITH...

TONE THE CHIEFROCCA

(Season 8)

'I SUCK AT REGULAR JOBS'

TONE THE CHIEFROCCA may one day make millions singing his catchy rap ditty "B- Double-O-T-Y." Until then, the aspiring one-hit-wonder needs to get himself a j-o-b! "I don't care where I work, I just need to make money," he says. "I'd get a job at Walmart. I'd be happy if I had a job at Home Depot. I don't care. I rap because I genuinely like to. But I need to get paid!"

Tone – whose real name is Anthony Granger – is currently on government assistance. "I'm goin' to the GR (General Relief) building right now," he told us days after his elimination. "I'll be the most popular person at the GR building."

"I got laid off, but honestly, it seems like everything I have ever done people are like 'You should be a comedian.' That is like the only thing I ever did well on is trying to make people laugh. That's why I am trying to do this. I suck at regular jobs. I sucked at Best Buy. I sucked at Ralph's [a west coast supermarket]. I worked at Ralph's for two years and people would ask me where stuff was, I'd be like "Man, I don't know." I hated workin' at Best Buy. People there they don't take no for an answer. They'd be like 'Can you help me find *Les Miserables*?' and I be like 'I don't think we have that.' And they'd say 'Can you look it up in the computer?' And I'd be like 'I don't know how to spell '*Les Miserables*!'

The rapper had more to share the day after his elimination:

You got a great reaction to the song!

That's all I wanted. I'm one of those people that will watch a television show like I did last year and say "I'm gonna go up on there." Initially for me it started out like I just wanted to make my homies laugh. I didn't even tell anybody I was gonna be on there until the last minute. For a lot of other people to ride with me and be there with me, I just appreciate that love, you know? Even if this was it for me, they can never take this away from me, 'cause I had so much fun. I felt like I was Dr. Dre for one day. Ninety seconds up there, that was just fun.

Will there be a follow up song?

There might be. I said I just want three songs. If you ever listen to the radio, they only play three songs from everybody. And I am cool with that. Even [with] one song, I can open up for anybody.

Who is the one hit wonder you would most like to be?

I wanna be like Psy. Even though I know he is not a one hit wonder. Or I could be like Rebecca Black. I could do a "Friday" song. That is all I need. People hated Rebecca Black all the way to the bank.

You wrote this song years ago. Why did it take so long for it to break? Did you ever try to get a record deal?

I never tried to do anything. Honestly, I was just trying to get on TV and make people laugh. I knew the song was a funky song, but... This is my peanut butter and jelly time.

What do you do when you are not singing this song?

I am a dad. I am with my lovely daughter and my family. She is one and a half. Her name is Lea Kitana – and yes, it is Kitana from *Mortal Kombat*.

One day she will go on the Internet...

...and she'll be so embarrassed because her daddy is the booty man! [laughs]

Are you married to her mom?

I got nothin' but respect for her bein' my baby's mom and all, but we are not really down like that. We had a real big fallout before all this happened. And I mean a real big fallout.

So there is no Mrs. Rocca?

No.

What does your mom think of your sudden reality TV success?

This whole experience has been so fun. For one moment, my mama was proud of me. You know what I mean? She knows what I want to do and this is what she wants me to do, too. The show is always tryin' to dig deep into your life. They always tryin' to get bad stuff out there. My story can really be sad. I don't have a job, but there is a lot of people goin' through the same crap I am goin' through. What I want to do is like, I want to bring life. Every time you see me, it is supposed to be a party.

How long ago did you decide to go on *AGT*?

This whole thing has been going on since November [2012], since the first audition. Initially it was me, my mom, my brother and my pops. He went to the initial audition too where you have to make it in front of the producers. My pops is one of the people who helped me write the lyrics to the song. Then three weeks later, my pops passed away out of nowhere. The day after Thanksgiving. I didn't tell them that and I didn't want to tell them that because honestly that hurt so bad to even talk about that. Honestly, it took so long for them to call me back that I was gonna tell them forget it. I didn't even want to do it no more. My mom is the one that kept telling me to do it. I almost didn't even go to my first audition, because it hurt so bad. But then on the [contrary], me getting there and acting the way I do, was therapy for me. I don't have to go to a psychologist or something like that because me gettin' up there and making other people laugh, I was makin' myself laugh. So that helped us all get through. It helped my brother get through. He just lost his pops at 14-years-old. So if I can make anybody feel better, put a smile on somebody's face, that is what it is all about.

Was your dad sick?

It was a blood clot.

And your brother Cody was only 14?

Yeah, that is my baby brother. He is 15 now. He gets all the honeys now... When I first did this all, he was only six. I couldn't imagine anyone better backin' me up. He has a band himself. He has an instrumental band.

What is your plan going forward? I bet you could make a couple of grand a night playin' clubs now?

I'm down! I don't care if it's $300. I will do a show right now for $50 just because I like doin' it.

Do you have any other talents besides singing and rapping?

My main talent is that I can get up on any stage and just rock it. I am also a big fan of comedy. I myself was even rooting for [comedian] Angela Hoover. I give her so much respect. That is what I really want to do. I been tryin' out goin' to an open mic night. I don't have the balls to get up there and do stand up, but I can do the "B-Double-O-TY." I love hip-hop and I love comedy. I always said if there is a way I could mix the two and make people laugh and dance that is what I really want to do.

WILLIAM CLOSE

(Season 7)

BACK ON TOP AFTER LOSING EVERYTHING IN MALIBU BRUSH FIRE

WILLIAM CLOSE LOST EVERYTHING HE HAD – including ten of his hand-built Earth Harps – in a 2009 Malibu, California brush fire. "It was pretty intense," he remembers. "Wildfires are quite scary. I woke up and the whole side of the hill was on fire, raging toward me. Winds were blowing at 70 miles per hour. It was pretty intense. I hightailed it out of there."

But nature's wrath didn't get in the way of his dreams. "I had a run in Hong Kong a month after that," he remembers. "I was already booked. So I had family members fly in and we rebuilt the whole set of instruments. I shipped off to Hong Kong to do the show a month after losing everything."

William, who married his girlfriend Sarah in early 2013, says he thought about moving to China for good after the fire. "But the piece of property is too special," he tells us. "It is up on this bluff, overlooking the ocean. It's very valuable. So there were a lot of reasons to rebuild. And they say the fires come every 20 years so, you know, hopefully I have got another 15 years before I have to worry about another fire."

So you rebuilt the house?
It took about four and a half years to get totally rebuilt. Now I am back in the house. I designed a studio in the house where the Earth Harp is in the studio and it shoots out through this open part of the wall and goes up to the top of a mountain. It is like an indoor-outdoor harp.

You got married since appearing on the show...
Yeah. So I rebuilt the house and then Sarah got pregnant. We ended up having Phoenix...he was actually born in the living room of the house.

Like a phoenix rising from the ashes?
That is where he got his name from.

When was the wedding?
We got married on his first birthday, just a few months ago. We got married in Connecticut at my mother's house and then we went over and did shows in Tel Aviv and had our honeymoon over there.

What does Sarah do?
She does a lot of graphics work and she performs with me sometimes. She does a lot of music direction for the company. We just released a new CD, so she helped with that. She comes from a very creative background.

Is the CD a lot of string music or is there another side to it?
It is pretty spectacular, actually. It is sort of a combination of recognizable pieces along with compositions that we have written or were written for us. We do a version

of "Love Reign O'er Me" by The Who that we did on *AGT*. Then we have Beethoven's "Moonlight Sonata" but it is all rocked out with a lot of fun drums. So there is some recognizable stuff.

So there is a lot more to your act than people got to see on the show?
Oh, yeah. We only did three pieces on the show.

You have also performed at Coachella and Lollapalooza.
We do a lot of festival work. It has to be the right type of festival. Definitely music and art festivals.

How did you develop the harp? Did it take years?
A lot of it comes out of combining my background, which is sculpture and architecture. The first Earth Harp I put resonators on both sides of a valley and ran the strings a thousand feet across to the other side and turned that valley into a giant harp. That is where it gets its name, Earth Harp. That was back in 1999 and I have been developing it ever since. It is always refining and coming up with new directions for it, new ways to set it up. A lot of it is actually dictated by travel. I developed a bunch of instruments that pack up and fit into regular airline baggage.

Why did it take so long for your instruments to come to the mass public's attention?
I don't know. I think there are a lot of interesting unique things out there, but it is rare to get such a large scale, public stage. That is one of the things that is really unique about the show. It features things that are unique and don't necessarily have a typical venue or a typical genre. I have definitely been cruising along with this for a long time. I started doing events with my instruments in the late 1990s and basically that has been my full-time job ever since. This was definitely the first time that it kicked off to such a large scale, international audience.

Did you approach the show or did the producers call you?
The producers found me. Not only were they interested in the act but they are also interested in the personality of people and making sure they are going to be good on the show and function well.

Had you considered auditioning in previous seasons?

I knew about it and it was in the back of my mind that it would be really cool to audition for it. But actually, my wife, Sarah, was the one that said, "You've gotta go down and meet with them."

How many Earth Harps are in existence now?

There are probably about 20 of them. I lost about 10 in a wildfire back in 2007, where I lost my house and studio. Basically everything I had ever built was lost in the fire. Then it was basically rebuild time. I did a lot of new experimenting and went in different directions with it.

Did you personally do all the building?

Yes. I build each one by hand. Every once in a while I will bring in a set builder or cabinet builder to help me with some of them. I pretty much build all of them.

Were you doing something different in architecture before this?

No. I studied at the Art Institute in Chicago. Started building these musical sculptures or sculptural instruments. When I got out of school there was a lot of interest in them right away, so I just kept going. The only other job I had was I worked at a bunch of museums and did some educational stuff.

Is selling the instruments what bought the house in Malibu?

It was more from performing. I also received a big commission from Cirque du Soleil. That helped.

The judges, at one point, essentially offered to finance your act. Did you take them up on that?

Nothing has come of that yet. Quite honestly I haven't asked them to. I gotta reach out to them.

Where do you go from here?

I have this one bigger show concept that I have been dying to do through the years and it seems to be coming more into fruition. It is to have 1,000 strings. Where the audience is brought into a theatre and there are literally a thousand strings all around them and over them and that turns into an epoch show evening of theatrical music. So that is one of my main goals now, to get that show off the ground. It would be something that would live somewhere for at least a couple of months.

Nick Cannon once wrote a song called "Can I Live?" which thanked his mother, Beth, for not having an abortion when she found out she was pregnant with him at age 17.

Photo: Helga Esteb (Shutterstock)

25 Things You Might Not Know About
America's Got Talent

1. **Neal E. Boyd**'s (s3) uncle is Dennis Ray "Oil Can" Boyd, a former major league baseball pitcher for the Boston Red Sox.

2. **Kaitlyn Maher** (s4) is the show's youngest-ever finalist. In 2013 she landed a role in the short-lived Fox TV comedy *The Goodwin Games*.

3. **Cjaiilon Andrade** (s6) got the name 'Snap' from his late uncle who danced with a local break-dancing group called the Floorlords. First using the name Snap2, which later turned into **Snap Boogie**.

4. **Mary Joyner** (s7) once tried out for *X Factor* and *American Idol*. "I actually didn't even get past the producer round," she tells us. "I was kind of bummed."

5. **Thia Megia** (s4) later made the Top 10 during season 10 of *American Idol*.

6. The *AGT* episode with the highest ratings to date was the season 5 finale. Over 16.4 million people watched Kevin Skinner be crowned the winner.

7. *American Idol* season 10 winner **Phillip Phillips** and *X Factor* season 2 runner-up **Carly Rose Sonenclar** both auditioned for *AGT* – but didn't make it.

8. Former judge **Sharon Osbourne** never finished high school. She dropped out at 15.

9. Judge **Howie Mandel** is a well-documented germophobe and OCD sufferer, but fellow judge **Howard Stern** also once battled the disease.

10. **Landau Eugene Murphy, Jr.** considered becoming a barber before winning *AGT*. He learned to cut hair on a blind man that paid him $1 a week to cut his hair for him.

11. In 2013, *Forbes* named **Terry Fator** (s2) as the second highest-earning comic in America, behind only Jerry Seinfeld.

12. Kid ballroom dancers **D'Angelo & Amanda** (s8) were winners of the only season of Paula Abdul's CBS competition *Live To Dance* in 2011.

13. Two members of **Recycled Percussion** (s4) both broke their ankles during the same performance, within 10 seconds of each other. They both had to play in casts for two months.

14. During a season 4 performance, pianist **Jeremy Ou**'s dancer accidentally kicked the cord of the mic that went to his piano. He played the last 20 seconds of his song in silence.

15. According to **Howie Mandel**, child dancers are filmed as wide shots and not close ups to keep their appearance more family-friendly. He has also said that he sometimes feels uncomfortable watching children perform such grown-up moves.

16. In March 2011 Nuttin' But Stringz were featured on *The Fresh Beat Band* in an episode called "The Mystery of the Missing Violin".

17. Contestants cannot interact or contact their family or friends while on the show, without the permission of production, per their contract.

18. The sound made when the judges "X" an act is the strike sound used in *Family Feud*.

19. The 2011 children's movie *Hop* features David Hasselhoff (as himself) hosting an *AGT* spoof show called *Hoff Knows Talent*.

20. Kid singing group **Avery and the Calico Hearts** (s6) have broken up. We got this update from Brooklyn in July 2013: "Shortly after our appearance on *Maury* (January 2012), our vocal teacher moved, so Avery switched to a different theater. So part of it was management issues. We could have still been together, but then Avery moved to Dallas (nine hours apart). Kassidy and I continue to sing duet as the Calico Hearts and Avery sings solo now. We don't talk to Avery much anymore. Since the show, we've basically just been having local performances."

Brooklyn Elbert (L) and Kassidy King are still best friends but no longer perform with Avery Winter.
Photo: Courtesy (Brooklyn Elbert)

21. **Zac "Horse" Gordon** (s7) also competed on season 4 of *American Ninja Warrior*.

22. **The Smage Brothers** (s6) have taught their pet goats to do tricks. Goat pal Karl can snowboard, flip and snow skate, while their other pet goat, Burwell, can "faint" on command.

23. *AGT* producers monitor contestants' websites and social media accounts to make sure they do not reveal spoilers during the pre-taped audition rounds.

24. **Donald Braswell II** (s3) worked for two years as a singing waiter at a haunted inn in Texas before making it big.

25. Goth opera singer **Andrew De Leon** (s7) used to be obsessed with Britney Spears music. "I did not know how I got addicted to her music, but then it turned into light rock and then, it turned into heavy metal and finally into opera," he said in 2013.

ABOUT THE AUTHORS

SEAN DALY is a Los Angeles-based journalist who has conducted over 2,000 celebrity interviews and contributed to *People, Us Weekly, In Touch* and other top publications. A former producer for *TMZ*, he graduated from Syracuse University and was the west coast television reporter for the *New York Post* from 2008 to 2013.

ASHLEY MAJESKI is the founder and editor of *TheAshleysRealityRoundup.com*, the premiere website for news and information about reality television. She is a graduate of California State University-Fullerton and a regular contributor to *Today.com*.

Their most recent collaboration, ***Teen Mom Confidential: Secrets & Scandals From MTV's Most Controversial Shows***, is on sale now.

36537019R00184

Made in the USA
Lexington, KY
23 October 2014